MOON

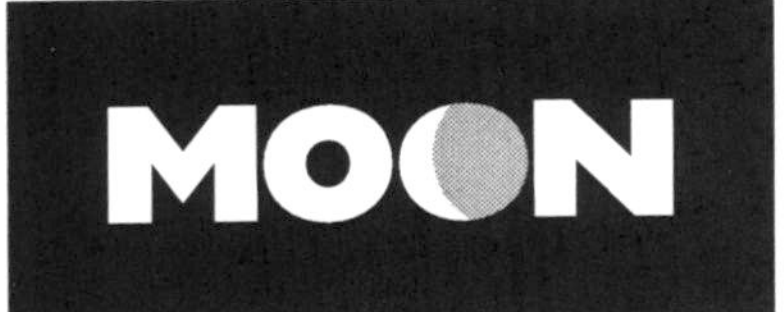

SPO

OREGON'S COLUMBIA RIVER GORGE CAMPING & HIKING

TOM STIENSTRA & SEAN PATRICK HILL

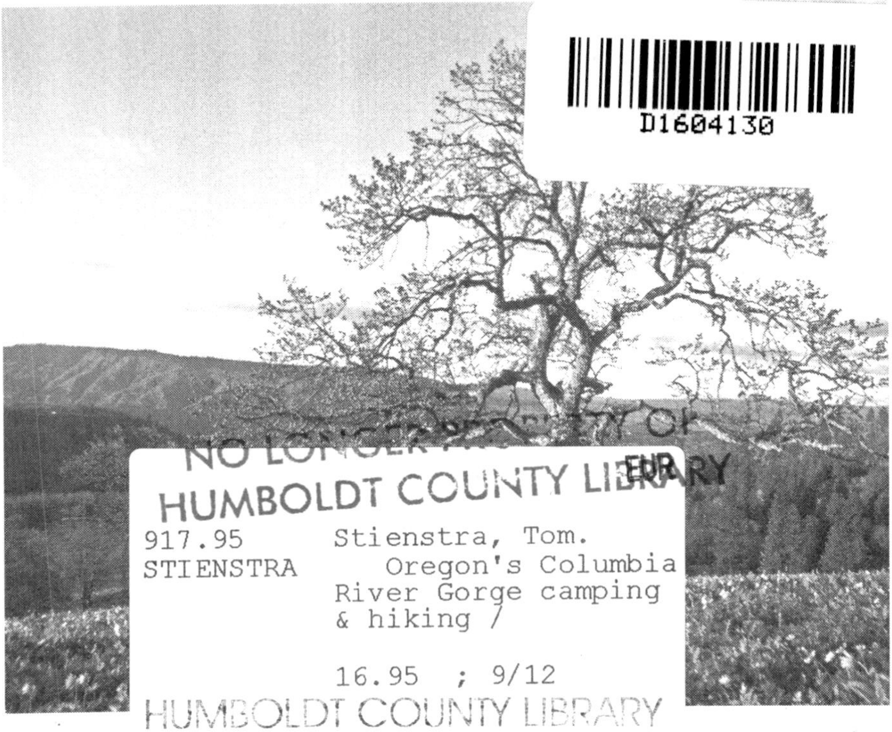

How to Use This Book

ABOUT THE CAMPGROUND PROFILES

The campgrounds are listed in a consistent, easy-to-read format to help you choose the ideal camping spot. If you already know the name of the specific campground you want to visit, or the name of the surrounding geological area or nearby feature (town, national or state park, forest, mountain, lake, river, etc.), look it up in the index and turn to the corresponding page. Here is a sample profile:

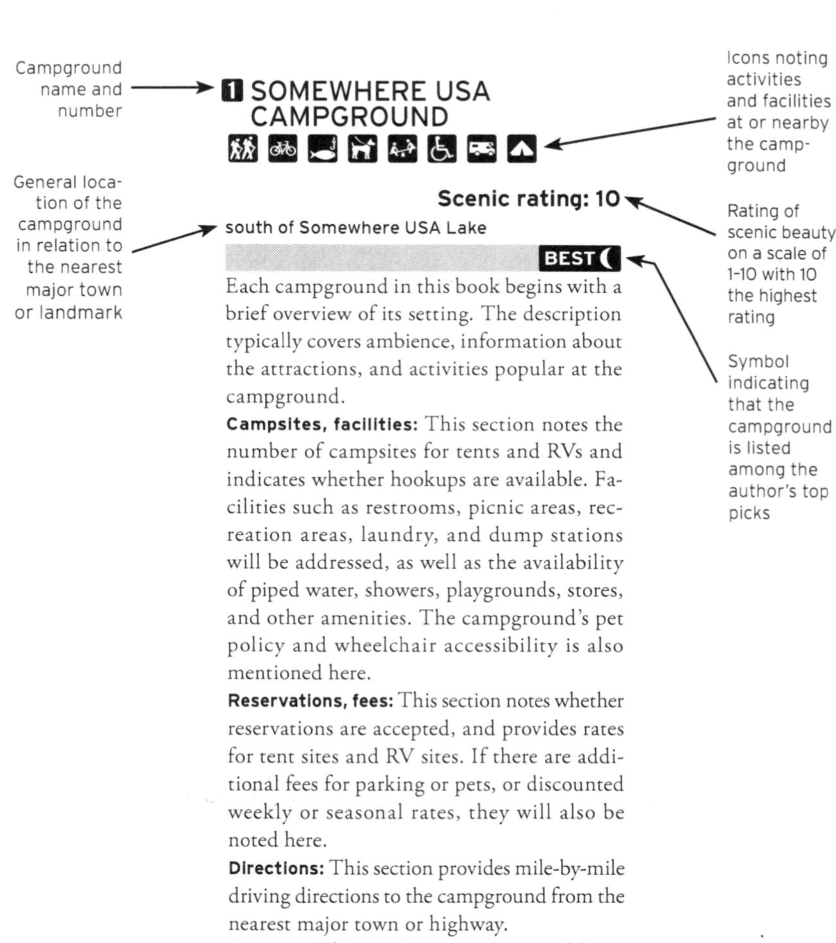

ABOUT THE ICONS

The icons in this book are designed to provide at-a-glance information on activities, facilities, and services available on-site or within walking distance of each campground.

- Hiking trails
- Biking trails
- Swimming
- Fishing
- Boating
- Canoeing and/or kayaking
- Winter sports
- Hot springs
- Pets permitted
- Playground
- Wheelchair accessible
- RV sites
- Tent sites

ABOUT THE SCENIC RATING

Each campground profile employs a scenic rating on a scale of 1 to 10, with 1 being the least scenic and 10 being the most scenic. A scenic rating measures only the overall beauty of the campground and environs; it does not take into account noise level, facilities, maintenance, recreation options, or campground management. The setting of a campground with a lower scenic rating may simply not be as picturesque that of as a higher rated campground, however other factors that can influence a trip, such as noise or recreation access, can still affect or enhance your camping trip. Consider both the scenic rating and the profile description before deciding which campground is perfect for you.

MAP SYMBOLS

Expressway	80 Interstate Freeway	Airfield
Primary Road	101 U.S. Highway	Airport
Secondary Road	21 State Highway	City/Town
Unpaved Road	66 County Highway	Mountain
Ferry	Lake	Park
National Border	Dry Lake	Pass
State Border	Seasonal Lake	State Capital

ABOUT THE TRAIL PROFILES

Each hike in this book is listed in a consistent, easy-to-read format to help you choose the ideal hike. From a general overview of the setting to detailed driving directions, the profile will provide all the information you need. Here is a sample profile:

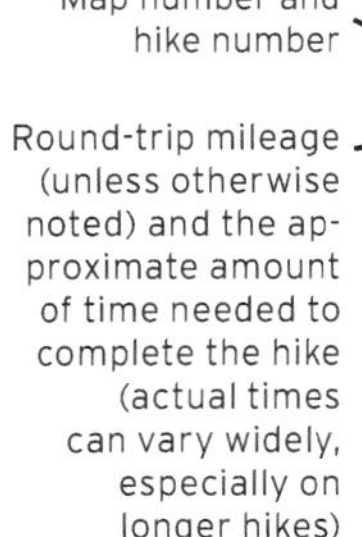

1 SOMEWHERE USA HIKE

9.0 mi/5.0 hrs 3 8

Difficulty and quality ratings

at the mouth of the Somewhere River

General location of the trail, named by its proximity to the nearest major town or landmark

BEST

Symbol indicating that the hike is listed among the author's top picks

Each hike in this book begins with a brief overview of its setting. The description typically covers what kind of terrain to expect, what might be seen, and any conditions that may make the hike difficult to navigate. Side trips, such as to waterfalls or panoramic vistas, in addition to ways to combine the trail with others nearby for a longer outing, are also noted here. In many cases, mile-by-mile trail directions are included.

User Groups: This section notes the types of users that are permitted on the trail, including hikers, mountain bikers, horseback riders, and dogs. Wheelchair access is also noted here.

Permits: This section notes whether a permit is required for hiking, or, if the hike spans more than one day, whether one is required for camping. Any fees, such as for parking, day use, or entrance, are also noted here.

Maps: This section provides information on how to obtain detailed trail maps of the hike and its environs. Whenever applicable, names of U.S. Geologic Survey (USGS) topographic maps and national forest maps are also included; contact information for these and other map sources are noted in the Resources section at the back of this book.

Directions: This section provides mile-by-mile driving directions to the trail head from the nearest major town.

Contact: This section provides an address and phone number for each hike. The contact is usually the agency maintaining the trail but may also be a trail club or other organization.

ABOUT THE ICONS

The icons in this book are designed to provide at-a-glance information on the difficulty and quality of each hike.

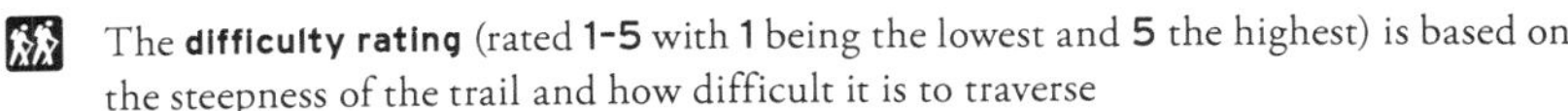

The **difficulty rating** (rated **1-5** with **1** being the lowest and **5** the highest) is based on the steepness of the trail and how difficult it is to traverse

The **quality rating** (rated **1-10** with **1** being the lowest and **10** the highest) is based largely on scenic beauty, but also takes into account how crowded the trail is and whether noise of nearby civilization is audible

ABOUT THE DIFFICULTY RATINGS

Trails rated 1 are very easy and suitable for hikers of all abilities, including young children.

Trails rated 2 are easy-to-moderate and suitable for most hikers, including families with active children 6 and older.

Trails rated 3 are moderately challenging and suitable for reasonably fit adults and older children who are very active.

Trails rated 4 are very challenging and suitable for physically fit hikers who are seeking a workout.

Trails rated 5 are extremely challenging and suitable only for experienced hikers who are in top physical condition.

MAP SYMBOLS

ABOUT THE MAPS

This book is divided into chapters based on major regions in the state; an overview map of these regions precedes the table of contents. Each chapter begins with a map of the region, which is further broken down into detail maps. Sites are noted on the detail maps by number.

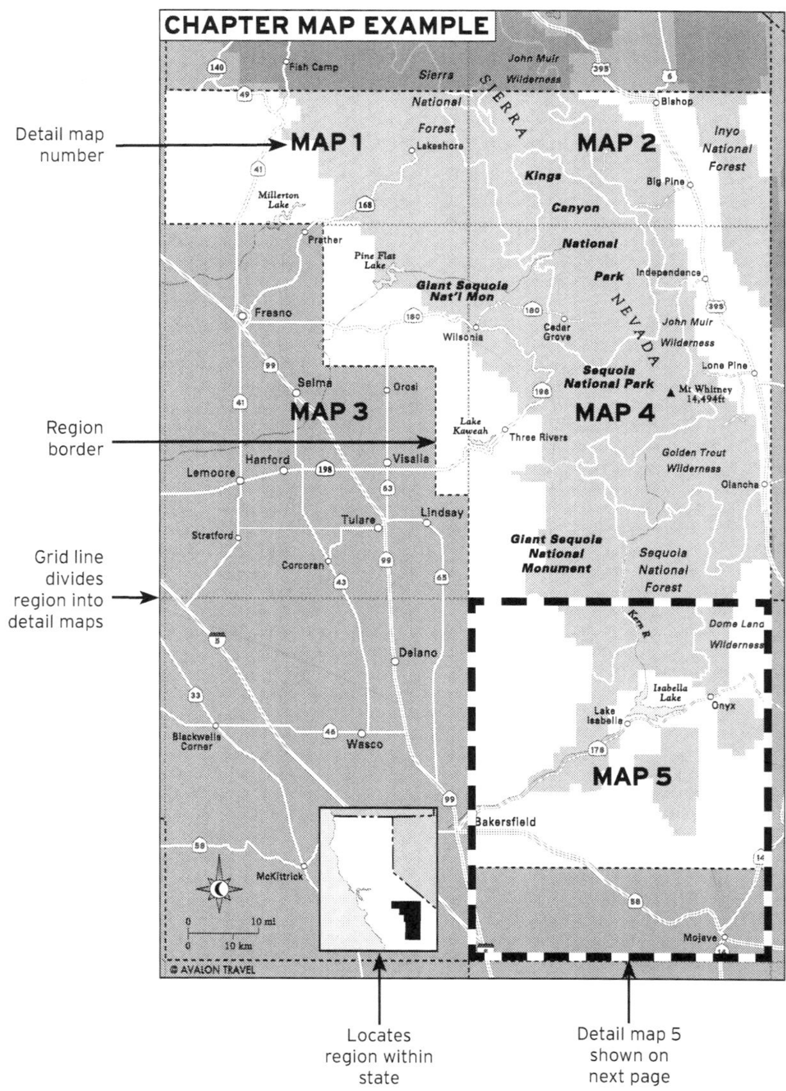

Locates detail map within region

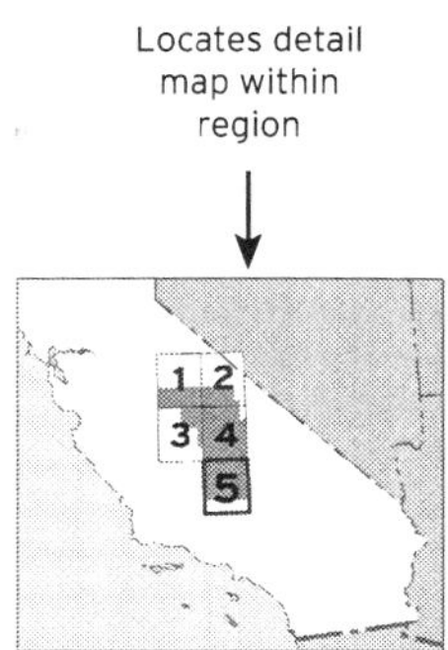

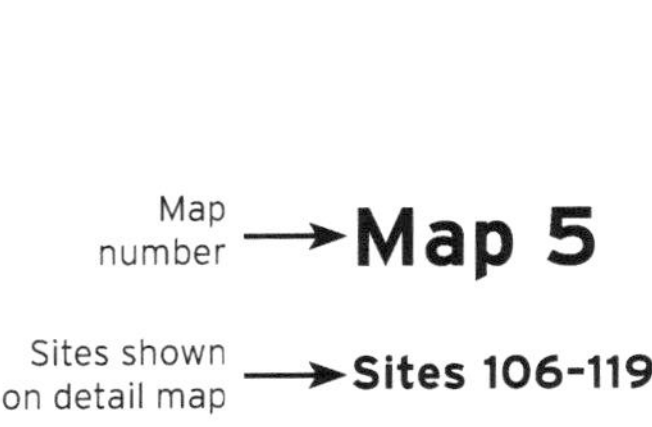

Site number

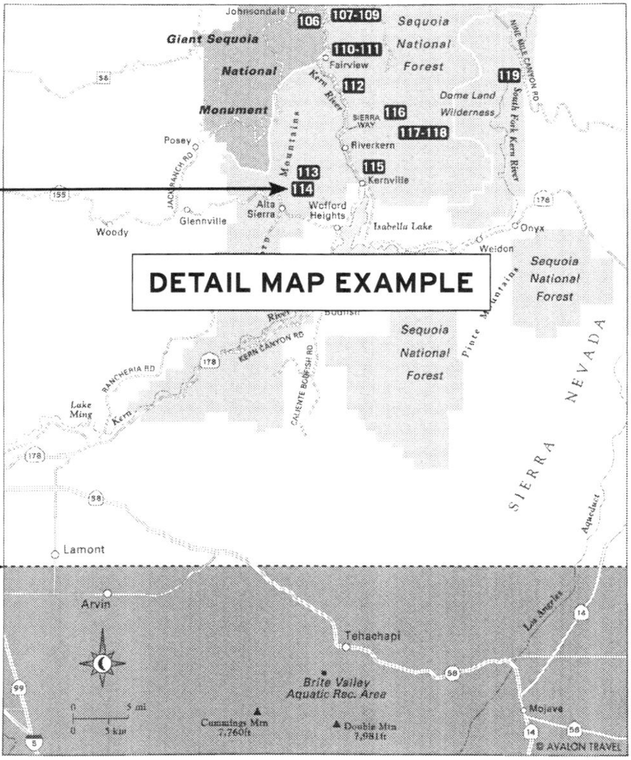

Region border

DETAIL MAP EXAMPLE

Camping and Hiking Tips

HIKING ESSENTIALS

In Oregon, there are those days when you get off work and want to head out for a couple hours of hiking. A day hike is a day hike, and you certainly don't need to lug 30 pounds of tents, stoves, and sleeping bags on your back. But this is absolutely no excuse not to be prepared. The forests resound with stories of people who got lost wandering off the trail, getting hurt or worse. The number one Boy Scout rule for the mountains, shorelines, and deserts of Oregon is *be prepared.* Here's a standard list any good outdoors person should adhere to.

Food and Water

Be sure to carry enough food on even the shortest hike, the reason being you never know if you'll get caught in the woods longer than anticipated. Outdoor stores, even grocery stores, carry a great abundance of high-energy trail food that is lightweight and easy to pack. As far as food goes, suit your tastes but also consider what your body needs. Salty foods replenish much needed sodium lost in sweat. Sugary foods maintain, well, your sugar levels, and they also give good bursts of energy (there are all sorts of great sugar-syrups in little packets for the big burst you need to make it up that final hill). Carbohydrates and proteins are a necessity, as your body will need them for energy and a little muscle repair. In general, bring more food than you think you'll need.

Though food is important, not to mention a great thing to have while you're sitting beside that mountain lake you've been walking for hours to get to, it is water that is far and away the real necessity. What will get you in the woods, even kill you, is not starvation but dehydration. Heat sickness, which can quickly degenerate into hyperthermia, can be damaging if not deadly. On a shorter, easier hike, play it safe and bring at least two quarts of water in your pack. An easy and novel solution is the CamelBak and other such products—small backpacks perfect for day hiking, with plenty of room for food, water, and the rest of the essentials. I swear by it, as does everyone I know who uses one. When I'm properly equipped, I'm carrying upwards of six quarts of water.

If you plan on backpacking and need to carry less weight, be sure to invest in a water filter or some other method of purifying. Never drink straight from the creek! Backcountry water has, unfortunately, largely been infected with *Giardia lamblia* and *Cryptosporidium,* two microscopic organisms that cause a plethora of terrible gastrointestinal problems, the likes of which hardly need to be discussed here. Iodine is still a staple for many backpackers, and there are all sorts of newfangled ways to purify water, including ultraviolet light.

Trail Map and Compass

You'd be surprised how empowering a map can be, especially when you can read it well. Never go on a hike without a map. Despite trail signs, getting confused in the backcountry is more common an occurrence than you'd think. Signs can disappear or get blown down. Trails, too, have a way of sometimes getting lost in certain areas, especially in places with many so-called "user trails" (made by people walking off the designated trail). The best maps are topographic, which can be used in conjunction with a compass to easily pinpoint your position. Plus, they give a good sense of the lay of the land—the more detailed the better. You can find nearby trails and even start adventuring cross-country into areas without trails. But it is imperative to know what you're doing first; one wrong adjustment of the compass can land you miles off track.

You can easily obtain maps from outdoors stores and from the management agencies of the area you are visiting. See the *Resources* chapter for names and contact information for those agencies and for USGS topographical maps, National Forest maps, and maps from commercial services.

A compass is an essential tool for keeping you on track. Take a class from an outdoor group, or a store like REI, and learn to use it correctly and effectively. Many people use GPS devices, but they may not work in some areas. A dense forest canopy may run you the risk of losing a signal, so why depend on it? Knowledge is power, and the compass and map make use of that knowledge.

SOCKS

You cannot underestimate the value of good socks, your cushion against blisters, moisture, and soreness. Hiking socks should be thick enough to fit snugly and cushion your feet all around. Buy plenty, especially for extended backpacking trips, or plan to wash the ones you do have. Dirty, damp, and worn-out socks will not do what they are meant to do. Never wear cotton socks!

Wool blend socks help to wick away moisture from your skin. They run around $15 a pair. Believe me, they're worth it. They are also, I have found, wonderfully warm for when you finally get your boots off at camp.

Extra Clothing

Oregon has a classic saying: Don't like the weather? Wait five minutes, it'll change. Those who say this aren't lying. Conditions fluctuate rapidly, so the right clothing is essential. Being wet and cold is not only uncomfortable, but also downright dangerous. Cotton is the worst clothing to wear: When it gets wet, it stays wet. Wool, the old standby, gets wet and heavy. Today's hiking clothes are manufactured to be waterproof and quick-drying, and even to wick moisture away from the skin. Many clothes are also UV resistant. And they're lightweight, to boot.

You should always carry a lightweight jacket that is both waterproof and wind-resistant. Breathable jackets control your heat, as well. Think ahead if your hike will change in altitude: the higher you go, the colder it may get, so bring a hat and gloves, too. And an extra pair of socks can't hurt, either, particularly ones that keep your feet warm and dry.

Flashlight

You know how sometimes in winter you find yourself saying, "Wow, how'd it get so dark so early?" Well, the *last* place you want to say that is on the trail. It happens.

There is some great and lightweight gear you can use. Headlamps are all the rage, and can cast quite a powerful beam; plus, they keep your hands free. No matter what kind of light source you use, make sure you have extra batteries and an extra bulb. You'll find them very handy around the campsite, as well.

Sunglasses and Sunscreen

One of the trickiest things about hiking near or on a mountain peak is that the air is thinner and therefore—don't ask me how it works—the sun gets stronger. Thus, the mountains are a great place to get sunburned, even on a cold day. Bring both sunscreen with a high SPF and sunglasses with good UV resistance. Put on that sunscreen liberally, and at least 30 minutes before you hike. Later, put on more. Other good accessories to have on hand: a wide-brimmed hat and SPF lip balm.

Insect Repellent

Oregon is famous for its mosquitoes. I mean it. Some of the best destinations, like the mountain wildflower meadows or the lakes and rivers, are overrun with mosquitoes in late spring and early summer. There are many ways to avoid this. One, of course, is to just stay home and wait for fall. The other is to equip yourself with one of the many brands of "bug dope" available in any decent store. The most powerful ones contain a toxic chemical called DEET, which some people prefer to avoid. DEET should not be used on children, and adults should use safe levels. There are also handy mosquito nets that can be pulled over the face, and these are available in outdoors stores.

Long sleeves and long pants will help protect you from the other pest: ticks. Ticks are known to carry nasty diseases like Rocky Mountain Spotted Fever, so it's best to tuck those long pants into your socks and check yourself often. The high desert of Oregon, especially along rivers, is one place ticks frequent.

First-Aid Kit

You really only need a few things here, so frugality is okay when you're dealing with minor cuts, blisters, and sore muscles. A little antibiotic ointment, some bandages, and an anti-inflammatory medication like ibuprofen or acetaminophen can be invaluable. Also be aware of who in your party may be allergic to bee stings, as Oregon has a local ground wasp that can be nasty. Be sure to bring an epinephrine pen or other medication for those with allergies.

It never hurts to learn a little CPR, or even have some Wilderness First-Aid training. When you've gained experience hiking among the rocks, cliffs, and swift rivers, you will quickly see how many potential disasters lurk a little too close for comfort. Be prepared!

Swiss Army-Style Pocket Knife

In Oregon, say "Leatherman" and everyone will know what you're talking about. The Leatherman is a modern equivalent of the famous Swiss Army knife, and a good one has the essentials: a few blades, a can opener, scissors, and tweezers. Whether removing splinters or ticks, or cutting moleskin for that blister, this is a must-have tool.

Firestarter

At night, cold can come on quick in the Oregon mountains, and especially the desert. Starting a fire may be the ultimate necessity in an emergency, for warmth as well as a distress signal, and no hiker should be without either a butane lighter or waterproof matches—and in a state as rainy as Oregon, they should be carried in a waterproof container.

HIKING GEAR

Having the right clothing makes for a comfortable hike. Long gone are the days of climbing mountains in wool pants and hiking to the lake in a pair of cut-off jeans. Today's hiking clothes are made from largely synthetic materials designed to do breathe, meaning to release heat away from the body, and stay dry: that is, they both wick moisture away from the body and dry quickly.

Then, too, there are the feet, which are of course the most heavily used body part while hiking. Caring for your feet is the single most important thing you can do, since nothing makes for a more miserable walk than wet, cold feet or blisters. Take care when choosing footwear and don't worry about frugality: A good pair of hiking shoes or boots is one of the best investments you'll make.

Clothing

Synthetic material, as mentioned above, is what it's all about. So what to bring? With a visit to a good outdoors store, you should walk away with ten articles: synthetic T-shirts, both long sleeve and short sleeve; synthetic hiking shorts and pants (and many companies, like Columbia Sportswear, make those wonderful pants with removable leggings—instant shorts!); a fleece pullover, lightweight and medium-weight; lightweight thermal underwear; synthetic-blend socks that wick away moisture and stay dry; rain jacket and pants; lightweight fleece gloves; waterproof gloves; wide-brimmed sun hat; a warm pullover hat. Snug clothes are better than loose, so make sure they fit properly.

Footwear

In general, you should consider three things when looking for good hiking footwear. For one, there is **support:** a good shoe or boot needs to offer both the foot and ankle ideal support, so as to make those rocky crossings safer and less strenuous. The **weight** of footwear is as important; heavy footwear means tiresome walking, especially if you are considering a long-distance jaunt. Talk about dragging your feet! **Flexibility** will save you from that painful culprit: the blister. Flexibility must balance itself with overall boot fit, since slippage is what generally exacerbates the formation of blisters.

You should fit boots in relation to socks: the combination of the two, once mastered, will save you from sitting around the campfire at night, cutting moleskin for those welts.

There are many options for footwear, from trail running shoes and lightweight hiking boots to sturdier backpacking boots. Consider the tread on the boot, the ankle support, and whether the material is waterproof or water-resistant. Once you purchase new footwear, be sure to take a few test runs and break them in before that big backpacking trip. Your feet will applaud you.

CLIMATE AND WEATHER PROTECTION

Weather in Oregon is diverse and unpredictable. Wind, pouring rain, snow and ice, blazing sun, high and low humidity, all of these are part of the Oregon experience. It is essential to be prepared. Weather reports, especially those from the National Weather Service, help greatly, but be ready for sudden changes—especially along the coast, in the high desert, and in the mountains.

THE PACIFIC CREST TRAIL

The most famous long-distance trail through Oregon is the Pacific Crest Trail (PCT), part of the 2,650-mile trail that passes through three states between Canada and Mexico. The Beaver State has its fair share of this historic and well-used National Scenic Trail, and its 430-mile stretch is usually snow-free between July and September. There's a lot to see: the Siskiyou Mountains, Crater Lake National Park, the Oregon Cascades with its long line of volcanic peaks, and the Columbia Gorge National Scenic Area.

The PCT accounts for a number of popular day hikes, especially in Oregon's famed wilderness areas: Mount Hood, Three Sisters, and Sky Lakes to name a few. Along the way, the trail passes everything from errant graves to lava fields to the incredible Timberline Lodge.

Seasons

Oregon has roughly four seasons, and each region reflects those seasons differently. Everywhere in the state, summer, the peak season, tends to have higher temperatures (though the people of Bend, Oregon, still talk about the time it snowed on the Fourth of July). As late summer approaches, so does the occasional rain and sleet.

Autumn, too, makes for beautiful days, and is my favorite time to hike. The color displays are at a height, and days can be significantly cooler, thus making for a sweat-free ramble.

As winter approaches, so does the wind, rain, and snow. For the most part, a significant number of Oregon's mountains are snowed-in and inaccessible all winter long: check with local agencies before trying a hike in an unfamiliar place. Roads, too, tend to be snowed in, and access to trailheads can be nonexistent. Winter in Oregon, at least in the mountains (including the Cascades, the Blues, the Wallowas, and the high elevations of the Siskiyous), can stretch from November to July.

Spring brings mud and more rain, but also increasing wildflower shows.

Rain Gear

What more needs to be said? Oregonians aren't said to have webbed feet for nothing. Rain gear is crucial, and this is largely why Oregonians tend to not care if it's raining. It's not like hikers are the little kids in front of the window, glumly watching the rain, wishing they could go out. On the contrary, nothing stops hikers in Oregon.

Durable, breathable rain gear (along with waterproof or water-resistant footwear) is an investment that will allow access to many places in Oregon year-round. For the most part, the Oregon coast, the foothills of the Cascades, most of the Columbia River Gorge, and low-elevation valleys are open year-round. Take advantage of it! Much of Oregon's beauty is due to the rains. What else keeps Oregon so green?

SAFETY

Like many Western U.S. states, it is possible to run into rattlesnakes, mountain lions, and bears—not to mention poison oak and biting bugs. Here's a little information about the locals.

NON-TECHNICAL SUMMIT HIKES

Oregon is a mountain climber's dream. With numerous peaks exceeding the 10,000-foot elevation range, there are plenty of opportunities to get on top of the world and enjoy the stunning views that come with them. That being said, it is important to differentiate the kind of mountain climbs featured in this book as available to the common hiker.

A "technical" summit climb requires not just skill but equipment such as ropes, harnesses, protection gear, and other specialized tools like ice axes and crampons. Mount Hood is the most popular of all technical climbs in Oregon, and a summit climb of this kind should never be done without experienced partners and a great deal of training and conditioning. It is a sport unto itself.

Hikes recommended in this book are "non-technical" summits, meaning climbing gear is not required. The mountain hikes covered in this book are those that can be summited on trails recognized by management agencies and detailed on maps. They are generally a long, steep climb, but far safer than climbing extremely steep slopes and crossing glaciers. Think of a non-technical climb, also known as "scrambling," as a really tough hike, where the path may get arduous and you may have to cross some snow now and again.

No matter the climb – whether it be South Sister, Mount McLoughlin, or Eagle Cap – always be prepared as you would for any other hike, if not more so. Be sure to carry more than enough food, water, and clothing, and remember that any change in weather can prove disastrous. Also, pace yourself; any non-technical climb can be especially taxing if you are out-of-shape or tired. Practice on smaller climbs before attempting to bag the big peaks.

Wildlife

Rattlesnakes

Of the 15 species of snakes in Oregon, only *Crotalus viridis,* the Western Pacific Rattlesnake, is poisonous. They are most active in the spring, summer, and early fall and can be found in parts of the Willamette Valley, the Cascade Mountain foothills, the Siskiyou Mountains, and parts of Eastern Oregon. Their most easily identifiable characteristic, of course, is that heart-stopping rattle. And it's good to stop, because once it has warned you, a rattlesnake is going to try to retreat from you. Stand still; rattlers rarely attack a nonmoving object.

Although rattlesnake bites are certainly painful, they are rarely lethal. Not all rattlesnake bites contain venom, either. If you are bitten, the best thing you can do is call 911 and drive to a hospital. Remove any restrictive clothing and don't attempt to apply a tight tourniquet. Remain calm and avoid running, which can speed venom through the body.

Mountain Lions

Cougars, also known as mountain lions, are the largest of the big cats in Oregon. They range pretty much anywhere, and have even passed through towns and cities in the state, especially when following migrating prey such as elk. However, in all likelihood, you will never see one. Cougars will usually avoid humans at all cost. In fact, many people have been near one and never realized it.

In mountain lion country, keep children and pets close. Should you encounter a cougar, don't turn away and don't run. Instead, make yourself appear as large as possible by raising your arms, waving a stick, and opening your coat. Back away slowly, maintaining your pose and speaking loudly.

Black Bears

Like cougars, black bears range widely and try to steer clear of humans. Be alert and make a little noise in bear country to let them know you're coming. If you do see one—which is unlikely, but not impossible—you'll know what it is, since black bears are the only species of bear in Oregon.

If you do encounter a bear, don't run and don't look it in the eye: bears interpret this as a sign of aggression. Instead, back away slowly. If a bear does happen to charge you, stay calm and be prepared to fight back. You can make yourself look bigger by waving your arms and opening your coat. If you have a dog, keep it leashed; an over-protective dog can put a bear on the defensive. One of the worst-case scenarios is to come between a mother bear and her cubs.

A more common way to run into a bear is at camp. Bears are attracted by not only food, and sweet food at that, but by fragrances like toothpaste and perfume. Really. If bears know, or think, that there's something tasty in your tent or your bag, like that honey-almond granola you brought, they'll have at it. Though Oregon doesn't have the same issues with bears as, say, Yosemite National Park in California, it's still wise to hide your food. Backpackers should use a bear-proof canister for overnight trips. You can also make use of a food-hang, where you hang your food by rope from a tree limb, a minimum of 20 feet off the ground and 10 feet from the tree trunk. Tie your rope to a rock and throw it over a branch at least one inch in diameter and four inches at the trunk to accomplish this.

Insects and Plants

Aside from the large mammals and reptiles, it's the little things that get you: mosquitoes, ticks, poison oak, and stinging nettles. Here's how to avoid them.

Mosquitoes

Mosquitoes in Oregon are by far the peskiest pest of all. Come spring and summer, the valleys and mountains—even the deserts—bloom with the obnoxious buzzing and incessant biting. All this can make for a thoroughly annoying outdoor experience spent swatting and slapping.

Mosquitoes are not merely annoying; they may even be dangerous. As with other states, Oregon has had its first few experiences with West Nile Virus, though it has mostly been confined to a few infections in people, birds, and horses. Better safe than sorry. Know before you go: As snows melt in the mountains, mosquitoes are born, and this typically happens from June to August. Visiting a marshy wildlife refuge in spring? Expect skeeters. Even in deserts, you can expect hordes of them along rivers.

The worst of the worst is the Asian tiger mosquito, a non-native species thought to have been brought to America in automobile tires that contained stagnant water. You'll know them when you see them by their stripes. It's best to carry repellent and netting, or even to avoid certain areas in the peak hatching season.

Ticks

You'll want to corral a friend into a good old "tick check." Ticks find their way into the weirdest of places in an effort to lock in and draw from your blood. The frontline defense is long pants and long sleeves, and to check both your skin and your clothing after hiking. If you find a tick burrowed in, pull it straight out carefully with tweezers, grasping it firmly from the surface of the skin. It's important to get the body and head out, or you can risk infection.

Ticks are most active in spring and summer, in areas of tall grasses and shrubs. Of the four varieties of ticks in Oregon, only the Western black-legged tick is a carrier of Lyme disease. This little tick is mostly black; the larger brown ones are harmless. It's generally said that if you can save a removed tick and take it to a doctor for testing, that's a safe bet. If within a few days or a few weeks you begin to experience flu-like symptoms, see a doctor post-haste.

Dogs, too, are susceptible to ticks, so make sure to check them carefully when you've been hiking in susceptible areas.

Poison Oak

It's been said many times before, but let's say it again: "Leaves of three, let them be." Once you learn to recognize *Toxicodendron diversilobum*, it will become very familiar to you, especially in areas like southern Oregon, the Willamette Valley, and the Columbia Gorge. Otherwise, the brutal rash that can itch for weeks will teach you the hard way to remember. Even as the leaves dry, they still contain the chemical that affects us. Should you come into contact with poison oak, or think you may have, wash thoroughly with warm water and soap as soon as possible. There are several products and soap available that can deal with exposure to poison oak on the trail. As I've learned from experience, dogs pick it up on their fur. Rather than petting, offer your pooch a nice, hot bath.

Avoiding Poison Oak: Remember the old Boy Scout saying: "Leaves of three, let them be."

Stinging Nettles

This member of the nettle family likes to grow in clumps in the Coast Range and in the desert. Heart-shaped, coarse-toothed leaves on a stem bristling with little white hairs gives it away. If you come in contact with those hairs, the resulting sting will let you know immediately that your identification is successful. You'll have to ride out the sting for 24 hours, wondering all the while how it is possible—and delectable—to boil and eat nettles safely!

Safety on the Trail

Stories abound of unfortunate mishaps where people get lost in the wilderness for days on end, and every year seems to bring a new tale of woe. Most of these stories involve two kinds of hikers: the one who hikes alone, and the one who gets separated from a larger group. One wrong turn off a trail, or simply not paying attention in the midst of a huge mountain meadow, can have dire consequences. Weather, too, can have an impact on your safety—for example, getting caught on a ridgeline in a lightning storm (and this one comes from experience!) calls for quick thinking.

Should you find yourself lost, your first priority is to remain calm. Know that it's far better to stay put where you are than to try to keep moving; rescuers will be looking for where you were last known to be (this is why it's so important to fill out wilderness permits at trailheads). Emergency gear, especially a whistle and signaling device, will come in handy here, since rescuers will be listening and looking for signs.

What's the best way to avoid trouble? Simply this: Always tell someone where you'll be. Tell someone at home your travel plans and register with a local ranger station, especially if your plan is to hike into a remote wilderness area. Be specific and detail the area you're visiting, the times you intend to travel, and how long you think you'll be out. It's the responsible thing to do, and it saves searchers much time and effort should you become lost.

Driving Safely

If you think weather can wreak havoc on a trail, try a road. Many of the approaches to trailheads in Oregon require driving on dirt roads that can quickly turn to mud or, worse, can result in a washout. Always check road conditions before you go by calling the Oregon Department of Transportation at 511 or checking www.tripcheck.com. Detailed weather reports and forecasts are available through the National Weather Service online at www.nws.noaa.gov.

Make sure that your car is properly equipped. Fuel up often, check the oil and the brakes, and make sure you've got a spare tire. Have emergency road equipment like snow chains, flashers, and a cell phone.

Make sure your directions are accurate (even mine!). Carry a good atlas of Oregon, like the DeLorme or Benchmark, and don't rely exclusively on Internet maps or GPS devices. If all else fails, ask directions.

Check snow levels. Every year in recent memory has seen individuals or families getting trapped in the snow in the mountains. Just because it's raining in Portland doesn't mean it is at Mount Hood; most likely, it's piling up snow quick. Avoid roads closed in winter or otherwise impassable. Forest Service roads are not shortcuts; stick to main routes and get there safely.

HIKING ETHICS

Trail Etiquette

As wonderful as it is to think like Henry David Thoreau and head for the woods for a little soul-searching solitude, don't expect to find it all the time. Expect instead a lot of other intrepid hikers looking for their own Walden Pond, too. Here are some simple rules to follow to assure a good time for everyone.

WILDERNESS ETHICS

Congressionally designated Wilderness Areas are unique, and are preserved under certain criteria. It's important to maintain the wilderness experience for everyone by limiting human impact. Here are some basic guidelines:

Campfires: Gone are the days of singing around the campfire. For the most part, campfires are discouraged – if not outright prohibited – due to catastrophic forest fires rampant in the Western United States. Land management agencies have decreed that cooking is best done on a backpacking stove. Lighting can be provided by a variety of devices, from flashlights to headlamps.

Water sources: It is imperative to keep Oregon's waters clean. When camping near any lake, stream, or river, give yourself at least 100 feet distance from the waterline before pitching that tent. Likewise, wash all your cooking gear, socks, and hands by carrying water at least 100 feet away from the water source.

Campsites: When you pitch a tent, be aware of where you are plopping down. A misplaced tent can crush sensitive flowers and damage an area for years. You should always camp on a durable surface, such as rock, or even on sand or dead and dry organic matter – never on live vegetation. This helps maintain the environment for all and prevents area closures for rehabilitation.

Garbage: No one is impressed by a trashed campsite. Who wants to see another campfire ring filled with broken glass and blackened cans, or a campsite ringed by toilet paper wads? No matter what you bring, pack out your garbage. Neither burn nor bury it. That goes for human waste, too.

Maintain the silence. You and everyone else come to the wilderness to get away from the usual hustle and bustle of civilization. Be courteous to all the other hikers by refraining from undue noise. Avoid loud conversations, shouting, and above all, cell phones. This way, too, you're more likely to encounter wildlife and hear the falling water and wind in the trees.

Yield to other users accordingly. Standard rules on yielding apply for the three main user groups—hikers, horses, and bikers. In general, bikes must yield to everyone, and hikers should yield to horses.

Stay on maintained trails. Evidence of breaking this rule is everywhere. Degraded switchbacks and the ubiquitous "user trail" show for certain that people are taking shortcuts and wandering off-trail. Don't use closed trails or enter closed areas; often, they have been closed for restoration or because of overuse. Wandering off-trail tramples vegetation and in the end may force management agencies to limit access for everyone.

Hiking with Children

Always keep children close, especially in areas with cliffs and fast-moving water. Consider the trail carefully before taking children, as many routes are too difficult for them. By choosing appropriate trails, you'll make trips memorable and enjoyable for everyone.

Hiking with Dogs

It's possible that there's no more dog-friendly state than Oregon. That being so, you're sure to run into dogs on the trail or to want to bring your own. And what could be more charming than a dog carrying its own pack with little mitts on its paws?

Regardless, dogs open a whole new can of worms in the outdoors. For one thing, chasing wildlife is a leading reason why dogs get lost in the wilderness. A dog on a leash is a dog that goes home again.

Because of conflicts between hikers and pets, dogs are no longer allowed on many trails in Oregon, or are restricted to a leash on others. Some trails, like the Deschutes River Trail in Central Oregon, no longer allow dogs off-leash, but this may not be obvious at the trailhead. It's best to call the area's managing agency for up-to-date rules. If a posted sign says that dogs must be on a leash, follow it strictly. Otherwise, you could well end up with a ticket.

If a dog is allowed off-leash, as in many forest and wilderness areas, take care that your dog responds appropriately to verbal commands, for the dog's own safety. Why worry? Carry a leash or get good dog training and just enjoy the trip for you and your dog both.

Avoiding Crowds

On the one hand, you can hike into a place like Big Indian Gorge on a summer weekend and not see a soul but for a few deer. On the other hand, you can go to Multnomah Falls, trying to get to the top to hike on up to Larch Mountain and fight your way through throngs of tourists, day-trippers, kids with ice cream cones, and parents in flip-flops pushing strollers. What to do? With a little foresight, you can find a bit of solitude after all.

Avoid the weekends. Weekends are notorious for the so-called "weekend warrior" out for a Saturday afternoon. If you get the chance, take your hike when everyone else is at work. From Tuesday through Thursday seems to be the best, and quietest, time.

Be the first one at the trailhead. If you arrive at a trailhead at around 10 or 11 A.M. like most people do, you'll have trouble finding a parking spot and staying out of the parade. But get there at 6 A.M.? Now you're talking. More than likely, you'll be the only one there.

Hike more than just summer. For most of Oregon, the on-season is summer. Memorial Day (which can be horrendous) and Labor Day (even worse) and everything in between means everyone is out for that brief respite between rains. But once the kids are in school and everyone is secure in the usual routine, *now* is the time to get out.

Avoid the popular hikes. If you have a need for peace and quiet on an August weekend afternoon, then maybe Crater Lake is not your best bet. But then nearby Mount Bailey might be. Choose off-the-beaten-path journeys and you're less likely to see the casual tourist.

Hike in the rain. Any bad weather will do, and if you have good gear you can be out looking at wildflowers in the spring rain while the rest of the world is home keeping their feet warm. Oregon is a place of many moods: gale-force winds, fog, clouds, and rain. These make life more interesting—and memorable.

Leave No Trace

As Henry David Thoreau once said, "In wilderness is the preservation of the world." So how do we preserve our wilderness? The Center for Outdoor Ethics offers these simple dictums to "Leave only footprints and take only pictures":

Plan ahead and prepare. Know the special regulations of the area you are visiting. Be prepared. Schedule your trips to avoid high-use times. Visit in small groups. Repackage your food to minimize waste.

Travel and camp on durable surfaces. Use established trails and campsites. Keep campsites small. In pristine areas, disperse use to prevent the creation of camps or trails.

Dispose of waste properly. Pack it in, pack it out. Deposit human waste in a "cathole" dug 6–8 inches at least 200 feet from water, camp, and trails; cover and disguise when finished. Pack out toilet paper and hygiene products. To wash yourself or dishes, carry water 200 feet away from streams and lakes. If you must use soap, make sure it's biodegradable. Scatter the water when done.

Leave what you find. Examine, but do not touch or remove, cultural or historic structures and artifacts. Leave rocks, plants, and natural objects as you find them. Avoid introducing non-native species. Do not build structures or furniture or dig trenches.

Minimize campfire impacts. Use a stove for cooking, a candle for lighting. Where fires are permitted, use established fire rings, pans, or mounds. Keep fires small and use only ground material to burn. Burn wood and coals to ash, douse completely, and scatter the cool ashes.

Respect wildlife. Remember that you are only a visitor in the wilderness, but it is home to animals. Observe wildlife from a distance, and do not approach or follow. Never feed animals. Store your food securely and control your pets. Avoid wildlife during times of mating, nesting, and raising young.

Be considerate of other visitors. Respect others and protect the quality of their experience. Be courteous. Camp away from other people. Let nature's sounds prevail.

This copyrighted information has been reprinted with permission from the Leave No Trace Center for Outdoor Ethics. For more information or materials, please visit www.lnt.org or call 303/442-8222 or 800/332-4100.

Permits and Land Use

There are different permits you'll need for each of Oregon's 115 state parks, 13 national forest, and five state forests. Many trails on National Forest land, but not all, require the Northwest Forest Pass to park within a quarter-mile of a posted trailhead. These cost $5 a day or $30 for a yearly pass.

Most wilderness areas on National Forest land require a free wilderness permit (available at trailheads) to enter. There are exceptions, such as the Obsidian Trail or the Pamelia Lake area, which require a free special permit beforehand, secured simply by calling the ranger station.

Oregon State Parks vary widely. Some require a day-use fee, while others are free. Many of the more popular parks require a day-use fee, but the waysides—especially along beaches—tend to be free.

The Bureau of Land Management, National Forest Service, and National Park Service manage Oregon's national monuments, national recreation areas, Crater Lake National Park, and the Columbia Gorge National Scenic Area. In addition to the information provided in this book, be sure to contact the appropriate agency for up-to-date information on fees and permits.

OREGON'S COLUMBIA RIVER GORGE CAMPING

© OSCAR WILLIAMS/123rf.com

BEST CAMPGROUNDS

Most Scenic
Piety Island Boat-In, **page 63.**
Cove Creek, **page 64.**
Paul Dennis, **page 67.**

Families
Cascade Locks Marine Park, **page 39.**
Hoover Group Camp, **page 64.**

Fishing
Trillium Lake, **page 48.**
Gone Creek, **page 54.**
Pelton, **page 71.**

Hiking
Eagle Creek, **page 38.**
Toll Gate, **page 45.**

Waterfalls
Ainsworth State Park, **page 31.**

Waterfront Campgrounds
Lost Lake, **page 42.**
Trillium Lake, **page 48.**
Meditation Point, **page 56.**

Wildlife-Viewing
Pelton, **page 71.**

The Columbia River area is a living history lesson, a geological wonder, and a recreation paradise. The waterway is probably best known as the route the Lewis and Clark expedition followed two centuries ago. It's also famous for carving out a deep gorge through the Cascade Range that divides Oregon. Nearby Mount Hood and its surrounding national forest and many lakes provide almost unlimited opportunities for camping, fishing, and hiking.

The Columbia spans hundreds of square miles and is linked to a watershed that in turn is connected to the Snake River, which covers thousands of square miles. I-84 provides a major route along the southern shore of the Columbia, but the river view is not what you will remember. After you depart the traffic of the Portland area, driving west to east, you will pass along the wooded foothills of the Cascade Range to your south. When you pass Hood River, the world suddenly changes. The trees disappear.

In their place are rolling grasslands that seem to extend for as far as you can see. It is often hot and dry here, with strong winds blowing straight down the river.

However, the entire time you are within the realm of Mount Hood. At 11,239 feet, Hood is a beautiful mountain, shaped like a diamond, its flanks supporting many stellar destinations with campsites and small lakes set in forest. Snowmelt feeds many major rivers as well as numerous smaller streams, which roll down Mount Hood in every direction.

The transformation of the Gorge-area landscape from forest to grasslands to high desert is quick and striking. Particularly remarkable is how the Deschutes River has cut a path through the desert bluffs. And while the Deschutes is one of Oregon's better steelhead streams, unless you're fishing, you are more likely to encounter a desert chukar on a rock perch than anything water-bound.

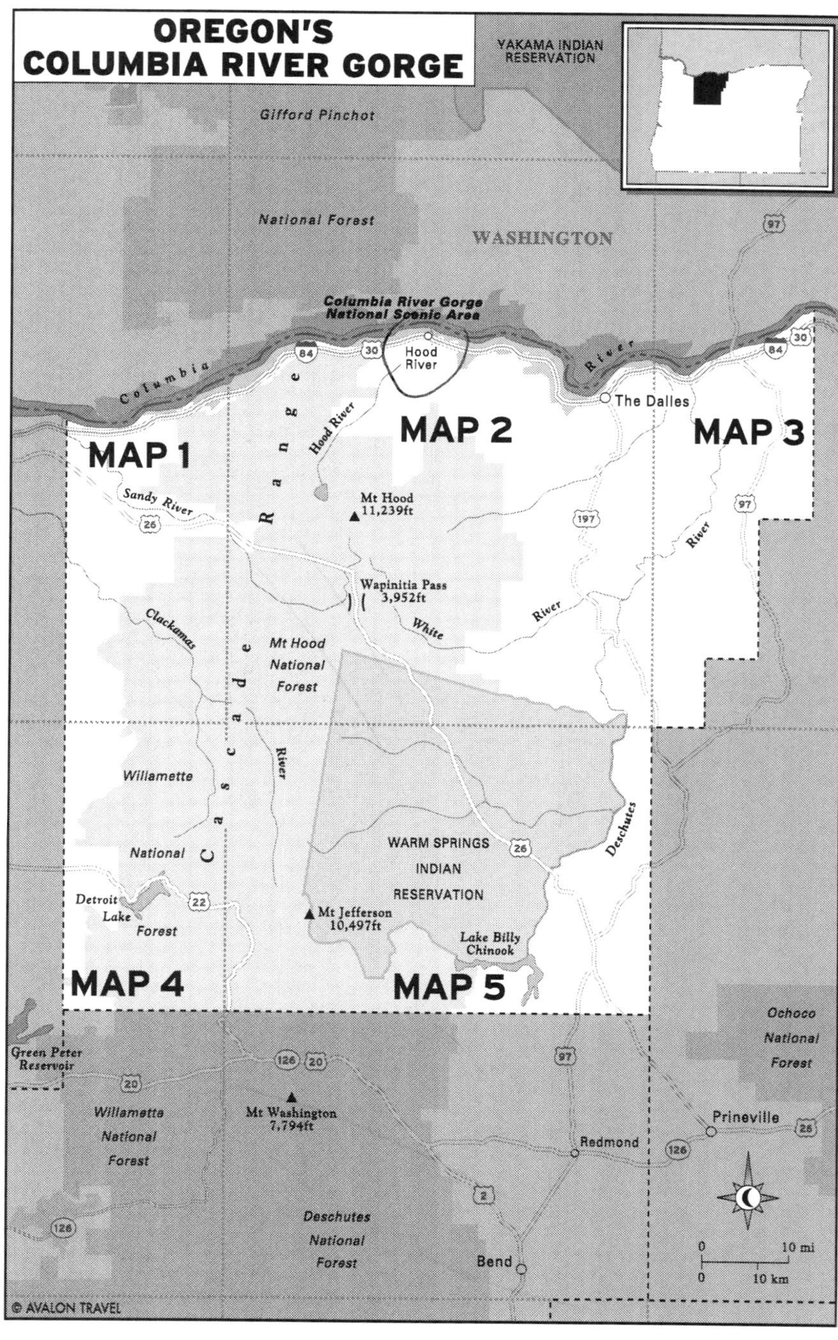

OREGON'S COLUMBIA RIVER GORGE
YAKAMA INDIAN RESERVATION
Gifford Pinchot
National Forest
WASHINGTON
Columbia River Gorge National Scenic Area
Columbia River
Hood River
The Dalles
MAP 1
MAP 2
MAP 3
MAP 4
MAP 5
Hood River
Sandy River
Mt Hood 11,239ft
Wapinitia Pass 3,952ft
White River
Clackamas
Cascade Range
Mt Hood National Forest
Willamette National Forest
River
Deschutes
WARM SPRINGS INDIAN RESERVATION
Detroit Lake
Mt Jefferson 10,497ft
Lake Billy Chinook
Green Peter Reservoir
Ochoco National Forest
Mt Washington 7,794ft
Willamette National Forest
Prineville
Redmond
Deschutes National Forest
Bend
0 10 mi
0 10 km
© AVALON TRAVEL

Map 1

Campgrounds 1-19

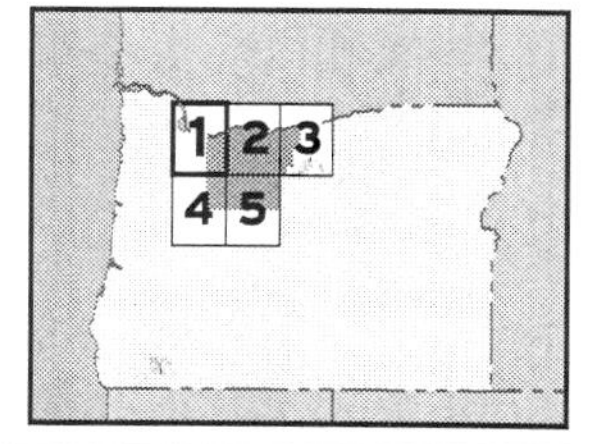

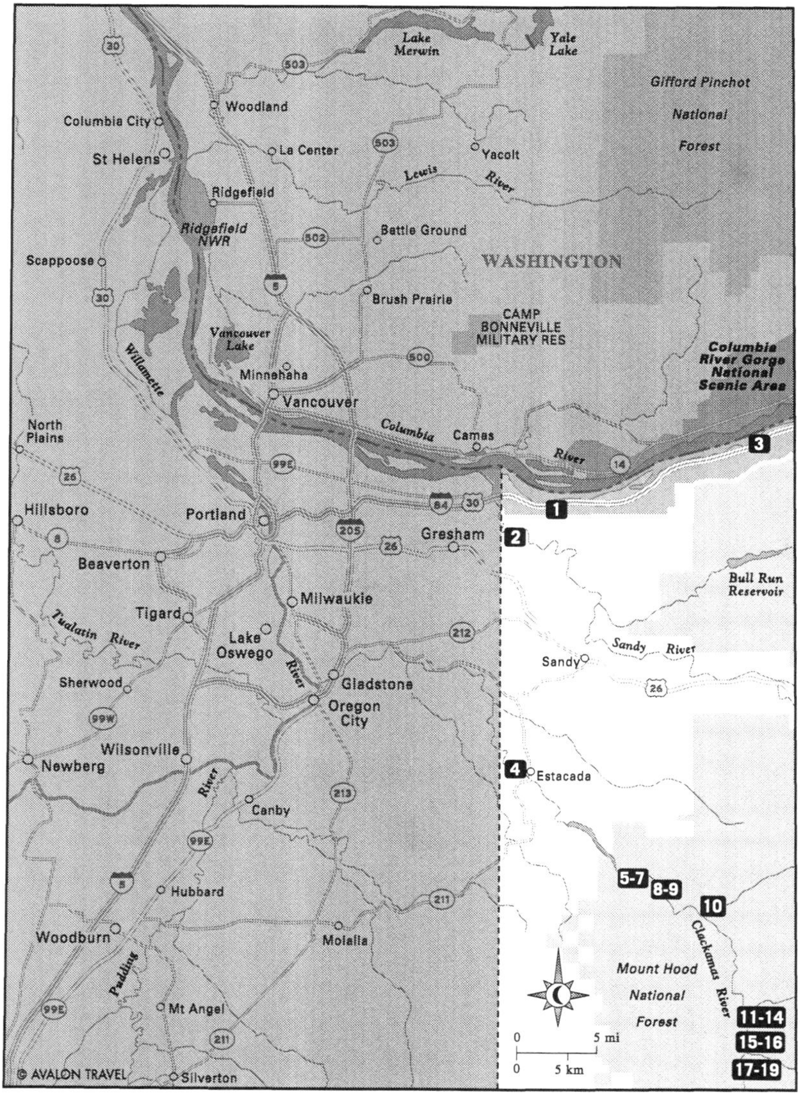

CAMPING

Map 2

Campgrounds 20-70

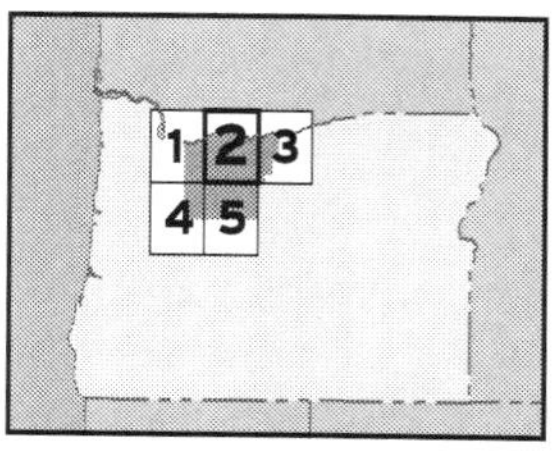

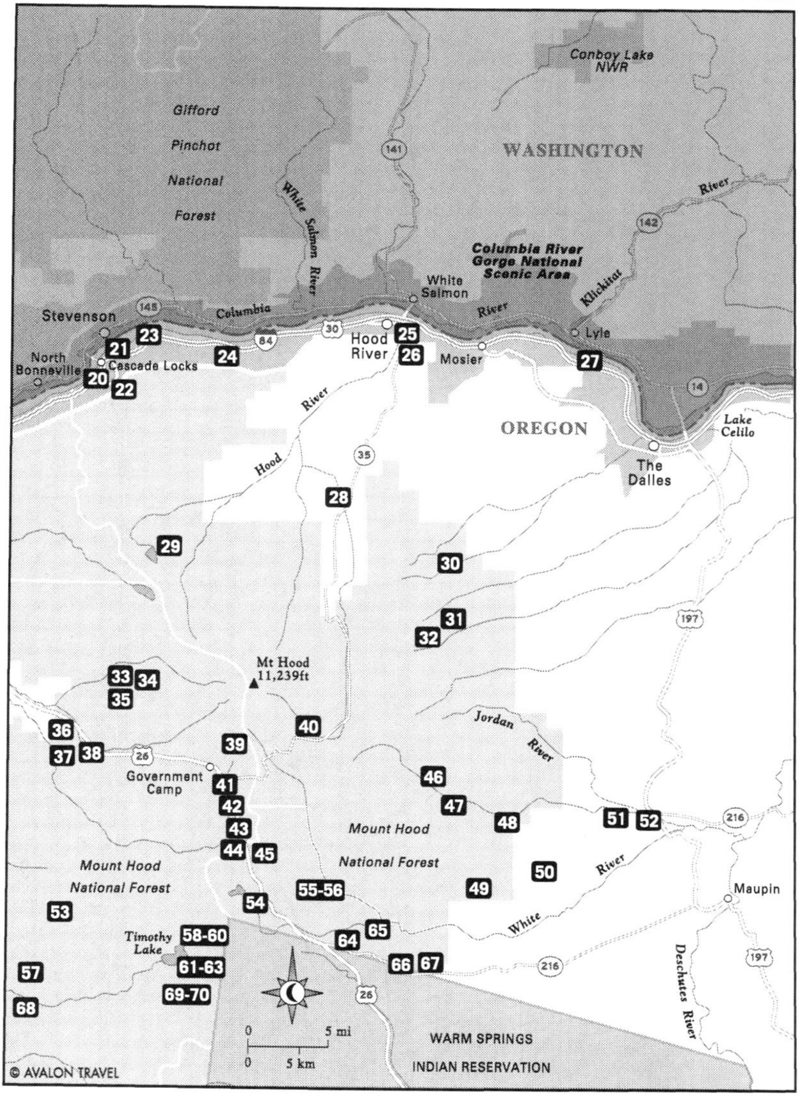

Gifford Pinchot National Forest
Conboy Lake NWR
WASHINGTON
White Salmon River
Klickitat River
Columbia River Gorge National Scenic Area
White Salmon
Columbia River
Stevenson
North Bonneville
Cascade Locks
Hood River
Mosier
Lyle
OREGON
Lake Celilo
The Dalles
Hood River
Mt Hood 11,239ft
Jordan River
Government Camp
Mount Hood National Forest
Mount Hood National Forest
White River
Maupin
Deschutes River
Timothy Lake
WARM SPRINGS INDIAN RESERVATION
0 5 mi
0 5 km
20 21 22 23 24 25 26 27 28 29 30 31 32 33 34 35 36 37 38 39 40 41 42 43 44 45 46 47 48 49 50 51 52 53 54 55-56 57 58-60 61-63 64 65 66 67 68 69-70

Map 3

Campgrounds 71-73

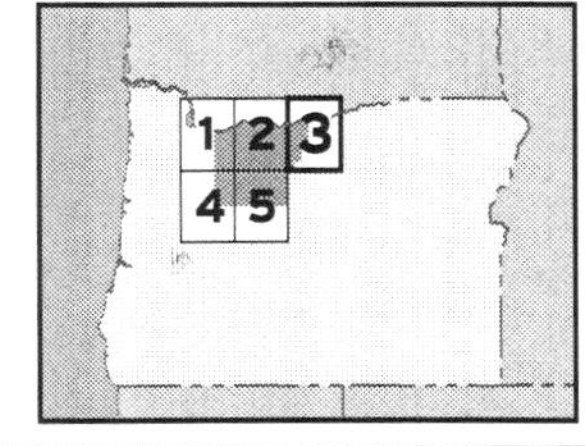

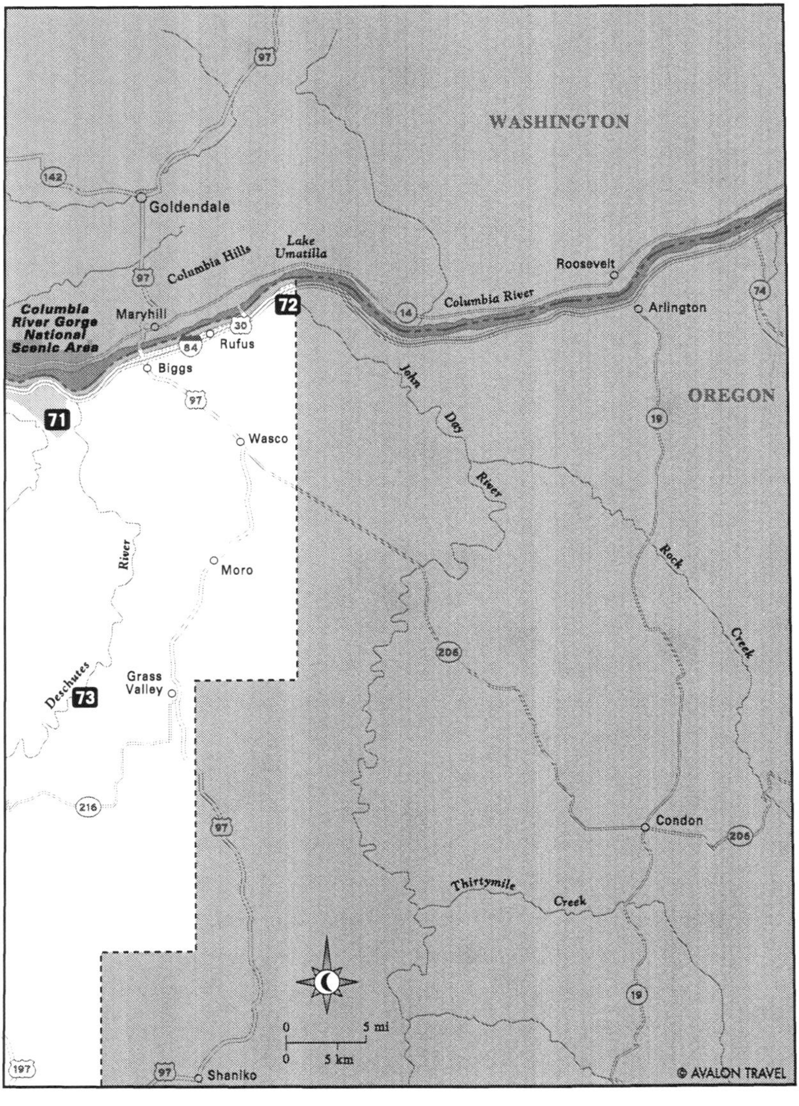

Map 4

Campgrounds 74-82

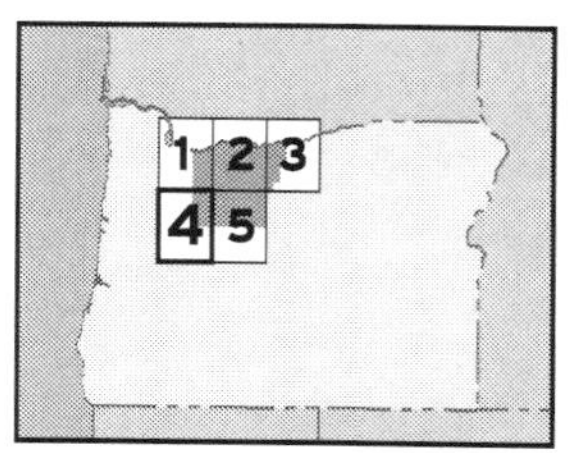

Four Corners
Pudding River
Turner
Stayton
Little North Santiam River
74
75
Lyons
Mill City
Gates
North Santiam River
76
Detroit
80-82
77-79
Detroit Lake
Scio
Thomas Creek
Santiam State Forest
Willamette National Forest
Lebanon
Middle Santiam River
Green Peter Reservoir
Willamette National Forest
Brownsville
Sweet Home
Calapooia River
McKenzie River
Belknap Springs
Leaburg
Cougar Reservoir
0 5 mi
0 5 km
Willamette National Forest
© AVALON TRAVEL

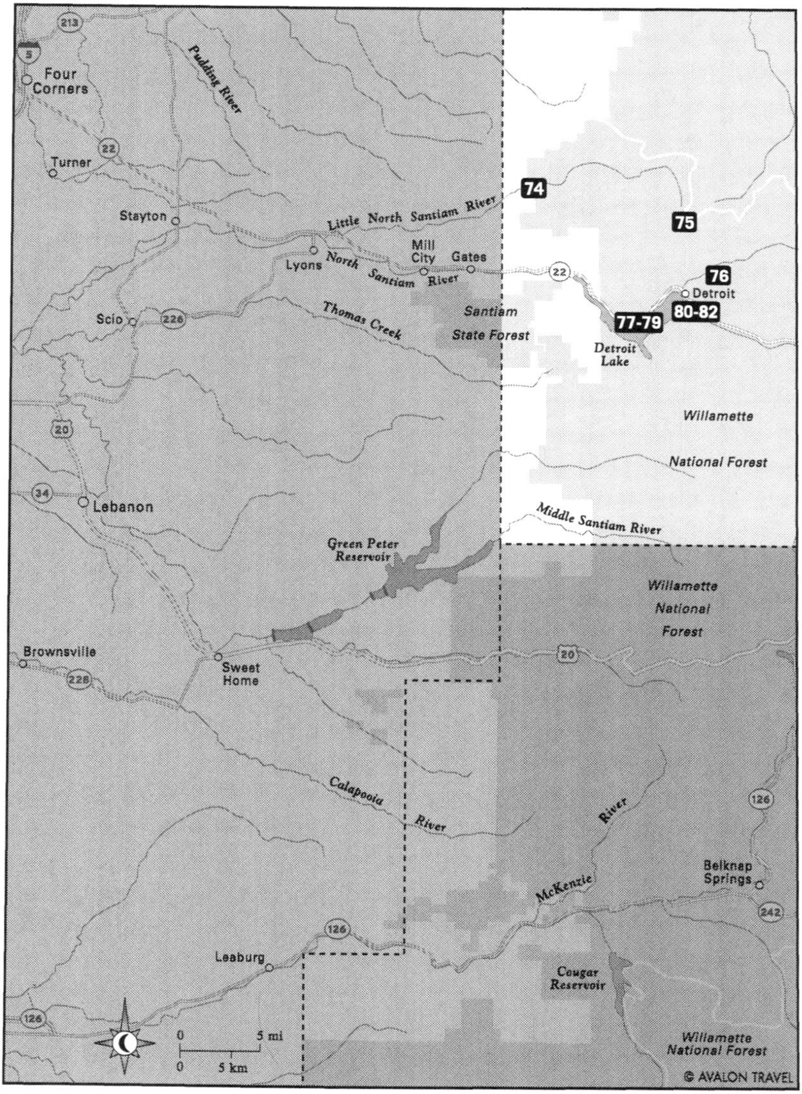

Map 5

Campgrounds 83-102

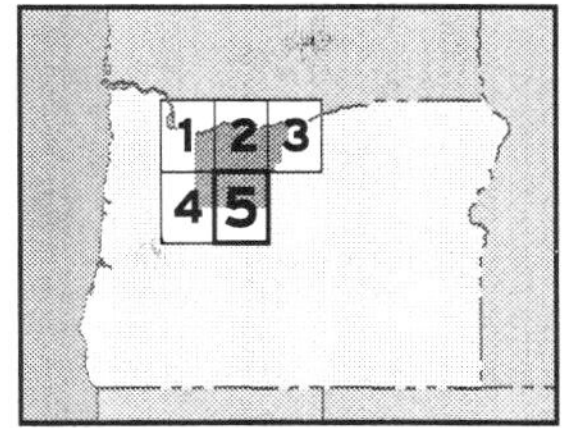

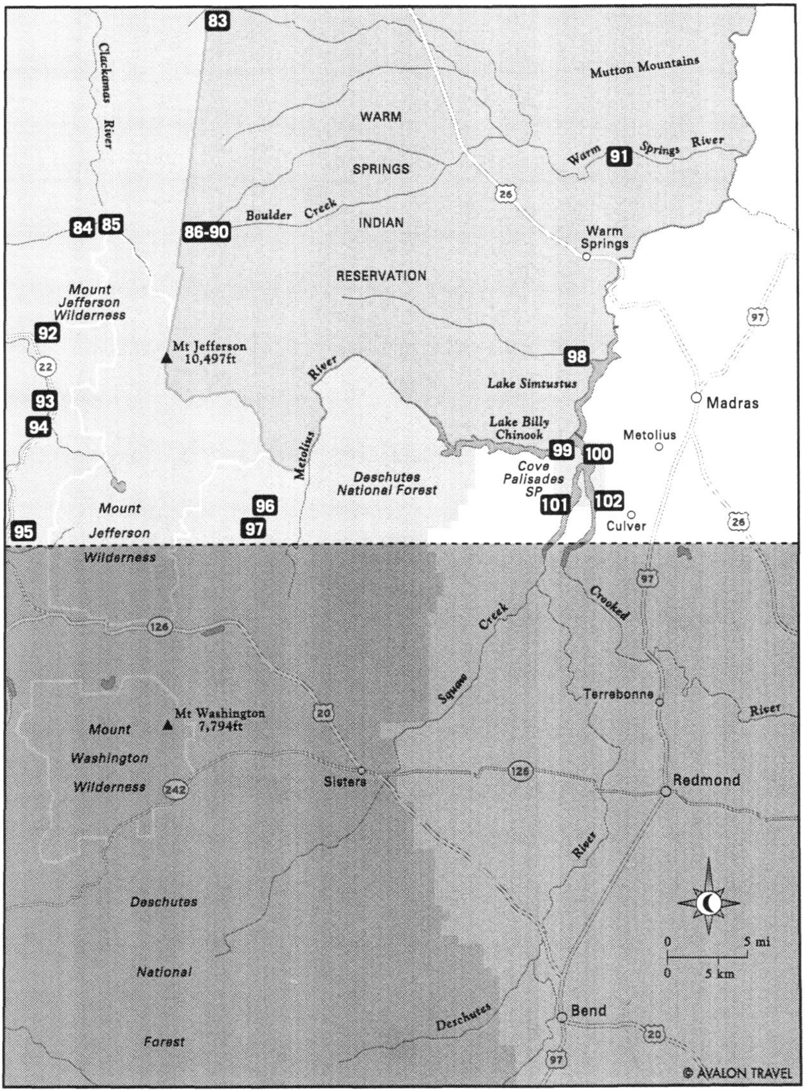

83
Clackamas River
Mutton Mountains
WARM
SPRINGS
INDIAN
RESERVATION
Warm Springs River
91
26
Boulder Creek
84 85
86-90
Warm Springs
Mount Jefferson Wilderness
92
22
Mt Jefferson 10,497ft
97
98
Lake Simtustus
Madras
Metolius River
93
94
Lake Billy Chinook
99
100
Metolius
Cove Palisades SP
Deschutes National Forest
101
102
96
97
Culver
26
95
Mount Jefferson Wilderness
97
Crooked River
126
Squaw Creek
Terrebonne
Mt Washington 7,794ft
20
Mount Washington Wilderness
242
Sisters
126
Redmond
River
Deschutes National Forest
0 5 mi
0 5 km
Deschutes
Bend
20
97
© AVALON TRAVEL

CAMPING

1 CROWN POINT RV PARK

Scenic rating: 6

near the Columbia River

This little park is located near the Columbia River along scenic U.S. 30. Nearby Crown Point State Park is open during the day and offers views of the Columbia River Gorge and the historic Vista House, a memorial built in 1918 to honor Oregon's pioneers. Multnomah Falls offers another possible side trip.

Campsites, facilities: There are 22 sites with full or partial hookups for RVs of any length; some sites are pull-through. Drinking water and picnic tables are provided. Restrooms with flush toilets and coin showers, modem access, horseshoe pits, a hair salon, and a coin laundry are available. A store and ice are within walking distance. Leashed pets are permitted.

Reservations, fees: Reservations are accepted. Sites are $30 per night. Open year-round.

Directions: From Portland on I-84 eastbound, drive 16 miles to Exit 22 and Corbett. Take that exit and turn right on Corbett Hill Road. Drive 1.5 miles to a Y intersection with East Historic Columbia River Highway. Bear left and drive 0.25 mile to the park on the right.

Note: The recommended route has a 10 percent grade for 1.5 miles. An alternate route: From Portland on I-84 eastbound, drive to Exit 18/Lewis and Clark State Park. Take that exit and drive to East Historic Columbia River Highway and continue seven miles to the park on the right.

Contact: Crown Point RV Park, 503/695-5207, fax 503/695-3217.

2 OXBOW REGIONAL PARK

Scenic rating: 7

on the Sandy River

This 1,200-acre park along the Sandy River, a short distance from the Columbia River Gorge, is a designated national scenic waterway. Fishing, non-motorized boating, and swimming are permitted here. The water is usually calm, and canoes, kayaks, and rafts are allowed. About 200 acres of the park are old-growth Douglas fir forest. There are several miles of hiking trails.

Campsites, facilities: There are 67 sites for tents or RVs up to 35 feet long; some sites are pull-through. Picnic tables, fire pits, and barbecues are provided. Drinking water, flush and vault toilets, coin showers, firewood, and a playground are available. Boat-launching facilities are nearby. Gates lock at sunset and open at 6:30 A.M. Services are approximately 10 miles away. Some facilities are wheelchair accessible. No pets are permitted.

Reservations, fees: Reservations are not accepted. Sites are $15 per night, $4 per night per additional vehicle. There is a park entrance fee of $4 per vehicle for the first day only. Open year-round.

Directions: From Portland on I-84, drive to Exit 17/Troutdale. Take that exit and drive on the frontage road for 0.5 mile to 257th Street. Turn right (south) on 257th Street and drive three miles to Division Street. Turn left and drive seven miles to the park entrance on the left.

Contact: Metro Regional Parks and Greenspaces, Oxbow Regional Park, 503/663-4708, www.oregonmetro.gov.

3 AINSWORTH STATE PARK

Scenic rating: 8

along the Columbia River Gorge

BEST

Set along the scenic Columbia River Gorge, Ainsworth State Park is waterfall central, with famous Multnomah Falls a highlight. A 1.3-mile trail leads from the campground to Horsetail Falls and the Nesmith Point Trail shares a great view of St. Peter's Dome. Anglers should check out the Bonneville Fish Hatchery about five miles away.

Campsites, facilities: There are 45 sites with full hookups for RVs up to 60 feet long and four walk-in tent sites. Picnic tables and fire grills are provided. Drinking water, restrooms with flush toilets and showers, garbage bins, a dump station, playground, camp host, amphitheater with occasional interpretive programs, and firewood are available. Some facilities are wheelchair accessible. Leashed pets are permitted.

Reservations, fees: Reservations are not accepted. Sites are $12–20 per night, $10–17 per night for walk-in tent sites, and $5 per night per additional vehicle. Some credit cards are accepted. Open mid-March–late October, weather permitting.

Directions: From Portland on I-84 eastbound, drive 35 miles to Exit 35. Turn southwest on the Columbia River Scenic Highway and continue a short distance to the park; the park is 17 miles east of Troutdale. An alternate route is to take the historic Columbia River Highway, a designated scenic highway, all the way from Portland (37 miles).

Contact: Ainsworth State Park, 503/695-2301 or 800/551-6949, www.oregonstateparks.org.

4 MILO McIVER STATE PARK

Scenic rating: 7

on the Clackamas River

Though only 45 minutes from Portland, this park is far enough off the beaten track to provide a feeling of separation from the metropolitan area. It sits along the banks of the Clackamas River and has a boat ramp. There is fishing for salmon and steelhead in season; check current regulations. Trails for hiking are available, and a 4.5-mile equestrian trail is also accessible; bicycles are not allowed on trails. A fish hatchery is a nearby point of interest. Every September, actors participate in a Civil War reenactment here.

Campsites, facilities: There are 44 sites with partial hookups for RVs up to 50 feet long, nine primitive tent sites, one hiker/bicyclist site, and three group tent areas for up to 50 people each. Picnic tables and fire grills are provided. Drinking water, garbage bins, restrooms with flush toilets and showers, a dump station, picnic shelters, and firewood are available. Boat-launching facilities (canoes, inflatables, and kayaks), a model airplane field, and a 27-hole disc golf course are nearby. Group facilities are available. Some facilities are wheelchair accessible. Leashed pets are permitted, and there is a designated area for off-leash dog runs.

Reservations, fees: Reservations are accepted at 800/452-5687 or www.oregonstateparks.org ($8 reservation fee). Tent sites are $11–18 per night, RV sites are $13–27 per night, $5 per night per each additional vehicle. Hiker/biker sites are $4 per person per night, and group sites are $64–128.25 per night in summer, $43–103 the rest of the year. Some credit cards are accepted. Open mid-March–October.

Directions: From Portland, drive east on U.S. 26 to Gresham. Continue 11 miles to Sandy and Highway 211. Turn right (south) and drive six miles to a junction. Turn south (still Highway 211) and drive one mile to Hayden Road.

Turn right and drive one mile to Springwater Road. Turn right and drive one mile to the park on the right.

Contact: Milo McIver State Park, 503/630-6147, 503/630-7150, or 800/551-6949, www.oregonstateparks.org.

5 PROMONTORY

Scenic rating: 7

on North Fork Reservoir

This Portland General Electric camp on North Fork Reservoir is part of a large recreation area and park. The reservoir, actually a dammed-up overflow of the Clackamas River, encompasses 350 acres. The water is calm and ideal for boating, and the trout fishing is excellent. A trail connects the campground to the marina. A one-acre lake is available for children's fishing.

Campsites, facilities: There are 35 sites for tents or RVs up to 35 feet long and 14 yomes (which are a cross between a yurt and a dome). There is also a group area for up to 35 people for tents or small self-contained RVs. There are no RV hookups. Picnic tables and fire rings are provided. Restrooms with flush toilets and showers, garbage bins, limited groceries, ice, a playground, horseshoes, covered picnic shelters, and snacks are available. A fish-cleaning station, a fishing pier, a children's fishing pond, boat ramp, dock, and boat rentals are also on-site. Some facilities, including the boat ramp and fishing pier, are wheelchair accessible. Leashed pets are permitted.

Reservations, fees: Reservations are accepted at 503/630-7229 or www.portlandgeneral.com. Sites are $16 per night, $25 per night for a yome. Some credit cards are accepted. Open mid-May–September.

Directions: From Portland, drive east on U.S. 26 to Gresham. Continue 11 miles to Sandy and Highway 211. Turn right (south) and drive six miles to a junction. Turn south (still Highway 211) and drive six miles to Estacada. Continue south on Highway 224 and drive seven miles to the campground on the right. The route is well signed.

Contact: Portland General Electric, 503/464-8515, fax 503/464-2944, www.portlandgeneral.com; store and marina, 503/630-5152; campground, 503/630-7229.

6 LAZY BEND

Scenic rating: 8

on the Clackamas River in Mount Hood National Forest

This campground is situated at 800 feet elevation along the banks of the Clackamas River near the large North Fork Reservoir. It's far enough off the highway to provide a secluded, primitive feeling, though it fills quickly on weekends and holidays. There's only catch-and-release fishing in the Clackamas.

Campsites, facilities: There are 23 sites for tents or RVs up to 52 feet long. Picnic tables, garbage service, and fireplaces are provided. Drinking water and flush toilets are available. Leashed pets are permitted.

Reservations, fees: Reservations are accepted at 877/444-6777 or www.recreation.gov ($10 reservation fee). Sites are $17 per night, $8 per night per additional vehicle. Open late early May–late September, weather permitting.

Directions: From Portland, drive south on U.S. 205 to the junction with Highway 24. Take the Highway 224/Estacada exit and turn left (south) onto Highway 224. Drive approximately 13 miles to Estacada. Continue south on Highway 224 for 10.5 miles to the campground on the right.

Contact: Mount Hood National Forest, Clackamas River Ranger District, 503/630-6861, fax 503/630-2299, www.fs.fed.us.

7 ARMSTRONG

Scenic rating: 5

on the Clackamas River in
Mount Hood National Forest

Armstrong campground is set at an elevation of 900 feet along the banks of the Clackamas River and offers good fishing access. Fishing is catch-and-release only.

Campsites, facilities: There are 11 sites for tents or RVs up to 40 feet long. Picnic tables and fire rings are provided. Vault toilets and drinking water are available. Garbage service is available in the summer only. Some facilities are wheelchair accessible. Leashed pets are permitted.

Reservations, fees: Reservations are accepted at 877/444-6777 or www.recreation.gov ($10 reservation fee). Sites are $16 per night, $8 per night per additional vehicle. Open year-round, with limited winter services.

Directions: From Portland, drive south on U.S. 205 to the junction with Highway 24. Take the Highway 224/Estacada exit and turn left (south) onto Highway 224. Drive approximately 13 miles to Estacada. Continue south on Highway 224 for 15 miles to the campground on the right.

Contact: Mount Hood National Forest, Clackamas River Ranger District, 503/630-6861, fax 503/630-2299, www.fs.fed.us.

8 CARTER BRIDGE

Scenic rating: 5

on the Clackamas River in
Mount Hood National Forest

This small, flat campground is popular with anglers. The Clackamas River flows along one end, and the other end borders the highway, with peripheral traffic noise.

Campsites, facilities: There are 15 sites for tents or RVs up to 28 feet long. Picnic tables and fire pits are provided. Vault toilets and garbage bins are available. There is no drinking water. Some facilities are wheelchair accessible. Leashed pets are permitted.

Reservations, fees: Reservations are not accepted. Sites are $14 per night, $7 per night per additional vehicle. Open late May–early September, weather permitting.

Directions: From Portland, drive south on U.S. 205 to the junction with Highway 24. Take the Highway 224/Estacada exit and turn left (south) onto Highway 224. Drive approximately 13 miles to Estacada. Continue south on Highway 224 for 15.2 miles to the campground on the left.

Contact: Mount Hood National Forest, Clackamas River Ranger District, 503/630-6861, fax 503/630-2299, www.fs.fed.us.

9 LOCKABY

Scenic rating: 6

on the Clackamas River in
Mount Hood National Forest

This campground sits at an elevation of 900 feet along the banks of the Clackamas River, next to Armstrong. Fishing in the Clackamas River is catch-and-release only.

Campsites, facilities: There are 30 sites for tents or RVs up to 15 feet long. Picnic tables, fireplaces, drinking water, garbage service, vault toilets, and firewood are available. A camp host is on-site. Leashed pets are permitted.

Reservations, fees: Reservations are accepted at 877/444-6777 or www.recreation.gov ($10 reservation fee). Sites are $16 per night, $8 per night per additional vehicle. Open late May–early September.

Directions: From Portland, drive south on U.S. 205 to the junction with Highway 24. Take the Highway 224/Estacada exit and turn left (south) onto Highway 224. Drive

approximately 13 miles to Estacada. Continue south on Highway 224 for 15.3 miles to the campground on the left.
Contact: Mount Hood National Forest, Clackamas River Ranger District, Estacada Ranger Station, 503/630-6861, fax 503/630-2299, www.fs.fed.us.

10 ROARING RIVER

Scenic rating: 8

on the Roaring River in Mount Hood National Forest

Set among old-growth cedars at the confluence of the Roaring and Clackamas Rivers at an elevation of 1,000 feet, this campground has access to the Dry Ridge Trail. The trail starts in camp, and it's a butt-kicker of an uphill climb. Several other trails into the adjacent roadless area are accessible from camp.
Campsites, facilities: There are 14 sites for tents or RVs up to 16 feet long. Picnic tables and fireplaces are provided. Garbage service, drinking water, and vault toilets are available. Leashed pets are permitted.
Reservations, fees: Reservations are accepted at 877/444-6777 or www.recreation.gov ($10 reservation fee). Sites are $16 per night, $8 per night per additional vehicle. Open mid-May–mid-September, weather permitting.
Directions: From Portland, drive south on U.S. 205 to the junction with Highway 24. Take the Highway 224/Estacada exit and turn left (south) onto Highway 224. Drive approximately 13 miles to Estacada. Continue south on Highway 224 for 18 miles to the campground on the left.
Contact: Mount Hood National Forest, Clackamas River Ranger District, 503/630-6861, fax 503/630-2299, www.fs.fed.us.

11 SUNSTRIP

Scenic rating: 3

on the Clackamas River in Mount Hood National Forest

This campground on the banks of the Clackamas River offers fishing and rafting access. One of several camps along the Highway 224 corridor, Sunstrip is a favorite with rafting and kayaking enthusiasts and can fill up quickly on weekends. The elevation is 1,000 feet. Note: This campground, squeezed between the river and the highway and traversed by power lines, may be a turnoff for those wanting another kind of experience.
Campsites, facilities: There are nine sites for tents or RVs up to 60 feet long. Picnic tables and fireplaces are provided. Garbage service, drinking water, firewood, and vault toilets are available. A camp host is on-site. Leashed pets are permitted.
Reservations, fees: Reservations are accepted at 877/444-6777 or www.recreation.gov ($10 reservation fee). Sites are $16 per night, $8 per night per additional vehicle. Open year-round, with limited winter services.
Directions: From Portland, drive south on U.S. 205 to the junction with Highway 24. Take the Highway 224/Estacada exit and turn left (south) onto Highway 224. Drive approximately 13 miles to Estacada. Continue south on Highway 224 for 19 miles to the campground.
Contact: Mount Hood National Forest, Clackamas River Ranger District, 503/630-6861, fax 503/630-2299, www.fs.fed.us.

12 RAINBOW

Scenic rating: 6

on the Oak Grove Fork of the Clackamas River in Mount Hood National Forest

Rainbow campground sits at an elevation of 1,400 feet along the banks of the Oak Grove Fork of the Clackamas River, not far from where it empties into the Clackamas River. The camp is less than a quarter mile from Ripplebrook Campground.

Campsites, facilities: There are 17 sites for tents or RVs up to 62 feet long. Picnic tables and fire grills are provided. Vault toilets are available. Garbage service is available during the summer. There is no drinking water. Leashed pets are permitted.

Reservations, fees: Reservations are accepted at 877/444-6777 or www.recreation.gov ($10 reservation fee). Sites are $14 per night, $8 per night per additional vehicle. Open year-round, with limited winter services.

Directions: From Portland, drive south on U.S. 205 to the junction with Highway 24. Take the Highway 224/Estacada exit and turn left (south) onto Highway 224. Drive approximately 13 miles to Estacada. Continue south on Highway 224 and drive 27 miles in national forest (the road becomes Forest Road 46). Continue south and drive about 100 yards to the campground on the right.

Contact: Mount Hood National Forest, Clackamas River Ranger District, 595 N.W. Industrial Way, Estacada, OR 97023, 503/630-6861, fax 503/630-2299, www.fs.fed.us.

13 INDIAN HENRY

Scenic rating: 8

on the Clackamas River in Mount Hood National Forest

One of the most popular campgrounds in the Clackamas River Ranger District, Indian Henry hugs the banks of the Clackamas River at an elevation of 1,250 feet and has a wheelchair-accessible trail. Group campsites and an amphitheater are available. The nearby Clackamas River Trail has fishing access.

Campsites, facilities: There are 84 sites for tents or RVs up to 40 feet long and eight group tent sites for up to 30 people. Picnic tables, garbage service, and fire grills are provided. Flush toilets, firewood, and drinking water are available. A camp host is on-site. Some facilities are wheelchair accessible. Leashed pets are permitted.

Reservations, fees: Reservations are accepted at 877/444-6777 or www.recreation.gov ($10 reservation fee). Sites are $17 per night, $8 per night per additional vehicle; group sites are $46–50 per night. Open late May–early September, weather permitting.

Directions: From Portland, drive south on U.S. 205 to the junction with Highway 24. Take the Highway 224/Estacada exit and turn left (south) onto Highway 224. Drive approximately 13 miles to Estacada. Continue south on Highway 224 for 23 miles to Forest Road 4620. Turn right and drive 0.5 mile southeast to the campground on the left.

Contact: Mount Hood National Forest, Clackamas River Ranger District, 503/630-6861, fax 503/630-2299, www.fs.fed.us.

14 RIPPLEBROOK

Scenic rating: 7

on the Oak Grove Fork of the Clackamas River in Mount Hood National Forest

Shaded sites with river views are a highlight at this campground along the banks of the Oak Grove Fork of the Clackamas River, where anglers are limited to artificial lures and catch-and-release only. Note: The road to this camp experiences slides and washouts; check current status before making a trip.

Campsites, facilities: There are 14 sites for RVs up to 45 feet long. Picnic tables, garbage service, and fire grills are provided. Vault toilets are available, but there is no drinking water. Leashed pets are permitted.

Reservations, fees: Reservations are accepted at 877/444-6777 or www.recreation.gov ($10 reservation fee). Sites are $14 per night, $8 per night per additional vehicle. Open late April–late September, weather permitting.

Directions: From Portland, drive south on U.S. 205 to the junction with Highway 24. Take the Highway 224/Estacada exit and turn left (south) onto Highway 224. Drive approximately 13 miles to Estacada. Continue south on Highway 224 for 26.5 miles to the campground entrance on the left.

Contact: Mount Hood National Forest, Clackamas River Ranger District, 503/630-6861, fax 503/630-2299, www.fs.fed.us.

15 ALDER FLAT HIKE-IN

Scenic rating: 9

on the Clackamas River in Mount Hood National Forest

This secluded hike-in campground is set along the banks of the Clackamas River in old-growth forest. If you want peace and quiet and don't mind a short walk to get there, this is the spot. Be sure to pack out whatever you bring in, and remember that fishing in the Clackamas River is catch-and-release only.

Campsites, facilities: There are six tent sites at this hike-in campground. Picnic tables and fire grills are provided. There is no drinking water and no toilet. Garbage must be packed out. Leashed pets are permitted.

Reservations, fees: Reservations are not accepted. There is no fee for camping. Open year-round.

Directions: From Portland, drive south on U.S. 205 to the junction with Highway 24. Take the Highway 224/Estacada exit and turn left (south) onto Highway 224. Drive approximately 13 miles to Estacada. Continue south on Highway 224 for 26 miles to the Ripplebrook Ranger Station. Parking for the camp is about half a mile west of the ranger station at the Alder Flat Trailhead. Hike one mile to the campground.

Contact: Mount Hood National Forest, Clackamas River Ranger District, 503/630-6861, fax 503/630-2299, www.fs.fed.us.

16 RIVERSIDE

Scenic rating: 8

on the Clackamas River in Mount Hood National Forest

The banks of the Clackamas River are home to this campground (elevation 1,400 feet). A worthwhile trail leaves the camp and follows the river for four miles north. Fishing is another option here, and several old forest roads in the vicinity make excellent mountain-biking trails.

Campsites, facilities: There are 16 sites for tents or RVs up to 40 feet long. Picnic tables, garbage service, and fire grills are provided. Vault toilets and drinking water are available. Some facilities are wheelchair accessible. Leashed pets are permitted; no horses are allowed in the campground.

Reservations, fees: Reservations are accepted at 877/444-6777 or www.recreation.gov ($10 reservation fee). Sites are $16 per night, $8 per night per additional vehicle. Open mid-May–late September, weather permitting.

Directions: From Portland, drive south on U.S. 205 to the junction with Highway 24. Take the Highway 224/Estacada exit and turn left (south) onto Highway 224. Drive approximately 13 miles to Estacada. Continue south on Highway 224 for 27 miles and into national forest (Highway 224 becomes Forest Road 46). Continue 2.5 miles south on Forest Road 46 to the campground on the right.

Contact: Mount Hood National Forest, Clackamas River Ranger District, 503/630-6861, fax 503/630-2299, www.fs.fed.us.

17 RIVERFORD

Scenic rating: 4

on the Clackamas and Collawash Rivers in Mount Hood National Forest

This campground, just a two-minute walk from the confluence of the Clackamas and Collawash Rivers, offers access to good fishing. Otherwise, it's small, and the sites provide little privacy. It is set at an elevation of 1,500 feet. Although there is no drinking water at this camp, drinking water is available 0.75 mile away at Riverside Campground.

Campsites, facilities: There are eight sites for tents and two sites for RVs up to 20 feet long. Picnic tables and fire grills are provided. Vault toilets are available. Garbage service is provided in the summer. There is no drinking water. Leashed pets are permitted.

Reservations, fees: Reservations are not accepted. Sites are $16 per night, $7 per night per additional vehicle. Open year-round, with limited winter services.

Directions: From Portland, drive south on U.S. 205 to the junction with Highway 24. Take the Highway 224/Estacada exit and turn left (south) onto Highway 224. Drive approximately 13 miles to Estacada. Continue south on Highway 224 for 27 miles in national forest (the road becomes Forest Road 46). Continue south on Forest Road 46 for 3.5 miles to the campground on the right.

Contact: Mount Hood National Forest, Clackamas River Ranger District, 503/630-6861, fax 503/630-2299, www.fs.fed.us.

18 RAAB GROUP

Scenic rating: 7

on the Collawash River in Mount Hood National Forest

Raab Group camp (1,500 feet elevation) is located along the banks of the Collawash River, about a mile from its confluence with the Clackamas River. Raab gets moderate use, but it's usually quiet and has a nice, secluded atmosphere with lots of privacy among the sites.

Campsites, facilities: There are 27 sites for tents or RVs up to 16 feet long. Picnic tables, garbage service, and fire grills are provided. Vault toilets are available. There is no drinking water in the campground; water is available one mile away at Two Rivers Picnic Area. Leashed pets are permitted.

Reservations, fees: Reservations are accepted at 877/444-6777 or www.recreation.gov ($10 reservation fee). Sites are $35–42 per night. Open late May–early September, weather permitting.

Directions: From Portland, drive south on U.S. 205 to the junction with Highway 24. Take the Highway 224/Estacada exit and turn left (south) onto Highway 224. Drive approximately 13 miles to Estacada. Continue south on Highway 224 for 27 miles in national forest (the road becomes Forest Road 46). Continue south on Forest Road 46 for 2.5 miles to Forest Road 63. Turn right and drive 1.5 miles to the campground on the right.

Contact: Mount Hood National Forest, Clackamas River Ranger District, 503/630-6861, fax 503/630-2299, www.fs.fed.us; park concessionaire, 503/668-1700.

19 KINGFISHER

Scenic rating: 7

on the Hot Springs Fork of the Collawash River in Mount Hood National Forest

This pretty campground, surrounded by old-growth forest, sits on the banks of the Hot Springs Fork of the Collawash River and provides fishing access. It's about three miles from Bagby Hot Springs, a U.S. Forest Service day-use area. The hot springs are an easy 1.5-mile hike from the day-use area. The camp sits at 1,250 feet elevation.

Campsites, facilities: There are 23 sites for tents or RVs up to 66 feet long. Picnic tables and fireplaces are provided. Garbage service is provided during the summer. Vault toilets and drinking water are available. Leashed pets are permitted.

Reservations, fees: Reservations are accepted at 877/444-6777 or www.recreation.gov ($10 reservation fee). Sites are $16 per night, $8 per night per additional vehicle. Open year-round, weather permitting, with limited winter facilities.

Directions: From Portland, drive south on U.S. 205 to the junction with Highway 24. Take the Highway 224/Estacada exit and turn left (south) onto Highway 224. Drive approximately 13 miles to Estacada. Continue south on Highway 224 for 27 miles in national forest (the road becomes Forest Road 46). Continue south on Forest Road 46 for 3.5 miles to Forest Road 63. Turn right and drive three miles to Forest Road 70. Turn right again and drive one mile to the campground on the left.

Contact: Mount Hood National Forest, Clackamas River Ranger District, 503/630-6861, fax 503/630-2299, www.fs.fed.us.

20 EAGLE CREEK

Scenic rating: 8

near the Columbia Wilderness in Mount Hood National Forest

BEST

Eagle Creek is the oldest Forest Service Camp in America. Set at 400 feet elevation among old-growth Douglas fir and hemlock, it makes a good base camp for a hiking trip. The Eagle Creek Trail leaves the campground and travels 13 miles to Wahtum Lake, where it intersects with the Pacific Crest Trail. A primitive campground sits at the 7.5-mile point. The upper seven miles of the trail pass through the Hatfield Wilderness.

Campsites, facilities: There are 20 sites for tents or RVs up to 20 feet long and one group site for up to 90 people. Picnic tables and fire grills are provided. Drinking water, garbage bins, and flush toilets are available. A camp host is on-site. Boat docks and launching facilities are nearby on the Columbia River. Some facilities are wheelchair accessible. Leashed pets are permitted.

Reservations, fees: Reservations are not accepted for single sites, but are required for the group site at 877/444-6777 or www.recreation.gov ($10 reservation fee). Sites are $10 per night, $5 per night per additional vehicle; the group site is $75–125. Open May–September.

Directions: From Portland, drive east on I-84 for 41 miles to Bonneville. Continue east for two miles to the campground.

Contact: Columbia River Gorge National Scenic Area, 541/308-1700, fax 541/386-1916, www.fs.fed.us/r6/columbia.

21 CASCADE LOCKS MARINE PARK

Scenic rating: 8

in Cascade Locks

BEST

This public riverfront park covers 23 acres and offers a museum and boat rides. The salmon fishing is excellent here. Stern-wheeler dinner cruises are available. Hiking trails and tennis courts are nearby; the Pacific Crest Trail is within one mile.

Campsites, facilities: There are 16 sites for tents or RVs of any length; some sites have partial hookups. Picnic tables are provided. Drinking water, restrooms with flush toilets and showers, a dump station, boat docks, launching facilities, a picnic area, and a playground are available. A camp host is on-site. Propane gas, gasoline, a store, café, coin laundry, and ice are within one mile. Some facilities are wheelchair accessible. Leashed pets are permitted.

Reservations, fees: Reservations are accepted at 541/374-8619. Sites are $15–25 per night. Some credit cards are accepted. Open year-round, with limited winter facilities.

Directions: From Portland, drive east on I-84 for 44 miles to Cascade Locks. Take Exit 44/Cascade Locks to Wanapa Street. Turn left and drive 0.5 mile to the sign for the park on the left (well signed).

Contact: Port of Cascade Locks, Cascade Locks Marine Park, 541/374-8619, fax 541/374-8428, www.portofcascadelocks.org.

22 KOA CASCADE LOCKS

Scenic rating: 5

near the Columbia River

This KOA is a good layover spot for RVers touring the Columbia River corridor. The campground offers level, shaded RV sites and grassy tent sites. A pancake breakfast is available on weekends during the summer season. Nearby recreation options include bike trails, hiking trails, and tennis courts. The 200-acre Cascade Locks Marine Park is close by and offers everything from museums to boat trips.

Campsites, facilities: There are 33 sites for tents, 78 sites with full or partial hookups for RVs of any length, nine cabins, and two cottages. Most RV sites are pull-through. Picnic tables and fire pits are provided. Restrooms with flush toilets and showers, drinking water, propane gas, a dump station, firewood, a spa, cable TV, wireless Internet service, a recreation hall, convenience store, coin laundry, ice, a playground, bicycle rentals, and a heated seasonal swimming pool are available. A café is within one mile. Some facilities are wheelchair accessible. Leashed pets are permitted.

Reservations, fees: Reservations are accepted at 800/562-8698. Sites are $27–36 per night, $5 per person per night for more than two people. Cabins are $45–55 per night; cottages are $55–89 per night. Some credit cards are accepted. Open February–November.

Directions: From Portland, drive east on I-84 for 44 miles to Cascade Locks and Exit 44. Take that exit to Forest Lane. Turn east on Forest Lane and drive one mile to the campground on the left.

Contact: KOA Cascade Locks, 541/374-8668, www.koa.com.

23 HERMAN CREEK HORSE CAMP

Scenic rating: 9

near the Pacific Crest Trail in Mount Hood National Forest

This rustic campground sits at 300 feet elevation and is about half a mile from Herman Creek, not far from the Pacific Crest Trail. This area, separated from Washington by the Columbia River, is particularly beautiful. The campsites are spacious, and the many recreation options include biking, boating, fishing, and hiking. Note that new rules regarding stock feed require certified weed-free hay, feed, and crop products on national forest land.

Campsites, facilities: There are seven sites for tents or RVs up to 20 feet long. Drinking water, garbage bins, fire grills, and picnic tables are provided. Restrooms with flush toilets and showers, stock-handling facilities, a store, a café, a coin laundry, and ice are available. Leashed pets are permitted.

Reservations, fees: Reservations are not accepted. Sites are $10 per night, $5 per night per additional vehicle. Open May–September.

Directions: From Portland, drive east on I-84 for 44 miles to Cascade Locks and Exit 44. Take that exit and drive straight ahead (east) onto Wanapa Street and drive back under the highway. Continue 1.5 miles (the road becomes Herman Creek Road) to the campground on the right.

Contact: Columbia River Gorge National Scenic Area, 541/308-1700, fax 541/386-1916, www.fs.fed.us/r6/columbia.

24 WYETH

Scenic rating: 5

on Gordon Creek in Mount Hood National Forest

Wyeth makes a good layover spot for Columbia River corridor cruisers. The camp (100 feet elevation) borders Gordon Creek, near the Columbia River. Recreation options include biking, boating, fishing, and hiking.

Campsites, facilities: There are 16 sites for tents or RVs up to 30 feet long and three group sites. Fire grills and picnic tables are provided. Drinking water and flush toilets are available. A camp host is on-site. Leashed pets are permitted.

Reservations, fees: Reservations are not accepted. Sites are $15 per night, $5 per night per additional vehicle, group sites are $30 per night. Open April–mid-October.

Directions: From Portland, drive east on I-84 for 44 miles to Cascade Locks. Continue east on I-84 for seven miles to Wyeth and Exit 51. Turn right and drive 0.25 mile to the campground entrance.

Contact: Columbia River Gorge National Scenic Area, 541/308-1700, fax 541/386-1916, www.fs.fed.us/r6/columbia.

25 VIENTO STATE PARK

Scenic rating: 8

along the Columbia River Gorge

This park along the Columbia River Gorge offers scenic hiking trails and some of the best windsurfing in the Gorge. Just 12 miles to the east, old U.S. 30 skirts the Columbia River, offering a picturesque drive. Viento has a day-use picnic area right next to a babbling creek. Look for weekend interpretive programs during the summer. There are several other day-use state parks along I-84 just west of Viento, including Seneca Fouts, Vinzenz Lausmann, and Wygant. All offer quality hiking trails and scenic views.

Campsites, facilities: There are 56 sites with partial hookups for RVs up to 30 feet long (with some up to 40 feet long) and 18 tent sites. Picnic tables and fire grills are provided. Drinking water, garbage bins, restrooms with flush toilets and showers, firewood, and a playground are available. Some facilities are wheelchair accessible. Leashed pets are permitted.

Reservations, fees: Reservations are not accepted. RV sites are $12–20 per night, tent sites are $10–17 per night, $5 per night per additional vehicle. Some credit cards are accepted. Open mid-March–October, weather permitting.

Directions: From Portland, drive east on I-84 for 56 miles to Exit 56 (eight miles west of

Hood River). Take Exit 56 and drive to the park entrance. The park is set on both sides of I-84.

Contact: Viento State Park, 541/374-8811 or 800/551-6949, www.oregonstateparks.org.

26 TUCKER COUNTY PARK

Scenic rating: 6

on the Hood River

This county park along the banks of the Hood River is just far enough out of the way to be missed by most of the tourist traffic. Many people who choose this county park come for the windsurfing. Other recreation opportunities include rafting and kayaking. Fishing is not allowed at the park.

Campsites, facilities: There are 84 tent sites and 14 sites with partial hookups for tents or RVs up to 30 feet long. Picnic tables and fire rings are provided. Drinking water, restrooms with flush toilets and showers, and a playground are available. A store, café, gasoline, and ice are within two miles. Leashed pets are permitted.

Reservations, fees: Reservations are not accepted. Sites are $18–20 per night, and it costs $8 per night per additional tent and $5 per night per additional vehicle. Open April–October.

Directions: From Portland, turn east on I-84 and drive about 65 miles to the town of Hood River and Exit 62. Take the exit and drive east on Cascade Street, continuing to 13th Street (first light). Turn right (south) and drive through and out of town; 13th Street becomes Tucker Road and then Dee Highway (Highway 281). Follow the signs to Parkdale. The park is four miles out of town on the right.

Contact: Hood River County Parks, 541/387-6889 or 541/386-4477, fax 541/386-6325, www.co.hood-river.or.us.

27 MEMALOOSE STATE PARK

Scenic rating: 7

in the Columbia River Gorge

This park borrows its name from nearby Memaloose Island, which Native Americans used as a sacred burial ground. Situated along the hottest part of the scenic Columbia River Gorge, the campground makes a prime layover spot for campers cruising the Oregon/Washington border. Nature programs and interpretive events are held here. This popular camp receives a good deal of traffic, so plan on arriving early to claim a spot, even if you have a reservation.

Campsites, facilities: There are 66 tent sites and 44 sites with full hookups for RVs up to 60 feet long. Picnic tables and fire grills are provided. Drinking water, garbage bins, restrooms with flush toilets and showers, a dump station, playground, and firewood are available. Leashed pets are permitted.

Reservations, fees: Reservations are accepted at 800/452-5687 or www.oregonstateparks.org ($8 reservation fee). RV sites are $16–20 per night, tent sites are $12–24 per night, $5 per night per additional vehicle. Some credit cards are accepted. Open mid-March–October.

Directions: Memaloose State Park is accessible only to westbound traffic on I-84. From The Dalles, drive west on I-84 for 11 miles to the signed turnoff. (The park is about 75 miles east of Portland.)

If eastbound on I-84, take Exit 76. Drive under the freeway to the I-84 west on-ramp. Once on I-84 west, drive 2.5 miles to the sign for Rest Area/Memaloose State Park. Drive into the rest area and take an immediate right into the campground.

Contact: Memaloose State Park, 541/478-3008 or 800/551-6949, www.oregonstateparks.org.

28 KINNICKKINNICK

Scenic rating: 5

on Laurence Lake in Mount Hood National Forest

Kinnickkinnick campground sits on a peninsula that juts into Laurence Lake; only non-motorized boats are allowed on the lake. Campsite privacy varies because of the fairly sparse tree cover, and more than half of the sites are a short walk from your vehicle.

Campsites, facilities: There are 20 sites for tents or RVs up to 16 feet long. Picnic tables and fire rings with fire grills are provided. There is no drinking water. Vault toilets, garbage bins, and a boat ramp are available. Some facilities are wheelchair accessible. Leashed pets are permitted.

Reservations, fees: Reservations are not accepted. Sites are $12 per night, $7 per night per additional vehicle. Open May–September, weather permitting.

Directions: From Portland, drive 62 miles west on I-84 to the city of Hood River. Take Exit 64 and drive about 14 miles south on Highway 35 to the town of Mount Hood and Cooper Spur Road. Turn right and drive three miles to Parkdale and Clear Creek Road. Turn left (south) and drive three miles to the Laurence Lake turnoff. Turn right on Forest Road 2840 (Laurence Lake Road) and drive four miles to the campground on the right.

Contact: Mount Hood National Forest, Hood River Ranger District, 541/352-6002, fax 541/352-7365, www.fs.fed.us.

29 LOST LAKE

Scenic rating: 9

on Lost Lake in Mount Hood National Forest

BEST

Only non-motorized boats are allowed on this clear, 240-acre lake set against the Cascade Range. The campground is nestled in an old-growth forest of cedar, Douglas fir, and hemlock trees at 3,200 feet elevation. Many sites have a lake view, and the campground affords a great view of Mount Hood.

Campsites, facilities: There are 125 sites for tents or RVs up to 32 feet long and several group sites. A horse camp with a corral is also available. Picnic tables and fire rings with grills are provided. Drinking water, vault toilets, garbage containers, a dump station, and a covered picnic shelter are available. Cabins, a grocery store, showers, beach picnic areas, a boat launch, and boat rentals are nearby. Some facilities are wheelchair accessible, including a barrier-free boat launch and fishing pier, as well as 3.5 miles of barrier-free trails. Leashed pets are permitted.

Reservations, fees: Reservations are not accepted for single sites but are required for the group sites at 541/386-6366. Single sites are $25 per night, $7 per night per additional vehicle. There are three group sites that can accommodate up to 15 people and five vehicles each. The group sites are $75–125 per night. Some credit cards are accepted. Open mid-May–mid-October, weather permitting.

Directions: From Portland, drive 62 miles east on I-84 to the city of Hood River. Take Exit 62/Westcliff to Cascade Street. Drive east on Cascade Street to 13th Street. Turn right on 13th Street and drive through Hood River Heights. The road turns into Dee Highway. Continue seven miles to Lost Lake Road/Forest Road 13. Turn right and drive seven miles to the campground.

Contact: Mount Hood National Forest, Hood River Ranger District, 541/352-6002, fax 541/352-7365; Lost Lake Resort, 541/6366, www.fs.fed.us.

30 KNEBAL SPRINGS

Scenic rating: 6

near Knebal Springs in Mount Hood National Forest

This spot (4,000 feet elevation) is in a semi-primitive area near Knebal Springs, an ephemeral water source. The Knebal Springs Trail begins at the campground. A nice, level family bike trail is available here. Another trail from the camp provides access to a network of trails in the area. A U.S. Forest Service map is advised.

Campsites, facilities: There are eight sites for tents or RVs up to 22 feet long. Picnic tables and fire grills are provided. There is no drinking water. Vault toilets and horse-loading and -tending facilities are available. Garbage must be packed out. Leashed pets are permitted.

Reservations, fees: Reservations are not accepted. Sites are $10 per night. Open mid-May–October, weather permitting.

Directions: From Portland, turn east on I-84 and drive about 90 miles to Exit 87. Take Exit 87 and turn south on U.S. 197; drive 13 miles to Dufur and Dufur Valley Road. Turn right on Dufur Valley Road and drive west for 12 miles to Forest Road 44. Continue west on Forest Road 44 for four miles to Forest Road 4430. Turn right and drive four miles to Forest Road 1720. Turn left (southwest) and drive one mile to the campground.

Contact: Mount Hood National Forest, Barlow Ranger District, 541/467-2291, fax 541/467-2271, www.fs.fed.us.

31 EIGHTMILE CROSSING

Scenic rating: 7

on Eightmile Creek in Mount Hood National Forest

This campground sits at an elevation of 4,200 feet along Eightmile Creek. Although pretty and shaded, with sites scattered along the banks of the creek, it gets relatively little camping pressure. From the day-use area, you have access to a nice hiking trail that runs along Eightmile Creek. In addition, a 0.75-mile wheelchair-accessible trail links Eightmile Campground to Lower Crossing Campground. The fishing can be good here, so bring your gear.

Campsites, facilities: There are 21 sites for tents or RVs up to 30 feet long. Picnic tables and fire grills are provided. Vault toilets are available. No drinking water is available, and garbage must be packed out. Some facilities are wheelchair accessible. Leashed pets are permitted.

Reservations, fees: Reservations are not accepted. Sites are $10 per night. Open June–mid-October, weather permitting.

Directions: From Portland, turn east on I-84 and drive about 90 miles to Exit 87. Take Exit 87 and turn south on U.S. 197; drive 13 miles to Dufur and Dufur Valley Road. Turn right on Dufur Valley Road and drive west for 12 miles to Forest Road 44. Continue west on Forest Road 44 for four miles to Forest Road 4430. Turn right and drive 0.5 mile to the campground.

Contact: Mount Hood National Forest, Barlow Ranger District, 541/467-2291, fax 541/467-2271, www.fs.fed.us.

32 PEBBLE FORD

Scenic rating: 6

in Mount Hood National Forest

This is just a little camping spot by the side of a gravel forest road. Primitive and quiet, it's an alternative to the better-known Eightmile Crossing. There are some quality hiking trails in the area if you're willing to drive two or three miles. The elevation is 4,200 feet.

Campsites, facilities: There are three sites for tents or RVs up to 16 feet long. Picnic tables and fire grills are provided. Vault toilets are available. There is no drinking water. Leashed pets are permitted.

Reservations, fees: Reservations are not accepted. Sites are $10 per night. Open June–early October, weather permitting.

Directions: From Portland, turn east on I-84 and drive about 90 miles to Exit 87. Take Exit 87 and turn south on U.S. 197; drive 13 miles to Dufur and Dufur Valley Road. Turn right on Dufur Valley Road and drive west for 12 miles to Forest Road 44. Continue west on Forest Road 44 for five miles to Forest Road 130. Turn left (south) and drive a short distance to the campground on the left.

Contact: Mount Hood National Forest, Barlow Ranger District, 541/467-2291, fax 541/467-2271, www.fs.fed.us.

33 McNEIL

Scenic rating: 5

on the Clear Fork of the Sandy River in Mount Hood National Forest

McNeil campground (2,040 feet elevation) is located in Old Maid Flat, a special geological area along the Clear Fork of the Sandy River. There's a good view of Mount Hood from the campground entrance. Several trails nearby provide access to the wilderness backcountry.

Campsites, facilities: There are 34 sites for tents or RVs up to 22 feet long. Picnic tables and vault toilets are provided. There is no drinking water. Leashed pets are permitted.

Reservations, fees: Reservations are not accepted. Sites are $12 per night, $6 per night per additional vehicle. Open May–October, weather permitting.

Directions: From Portland, drive 40 miles east on U.S. 26 to Zigzag. Turn left on County Road 18/East Lolo Pass Road and drive 4.5 miles to Forest Road 1825. Turn right on Forest Road 1825, drive less than one mile, bear right onto a bridge to stay on Forest Road 1825, and drive 0.25 mile to the campground on the left.

Contact: Mount Hood National Forest, Zigzag Ranger District, 503/622-3191, fax 503/622-5622, www.fs.fed.us.

34 RILEY HORSE CAMP

Scenic rating: 6

near the Clear Fork of the Sandy River in Mount Hood National Forest

Riley Horse Camp is close to McNeil and offers the same opportunities, except Riley provides stock facilities and is reserved for horse camping only on holidays. Secluded in an area of Douglas fir and lodgepole pine at 2,100 feet elevation, Riley is a popular base camp for horse-packing trips.

Campsites, facilities: There are 14 sites for tents or RVs up to 45 feet long. Picnic tables and fire grills are provided. Drinking water, vault toilets, garbage bins, and firewood are available. Corrals and hitching posts for horses are available. Leashed pets are permitted.

Reservations, fees: Reservations are accepted at 877/444-6777 or www.recreation.gov ($10 reservation fee). Sites are $16 per night, $8 per night per additional vehicle. Open May–September, weather permitting.

Directions: From Portland, drive 40 miles east on U.S. 26 to Zigzag. Turn left (northeast) on County Road 18/East Lolo Pass Road and drive 4.5 miles to Forest Road 1825. Turn right and drive 0.5 mile to Forest Road 380. Turn right and drive 100 yards to the camp.

Contact: Mount Hood National Forest, Zigzag Ranger District, 503/622-3191, fax 503/622-5622, www.fs.fed.us.

35 LOST CREEK

Scenic rating: 8

on Lost Creek in Mount Hood National Forest

This campground near McNeil and Riley has some of the same opportunities. Set in a cool, lush area on a creek at 2,600 feet elevation, it's barrier-free and offers an interpretive nature trail about one mile long, as well as a wheelchair-accessible fishing pier.

Campsites, facilities: There are 14 sites for tents or RVs up to 40 feet long, including some pull-through sites and some walk-in sites. Picnic tables and fire grills are provided. Drinking water, garbage service, and vault toilets are available. Some facilities are wheelchair accessible. Leashed pets are permitted.

Reservations, fees: Reservations are accepted at 877/444-6777 or www.recreation.gov ($10 reservation fee). Sites are $16 for a single site, $32 for a double site, and $8–9 per night per additional vehicle. Open May–late September.

Directions: From Portland, drive 40 miles east on U.S. 26 to Zigzag. Turn left (northeast) on County Road 18/East Lolo Pass Road and drive 4.5 miles to Forest Road 1825. Turn right and drive two miles to a fork. Bear right and drive 0.25 mile to the campground on the right.

Contact: Mount Hood National Forest, Zigzag Ranger District, 503/622-3191, fax 503/622-5622, www.fs.fed.us.

36 TOLL GATE

Scenic rating: 8

on the Zigzag River in Mount Hood National Forest

BEST

This shady campground along the banks of the Zigzag River near Rhododendron is extremely popular, and finding a site on a summer weekend can be next to impossible. Luckily, you can make a reservation. There are numerous hiking trails in the area. The nearest one leads east for several miles along the river. The campground features a historic Civilian Conservation Corps shelter from the 1930s, which can be used by campers for day use.

Campsites, facilities: There are 15 sites for tents or RVs up to 40 feet long. Picnic tables and fire grills are provided. Drinking water, garbage service, firewood, a group picnic area (available by reservation), and vault toilets are available. A camp host is on-site. Leashed pets are permitted.

Reservations, fees: Reservations are accepted at 877/444-6777 or www.recreation.gov ($10 reservation fee). Sites are $16 per night, $8 per night per additional vehicle. Open late May–early September, weather permitting.

Directions: From Portland, drive east on U.S. 26 for 40 miles to Zigzag. Continue 2.5 miles southeast on U.S. 26 to the campground entrance.

Contact: Mount Hood National Forest, Zigzag Ranger District, 503/622-3191, fax 503/622-5622, www.fs.fed.us.

37 GREEN CANYON

Scenic rating: 8

on the Salmon River in Mount Hood National Forest

Few out-of-towners know about this winner. But the locals do, and they keep the place hopping in the summer. The camp sits at 1,600 feet elevation along the banks of the Salmon River. A long trail cuts through the area and parallels the river, passing through a magnificent old-growth forest.

Campsites, facilities: There are 15 sites for tents or RVs up to 22 feet long. Picnic tables and fire grills are provided. Drinking water, garbage bins, and vault toilets are available. A store, café, and ice are within five miles. Leashed pets are permitted.

Reservations, fees: Reservations are not accepted. Sites are $16–18 per night, $8–9 per night per additional vehicle. Open May–October, weather permitting.
Directions: From Portland, drive east on U.S. 26 for 39 miles to Forest Road 2618 (Salmon River Road) near Zigzag. Turn right and drive 4.5 miles to the campground on the right.
Contact: Mount Hood National Forest, Zigzag Ranger District, 503/622-3191, fax 503/622-5622, www.fs.fed.us.

38 CAMP CREEK

Scenic rating: 8

near the Zigzag River in Mount Hood National Forest

This campground (2,200 feet elevation) sits along Camp Creek, not far from the Zigzag River. It looks similar to Toll Gate, but larger and farther from the road. A hiking trail runs through camp and along the river; another one leads south to Still Creek. This campground, along with Toll Gate to the west, is very popular—you'll probably need a reservation.
Campsites, facilities: There are 25 sites for tents or RVs up to 45 feet long. Picnic tables and fire grills are provided. Drinking water, vault toilets, and garbage bins are available. A camp host is on-site. Some facilities are wheelchair accessible. Leashed pets are permitted.
Reservations, fees: Reservations are accepted at 877/444-6777 or www.recreation.gov ($10 reservation fee). Sites are $16 per night, $32 for a double site, and $8 per night per additional vehicle. Open May–September, weather permitting.
Directions: From Portland, drive east on U.S. 26 for 40 miles to Zigzag. Continue southeast on U.S. 26 for about four miles to the camp on the right.
Contact: Mount Hood National Forest, Zigzag Ranger District, 503/622-3191, fax 503/622-5622, www.fs.fed.us.

39 ALPINE

Scenic rating: 8

near the Pacific Crest Trail in Mount Hood National Forest

The small Alpine campground is set on the south slope of Mount Hood at 5,400 feet elevation, one mile from the Timberline Ski Area lodge. If you can bear some traffic noise, you'll be rewarded with big trees, a mountain feel, and year-round skiing and snowboarding less than one mile away. The Pacific Crest Trail is accessible from the Timberline Lodge. It can get quite crowded here on weekends. In the shoulder seasons, come prepared for cold nights.
Campsites, facilities: There are 16 sites for tents or RVs up to 16 feet long. Picnic tables and fire grills are provided. Drinking water, a portable toilet, and garbage service are available. Some facilities are wheelchair accessible. Leashed pets are permitted.
Reservations, fees: Reservations are not accepted. Sites are $16 per night, $8 per night per additional vehicle. Open mid-July–September, weather permitting.
Directions: From Portland, drive east on U.S. 26 for 55 miles to the small town of Government Camp. Continue east for one mile to Timberline Road (Forest Road 173). Turn left and drive 4.5 miles to the campground on the left.
Contact: Mount Hood National Forest, Zigzag Ranger District, 503/622-3191, fax 503/622-5622, www.fs.fed.us.

40 NOTTINGHAM

Scenic rating: 7

near the East Fork of the Hood River

Nottingham campground, situated at 3,300 feet in elevation on the East Fork of the Hood River, has a variety of shady and sunny spots.

The primary tree cover is Douglas fir and ponderosa pine. The Tamanawas Falls Trail (near Sherwood Camp) is three miles away, and the Gumjuwac Trail is 1.5 miles north. Fishing is only fair because of the swift water and lack of pools.

Campsites, facilities: There are 23 sites for tents or RVs up to 32 feet long. Picnic tables and fire rings are provided. Vault toilets and garbage bins are available. There is no drinking water. Some facilities are wheelchair accessible. Leashed pets are permitted.

Reservations, fees: Reservations are not accepted. Sites are $12 per night, $7 per night per additional vehicle. Open May–October, weather permitting.

Directions: From Mount Hood, drive south on Highway 35 for 13 miles to the camp on the right.

Contact: Mount Hood National Forest, Hood River Ranger District, 541/352-6002, fax 541/352-7365, www.fs.fed.us.

41 STILL CREEK

Scenic rating: 6

on Still Creek in Mount Hood National Forest

This primitive camp, shaded primarily by fir and hemlock, sits along Still Creek where the creek pours off Mount Hood's south slope. Adjacent to Summit Meadows and the site of a pioneer gravesite from the Oregon Trail days, it's a great place for mountain views, sunsets, and wildlife. Anglers should bring along their rods: The fishing in Still Creek can be excellent. The camp sits at 3,600 feet elevation.

Campsites, facilities: There are 27 sites for tents or RVs up to 40 feet long. Picnic tables and fire grills are provided. Vault toilets, drinking water, and garbage service are available. Leashed pets are permitted.

Reservations, fees: Reservations are accepted at 877/444-6777 or www.recreation.gov ($10 reservation fee). Sites are $16–18 per night, $8–9 per night per additional vehicle. Open mid-June–mid-September, weather permitting.

Directions: From Portland, drive 55 miles east on U.S. 26 to Government Camp. Continue east on U.S. 26 for one mile to Forest Road 2650. Turn right and drive south for 500 yards to the campground.

Contact: Mount Hood National Forest, Zigzag Ranger District, 503/622-3191, fax 503/622-5622, www.fs.fed.us.

42 GRINDSTONE

Scenic rating: 7

near Barlow Creek in Mount Hood National Forest

This tiny campground, located at 3,400 feet elevation in a meadow along Barlow Creek, is a little-known and little-used spot. You won't find much out here but wind, water, and trees—but sometimes that's all you need. High-clearance vehicles are recommended. This camp was a site first used by the pioneers.

Campsites, facilities: There are three primitive sites for tents. Picnic tables and fire grills are provided. Vault toilets are available. There is no drinking water, and garbage must be packed out. Leashed pets are permitted.

Reservations, fees: Reservations are not accepted. There is no fee for camping. Open May–September, weather permitting.

Directions: From Portland, turn east on U.S. 26 and drive 57 miles (just past the town of Government Camp) to the junction with Highway 35. Take that exit, bear right onto Highway 35, and drive 4.5 miles to Forest Road 3530. Turn right and drive two miles to the campground on the right.

Contact: Mount Hood National Forest, Hood River Ranger District, 541/352-6002, fax 541/352-7365, www.fs.fed.us.

43 DEVIL'S HALF ACRE MEADOW

Scenic rating: 8

on Barlow Creek in
Mount Hood National Forest

On a site used by the pioneers, this campground is situated a few miles upstream from Grindstone Campground on Barlow Creek. Several hiking trails close to camp, including the Pacific Crest Trail, provide access to small lakes in the area. There are many historic points of interest in the vicinity. High-clearance vehicles are recommended. The camp is at 3,600 feet elevation.

Campsites, facilities: There are two sites for tents or RVs up to 16 feet long. Picnic tables and fire grills are provided. Vault toilets are available. There is no drinking water, and garbage must be packed out. Leashed pets are permitted.

Reservations, fees: Reservations are not accepted. There is no fee. Open May–October, weather permitting.

Directions: From Portland, drive east on U.S. 26 for 57 miles (just past the town of Government Camp) to the junction with Highway 35. Take that exit, bear right on Highway 35, and drive 4.5 miles to Forest Road 3530. Turn southeast and drive one mile to the campground.

Contact: Mount Hood National Forest, Hood River Ranger District, 541/352-6002, fax 541/352-7365, www.fs.fed.us

44 TRILLIUM LAKE

Scenic rating: 9

on Trillium Lake in
Mount Hood National Forest

BEST

This campground (3,600 feet elevation) hugs the shores of Trillium Lake, which is about half a mile long and a quarter mile wide. Fishing is good in the evening here, and the nearby boat ramp makes this an ideal camp for anglers. The lake is great for canoes, rafts, and small rowboats. Trillium Lake is an extremely popular vacation destination, so expect plenty of company. Reservations are highly recommended.

Campsites, facilities: There are 57 sites for tents or RVs of any length. Picnic tables and fire grills are provided. Vault toilets and drinking water are available. Boat docks and launching facilities are available on the lake, but no motors are allowed. Some facilities are wheelchair accessible. Leashed pets are permitted.

Reservations, fees: Reservations are accepted at 877/444-6777 or www.recreation.gov ($10 reservation fee). Sites are $17 per night; double sites are $34 per night, $8–9 per night per additional vehicle. Open late May–late September, weather permitting.

Directions: From Portland, drive east on U.S. 26 for 55 miles to the small town of Government Camp. Continue east on U.S. 26 for 1.5 miles to Forest Road 2656. Turn right and drive 1.3 miles to the campground on the right.

Contact: Mount Hood National Forest, Zigzag Ranger District, 503/622-3191, fax 503/622-5622, www.fs.fed.us.

45 FROG LAKE

Scenic rating: 6

near the Pacific Crest Trail in
Mount Hood National Forest

This classic spot in the Cascade Range is situated on the shore of little Frog Lake (more of a pond than a lake), at an elevation of 3,800 feet and a short distance from the Pacific Crest Trail. Several other trails lead to nearby lakes. Clear Lake, to the south, provides a possible day trip and offers more recreation options.

Campsites, facilities: There are 33 sites for

tents or RVs up to 35 feet long. Picnic tables and fire rings are provided. Drinking water, vault toilets, garbage bins, and firewood are available. A camp host is on-site. Boat-launching facilities are nearby; no motorized boats are allowed. Some facilities are wheelchair accessible. Leashed pets are permitted.

Reservations, fees: Reservations are accepted at 877/444-6777 or www.recreation.gov ($10 reservation fee). Sites are $15–18 per night, $8–9 per night per additional vehicle. Open mid-May–mid-September, weather permitting.

Directions: From Portland, drive east on U.S. 26 for 57 miles to the junction with Highway 35 (two miles past Government Camp). Take that exit, bear right onto Highway 35, and drive seven miles to Forest Road 2610. Turn left and drive 0.5 mile to the campground.

Contact: Mount Hood National Forest, Hood River Ranger District, 541/352-6002, fax 541/352-7365, www.fs.fed.us; park phone, 503/622-3191.

46 BADGER LAKE

Scenic rating: 8

on Badger Lake in Mount Hood National Forest

This campground (4,400 feet elevation) sits along the shore of Badger Lake. Nonmotorized boating is permitted if you can manage to get a boat in here over the rough roads. No trailers are allowed on the campground road. The camp is adjacent to the Badger Creek Wilderness, and numerous trails provide access to the backcountry. Badger Creek Trail heads out of camp, northeast along Badger Creek for several miles.

Campsites, facilities: There are four sites for tents only, accessible only by high-clearance vehicles. Picnic tables and fire grills are provided. Vault toilets are available. There is no drinking water, and garbage must be packed out. Leashed pets are permitted.

Reservations, fees: Reservations are not accepted. Some designated sites are $10 per night; others require a Northwest Forest Pass. Open June–September, weather permitting.

Directions: From Portland, drive east on I-84 for 65 miles to Hood River, Exit 64 and Highway 35. Turn right (south) on Highway 35 and drive 37 miles to Forest Road 48. Turn left and drive 16 miles to Forest Road 4860. Turn left (north) and drive eight miles to Forest Road 140. Bear right and drive four miles to the lake. The last two miles on this primitive road require a high-clearance vehicle.

Contact: Mount Hood National Forest, Barlow Ranger District, 541/467-2291, fax 541/467-2271, www.fs.fed.us.

47 BONNEY MEADOW

Scenic rating: 9

in Mount Hood National Forest

This primitive campground is on the east side of the Cascade Range at an elevation of 4,800 feet. As a result, there is little water in the area, and also very few people, so you're liable to have the place all to yourself. Bonney Meadow Trail leaves from the campground and travels 1.5 miles up to a group of small lakes. This trail provides great mountain views.

Campsites, facilities: There are six sites for tents or RVs up to 16 feet long. Picnic tables and fire grills are provided. Vault toilets are available. There is no drinking water and garbage must be packed out. Leashed pets are permitted.

Reservations, fees: Reservations are not accepted. Sites are $10 per night. Open June–early October, weather permitting.

Directions: From Portland, turn east on I-84 and drive 65 miles to the town of Hood River, Exit 64 and Highway 35. Turn right (south) on Highway 35 and drive 37 miles to Forest Road 48. Turn left and drive 14 miles to Forest Road 4890. Turn left and drive four miles north to

Forest Road 4891. Turn right and drive a short distance to the campground.

Contact: Mount Hood National Forest, Barlow Ranger District, 541/467-2291, fax 541/467-2271, www.fs.fed.us.

48 BONNEY CROSSING

Scenic rating: 7

on Badger Creek in
Mount Hood National Forest

Bonney Crossing campground at 2,200 feet elevation along Badger Creek is the trailhead for the Badger Creek Trail, which provides access to the Badger Creek Wilderness. The camp gets fairly light use and is usually very quiet. Fishing is available in the creek and is usually pretty good. Horse campers are welcome here.

Campsites, facilities: There are eight sites for tents or RVs up to 16 feet long. Picnic tables and fire grills are provided. Vault toilets are available. There is no drinking water, and garbage must be packed out. Stock facilities include horse corrals. Leashed pets are permitted.

Reservations, fees: Reservations are not accepted. Sites are $10 per night. Open mid-April–mid-October, weather permitting.

Directions: From The Dalles, drive south on U.S. 197 for 32 miles to Tygh Valley. Take the Tygh Valley exit to Tygh Valley Road. Turn west and drive 0.25 mile to Wamic Market Road (County Road 226). Turn right (west) and drive eight miles to Wamic. Continue through Wamic and drive seven miles to Forest Road 4810. Bear right and drive three miles to Forest Road 4811. Turn right and drive two miles to a junction with Forest Road 2710. Turn right and drive three miles to the campground on the right.

Contact: Mount Hood National Forest, Barlow Ranger District, 541/467-2291, fax 541/467-2271, www.fs.fed.us.

49 FOREST CREEK

Scenic rating: 6

on Forest Creek in
Mount Hood National Forest

This is a very old camp that borders Forest Creek on the original Barlow Trail, once used by early settlers. Shaded by an old-growth Douglas fir and ponderosa pine forest, you'll camp amid solitude. The elevation here is 3,000 feet. See a U.S. Forest Service map for specific roads and trails.

Campsites, facilities: There are eight sites for tents or RVs up to 16 feet long. Picnic tables and fire grills are provided. No drinking water is available. Vault toilets are available. Garbage must be packed out. Leashed pets are permitted.

Reservations, fees: Reservations are not accepted. Sites are $10 per night. Open June–early October, weather permitting.

Directions: From Portland, turn east on I-84 and drive 91 miles to The Dalles/Exit 87/Highway 197. Turn south and drive 31 miles to Tygh Valley and Wamic Market Road. Turn right and drive west for six miles to Forest Road 48. Continue west and drive 12.5 miles southwest to Forest Road 4885. Turn left and drive one mile to Forest Road 3530. Turn left and drive a short distance to the campground.

Contact: Mount Hood National Forest, Barlow Ranger District, 541/467-2291, fax 541/467-2271, www.fs.fed.us.

50 ROCK CREEK RESERVOIR

Scenic rating: 7

on Rock Creek Reservoir in
Mount Hood National Forest

Fishing is excellent, and the environment is perfect for canoes or rafts at this campground along the shore of Rock Creek Reservoir. Enjoy views of Mount Hood from the day-use area (Northwest Forest Pass required). No hiking trails are in the immediate vicinity, but there are many old forest roads that are ideal for walking or mountain biking. The camp sits at 2,200 feet elevation.

Campsites, facilities: There are 33 sites for tents or RVs up to 18 feet long. Picnic tables, garbage service, and fire grills are provided. Vault toilets, drinking water, and firewood are available. There are boat docks nearby, but no motorboats are allowed on the reservoir. Some facilities are wheelchair accessible. Leashed pets are permitted.

Reservations, fees: Reservations are accepted at 877/444-6777 or www.recreation.gov ($10 reservation fee). Sites are $14–16 per night, $7–8 per night per additional vehicle. Open late May–early October.

Directions: From Portland, turn east on I-84 and drive 91 miles to The Dalles/Exit 87/ Highway 197. Turn south and drive 31 miles to Tygh Valley and Wamic Market Road. Turn right and drive west for six miles to Forest Road 48. Turn west and drive one mile to Forest Road 4820. Turn west and drive a short distance to the campground.

Contact: Mount Hood National Forest, Barlow Ranger District, 541/467-2291, fax 541/467-2271, www.fs.fed.us.

51 PINE HOLLOW LAKESIDE RESORT

Scenic rating: 8

on Pine Hollow Reservoir

This resort on the shore of Pine Hollow Reservoir is the best game in town for RV campers, with some shaded lakefront sites and scenic views. Year-round boating, fishing, swimming, and waterskiing are some recreation options here.

Campsites, facilities: There are 35 tent sites, 78 sites with partial hookups for RVs of any length, and 10 cabins. Picnic tables and fire pits are provided. Drinking water, restrooms with flush toilets and coin showers, propane gas, a dump station, firewood, a convenience store, café, coin laundry, and ice are available. Boat docks, launching facilities, and boat and personal watercraft rentals are nearby. Leashed pets are permitted.

Reservations, fees: Reservations are accepted. Sites are $25 per night, $2 per person per night for more than two people, $2 per night per additional vehicle, and $2 per pet per night. Some credit cards are accepted. Open mid-March–October.

Directions: From Portland, turn east on I-84 and drive 91 miles to The Dalles/Exit 87/ Highway 197. Turn south on Highway 197 and drive 31 miles to Tygh Valley and Wamic Market Road. Turn right (west) and drive four miles to Ross Road. Turn right (north) and drive 3.5 miles to the resort on the right.

Contact: Pine Hollow Lakeside Resort, 541/544-2271, www.pinehollowlakeside.com.

52 HUNT PARK

Scenic rating: 6

near Badger Creek

This Wasco County campground is set near the confluence of Badger and Tygh Creeks. Hiking trails, marked bike trails, and tennis courts are nearby, and fishing and rafting are available on the Deschutes River.

Campsites, facilities: There are 150 tent sites, 120 pull-through sites with partial hookups for RVs of any length, and a group site for tents only. Picnic tables are provided. Drinking water, restrooms with flush toilets and coin showers, a dump station, garbage bins, a basketball court, wireless Internet, and picnic shelters (which can be reserved) are available. Horse facilities, including stalls and an arena, are also available. A camp host is on-site. A store, café, and ice are within one mile. Some facilities are wheelchair accessible. Leashed pets are permitted.

Reservations, fees: Reservations are accepted at 541/483-2288. Sites are $12–15 per night, $3 per night per additional vehicle. The group site is $5 per person per night for up to 100 people, $3 per person thereafter. Open May–October.

Directions: From Portland, turn east on I-84 and drive 91 miles to The Dalles/Exit 87/Highway 197. Turn south on Highway 197 and drive 31 miles to Tygh Valley and Main Street. Turn right on Main Street and drive two blocks to Fairgrounds Road. Turn right and drive one mile to the fairgrounds on the right.

Contact: Wasco County, 541/483-2288, http://co.wasco.or.us.

53 HIDEAWAY LAKE

Scenic rating: 9

near the Rock Lakes Basin in Mount Hood National Forest

This jewel of a spot features a small, deep lake where non-motorized boats are allowed, but they must be carried about 100 yards to the lake. The campsites are separate and scattered around the shore. At the north end of the lake, an 8.5-mile loop trail passes a number of lakes in the Rock Lakes Basin, all of which support populations of rainbow and brook trout. If you don't want to make the whole trip in a day, you can camp overnight at Serene Lake. See a U.S. Forest Service map for information.

Campsites, facilities: There are nine sites for tents or small RVs up to 16 feet long. Picnic tables and fire grills are provided. Vault toilets are available. There is no drinking water. Leashed pets are permitted.

Reservations, fees: Reservations are not accepted. Sites are $14 per night, $7 per night per additional vehicle. Open mid-June–late September, weather permitting.

Directions: From Portland, drive south on U.S. 205 to the junction with Highway 224/Estacada. Take the exit and turn left onto Highway 224, heading south. Drive approximately 13 miles to Estacada. Continue south on Highway 224 and drive 27 miles to Forest Road 57. Turn left (east) and drive 7.5 miles to Forest Road 58. Turn left (north) and drive three miles to Forest Road 5830. Turn left (northwest) and drive 5.5 miles to the campground on the left.

Contact: Mount Hood National Forest, Clackamas River Ranger District, 503/630-6861, fax 503/630-2299, www.fs.fed.us.

54 CLEAR LAKE

Scenic rating: 4

near the Pacific Crest Trail in Mount Hood National Forest

This campground is located along the shore of Clear Lake, a spot favored by anglers, swimmers, and windsurfers, but as a reservoir, it is subject to water-level fluctuations. The boating speed limit is 10 mph. This wooded camp features shady sites and is set at 3,600 feet elevation. The camp sometimes gets noisy from the revels of the party set. If you want quiet, this spot is probably not for you. A nearby trail heads north from the lake and provides access to the Pacific Crest Trail and Frog Lake, both good recreation options.

Campsites, facilities: There are 28 sites for tents or RVs up to 30 feet long and one lookout cabin. Picnic tables and fire grills are provided. Drinking water, garbage bins, firewood, and vault toilets are available. Some facilities are wheelchair accessible. Boat-launching facilities are nearby. Leashed pets are permitted.

Reservations, fees: Reservations are accepted at 877/444-6777 or www.recreation.gov ($10 reservation fee). Sites are $16–18 per night, $8–9 per night per additional vehicle. The lookout cabin is $30 per night. Open mid-May–late September, weather permitting.

Directions: From Portland, drive east on U.S. 26 for 57 miles to the junction with Highway 35 (two miles past Government Camp). Bear right (southeast) on U.S. 26 and drive nine miles to Forest Road 2630. Turn right (south) and drive one mile to the campground on the right.
Contact: Mount Hood National Forest, Hood River Ranger District, 541/352-6002, fax 541/352-7365, www.fs.fed.us.

55 BARLOW CREEK

Scenic rating: 7

on Barlow Creek in Mount Hood National Forest

One of several primitive U.S. Forest Service camps in the immediate vicinity, this campground is set along Barlow Creek at an elevation of 3,100 feet. It is on Old Barlow Road, which was the wagon trail for early settlers in this area. If this campground is full, Barlow Crossing Campground is one mile southeast on Forest Road 3530.
Campsites, facilities: There are three sites for tents. Picnic tables and fire grills are provided. Vault toilets are available. There is no drinking water, and garbage must be packed out. Leashed pets are permitted.
Reservations, fees: Reservations are not accepted. Sites are $10 per night. Open May–September, weather permitting.
Directions: From Portland, drive east on U.S. 26 for 57 miles to the junction with Highway 35 (two miles past Government Camp). Stay on U.S. 26 and continue 12 miles to Forest Road 43. Turn left and drive five miles to Forest Road 3530. Turn left (north) and drive 1.5 miles to the campground on the left.
Contact: Mount Hood National Forest, Hood River Ranger District, 541/352-6002, fax 541/352-7365, www.fs.fed.us.

56 WHITE RIVER STATION

Scenic rating: 9

on the White River in Mount Hood National Forest

This tiny campground is set along the White River at an elevation of 3,000 feet. It is on Old Barlow Road, an original wagon trail used by early settlers. One of several small, secluded camps in the area, White River Station is quiet and private, but with poor fishing prospects.
Campsites, facilities: There are five sites for tents or RVs up to 32 feet long. Picnic tables and fire grills are provided. Vault toilets are available. There is no drinking water, and garbage must be packed out. Leashed pets are permitted.
Reservations, fees: Reservations are not accepted. Sites are $10 per night, $5 per night per additional vehicle. Open May–September, weather permitting.
Directions: From Portland, drive east on U.S. 26 for 57 miles to the junction with Highway 35 (two miles past Government Camp). Stay on U.S. 26 and continue 12 miles to Forest Road 43. Turn left and drive five miles to Forest Road 3530. Turn right and drive approximately 1.5 miles to the campground on the left. (White River is less than one mile away from Barlow Creek.)
Contact: Mount Hood National Forest, Barlow Ranger District, 541/467-2291, fax 541/467-2271, www.fs.fed.us.

57 LAKE HARRIET

Scenic rating: 5

on Lake Harriet in Mount Hood National Forest

Formed by a dam on the Oak Grove Fork of the Clackamas River, this little lake is a popular spot during the summer. Rowboats and boats with small motors are permitted, but only non-motorized boats are encouraged. The lake is stocked regularly and can provide good fishing for a variety of trout, including brook, brown, cutthroat, and rainbow. Anglers often stand shoulder to shoulder in summer.

Campsites, facilities: There are 11 sites for tents or RVs up to 40 feet long. Picnic tables and fire grills are provided. Drinking water and vault toilets are available. Garbage service is provided in the summer. A fishing pier and boat-launching facilities are on the lake. Some facilities are wheelchair accessible. Leashed pets are permitted.

Reservations, fees: Reservations are accepted at 877/444-6777 or www.recreation.gov ($10 reservation fee). Sites are $16 per night, $8 per night per additional vehicle. Open year-round, weather permitting, with limited winter services.

Directions: From Portland, drive south on U.S. 205 to the junction with Highway 224/Estacada. Take the exit and turn left onto Highway 224, heading south. Drive approximately 13 miles to Estacada. Continue south on Highway 224 and drive 27 miles to Forest Road 57. Turn east and drive 7.5 miles to Forest Road 4630. Turn left and drive two miles to the campground on the left.

Contact: Mount Hood National Forest, Clackamas River Ranger District, 503/630-6861, fax 503/630-2299, www.fs.fed.us.

58 GONE CREEK

Scenic rating: 8

on Timothy Lake in
Mount Hood National Forest

BEST

This campground, set along the south shore of Timothy Lake at 3,200 feet elevation, is one of five camps at the lake. Timothy Lake provides good fishing for brook trout, cutthroat trout, kokanee salmon, and rainbow trout. Boats with motors are allowed, but a 10-mph speed limit keeps it quiet. Several trails in the area—including the Pacific Crest Trail—provide access to a number of small mountain lakes.

Campsites, facilities: There are 49 sites for tents or RVs up to 45 feet long. Picnic tables and fire grills are provided. Drinking water, garbage service, vault toilets, and firewood are available. A boat ramp is nearby. Leashed pets are permitted.

Reservations, fees: Reservations are accepted at 877/444-6777 or www.recreation.gov ($10 reservation fee). Sites are $17–18 per night, $8–9 per night per additional vehicle. Open mid-May–early September, weather permitting.

Directions: From Portland, drive on U.S. 26 for 55 miles (just past the town of Government Camp) to the junction with Highway 35. Bear southeast, staying on U.S. 26, and drive 15 miles to Forest Road 42 (Skyline Road). Turn right and drive eight miles to Forest Road 57. Turn right and drive one mile west to the campground on the right.

Contact: Mount Hood National Forest, Zigzag Ranger District, 503/622-3191, fax 503/622-5622, www.fs.fed.us.

59 OAK FORK

Scenic rating: 8

on Timothy Lake in
Mount Hood National Forest

Heavy timber and bear grass surround this forested camp along the south shore of Timothy Lake, where fishing is good for brook trout, cutthroat trout, kokanee salmon, and rainbow trout. Boats with motors are allowed, but a 10-mph speed limit is enforced. Oak Fork is located just east of Hoodview and Gone Creek campgrounds, at an elevation of 3,200 feet. Several area trails—including the Pacific Crest—provide access to various small mountain lakes.

Campsites, facilities: There are 46 sites for

tents or RVs up to 45 feet long. Picnic tables and fire grills are provided. Drinking water, firewood, and vault toilets are available. A boat ramp and launching facilities are nearby; the speed limit on the lake is 10 mph. Leashed pets are permitted.

Reservations, fees: Reservations are accepted at 877/444-6777 or www.recreation.gov ($10 reservation fee). Sites are $17–18 per night, $8–9 per night per additional vehicle. Open May–early October, weather permitting.

Directions: From Portland, turn east on U.S. 26 and drive 57 miles (just past the town of Government Camp) to the junction with Highway 35. Bear southeast, staying on U.S. 26, and drive 15 miles to Forest Road 42 (Skyline Road). Turn right and drive eight miles to Forest Road 57. Turn right and drive three miles to the camp on the right.

Contact: Mount Hood National Forest, Zigzag Ranger District, 503/622-3191, fax 503/622-5622, www.fs.fed.us.

60 PINE POINT

Scenic rating: 8

on Timothy Lake in Mount Hood National Forest

One of five camps on Timothy Lake, Pine Point spot sits at an elevation of 3,400 feet on the southwest shore. This camp has lake access and more open vegetation than the other Timothy Lake campgrounds. There's good fishing for brook trout, cutthroat trout, kokanee salmon, and rainbow trout, and a 10-mph speed limit keeps it pleasant for everyone. The trail that leads around the lake and to the Pacific Crest Trail passes along this campground.

Campsites, facilities: There are 25 sites for tents or RVs up to 45 feet long, including 12 single sites, eight double sites, and five group sites for up to 25 people each. Picnic tables, garbage service, and fire grills are provided. Drinking water and vault toilets are available. A boat ramp, launching facilities, and fishing pier are nearby; the speed limit on the lake is 10 mph. Leashed pets are permitted.

Reservations, fees: Reservations are accepted at 877/444-6777 or www.recreation.gov ($10 reservation fee). Single sites are $17 per night, $34 per night for a double site, and $8–9 per night per additional vehicle. Group sites are $50 per night. Open late May–mid-September, weather permitting.

Directions: From Portland, turn east on U.S. 26 and drive 57 miles (just past the town of Government Camp) to the junction with Highway 35. Bear southeast, staying on U.S. 26, and drive 15 miles to Forest Road 42 (Skyline Road). Turn right and drive eight miles to Forest Road 57. Turn right and drive four miles to the park on the right.

Contact: Mount Hood National Forest, Zigzag Ranger District, 503/622-3191, fax 503/622-5622, www.fs.fed.us.

61 HOODVIEW

Scenic rating: 9

on Timothy Lake in Mount Hood National Forest

Here's another camp along the south shore of Timothy Lake; this one is set at 3,200 feet elevation. Timothy Lake provides good fishing for brook trout, cutthroat trout, kokanee salmon, and rainbow trout. Motorized boats are allowed, and the speed limit is 10 mph. A trail out of camp branches south for a few miles and, if followed to the east, eventually leads to the Pacific Crest Trail.

Campsites, facilities: There are 41 sites for tents or RVs up to 45 feet long. Picnic tables and fire grills are provided. Vault toilets, drinking water, garbage service, and firewood are available. A boat ramp is nearby. Leashed pets are permitted.

Reservations, fees: Reservations are accepted at 877/444-6777 or www.recreation.gov ($10 reservation fee). Sites are $17–18 per night, $8–9 per night per additional vehicle. Open mid-May–mid-September, weather permitting.

Directions: From Portland, turn east on U.S. 26 and drive 57 miles (just past the town of Government Camp) to the junction with Highway 35. Bear southeast, staying on U.S. 26, and drive 15 miles to Forest Road 42 (Skyline Road). Turn right and drive eight miles to Forest Road 57. Turn right and drive three miles to the campground on the right.

Contact: Mount Hood National Forest, Zigzag Ranger District, 503/622-3191, fax 503/622-5622, www.fs.fed.us.

62 MEDITATION POINT

Scenic rating: 9

on Timothy Lake in Mount Hood National Forest

BEST

Accessible only by foot or boat, this remote and rustic camp sits at 3,200 feet elevation and offers the most secluded location along Timothy Lake. It's one of two campgrounds on the north shore of the lake, which means you'll get a quieter, less crowded environment, though you'll have to bring your own water. The lake has a 10-mph speed limit for boaters. Timothy Lake Trail makes a 14-mile loop around the lake.

Campsites, facilities: There are five boat-in or walk-in tent sites. Picnic tables and fire grills are provided. Vault toilets are available. There is no drinking water, and garbage must be packed out. Boat docks and launching facilities are nearby. Leashed pets are permitted.

Reservations, fees: Reservations are not accepted. Access from PGE Day Use Area requires a $5 fee or a Northwest Forest Pass. There is no fee for camping. Open late May–mid-September, weather permitting.

Directions: From Portland, drive east on U.S. 26 and drive 57 miles to the junction with Highway 35 (two miles past Government Camp). Bear right (southeast), staying on U.S. 26, and continue for 15 miles to Forest Road 42/Skyline Road. Turn right and drive eight miles south to Forest Road 57. Turn right and drive five miles, passing Pine Point Campground and crossing the Timothy Lake Dam. Park in the day-use area and hike one mile or take a boat to the north shore of the lake.

Contact: Mount Hood National Forest, Zigzag Ranger District, 503/622-3191, fax 503/622-5622, www.fs.fed.us.

63 LITTLE CRATER LAKE

Scenic rating: 7

on Clear Creek in Mount Hood National Forest

Little Crater campground (3,200 feet elevation) nestles against Crater Creek and scenic Little Crater Lake. This camp is popular with hunters in the fall. Both the drinking water and the lake water are spring fed, and the water is numbingly cold. The Pacific Crest Trail is located near camp, providing hiking trail access. Fishing is poor at Little Crater Lake. Little Timothy Lake lies about 10 miles away; note the 10-mph speed limit for boats. Bring your mosquito repellent—you'll need it.

Campsites, facilities: There are 16 sites for tents or RVs up to 35 feet long. Picnic tables, garbage bins, and fire grills are provided. Vault toilets, firewood, and drinking water are available. Leashed pets are permitted.

Reservations, fees: Reservations are accepted at 877/444-6777 or www.recreation.gov ($10 reservation fee). Sites are $16 per night, $8 per night per additional vehicle. Open May–mid-September, weather permitting.

Directions: From Portland, drive east on U.S. 26 for 57 miles to the junction with Highway 35 (two miles past Government Camp). Bear right (southeast), staying on U.S. 26, and drive 15 miles to Forest Road 42 (Skyline Road). Turn right and drive about six miles to Forest Road 58. Turn right and drive about 2.5 miles to the campground on the left.

Contact: Mount Hood National Forest, Zigzag Ranger District, 503/622-3191, fax 503/622-5622, www.fs.fed.us.

64 CLEAR CREEK CROSSING

Scenic rating: 7

on Clear Creek in Mount Hood National Forest

This secluded, little-known spot hugs the banks of Clear Creek at an elevation of 3,600 feet. Clear Creek Trail, a very pretty walk, begins at the campground. Fishing and hiking are two recreation options here.

Campsites, facilities: There are seven sites for tents or RVs up to 16 feet long. Picnic tables and fire grills are provided. Vault toilets are available. There is no drinking water, and garbage must be packed out. Leashed pets are permitted.

Reservations, fees: Reservations are not accepted. Sites are $10 per night. Open May–September, weather permitting.

Directions: From Portland, drive east on U.S. 26 for 55 miles to Government Camp. Continue three miles to a junction and bear right, staying on U.S. 26, and drive south for 12 miles to Highway 216. Turn left (east) on Highway 216 and drive two miles to Forest Road 2130. Turn left (north) on Forest Road 2130 and drive three miles to the campground.

Contact: Mount Hood National Forest, Barlow Ranger District, 541/467-2291, fax 541/467-2271, www.fs.fed.us.

65 KEEPS MILL

Scenic rating: 9

on Clear Creek in Mount Hood National Forest

This small, pretty campground is situated at the confluence of Clear Creek and the White River. No RVs are permitted. The elevation is 2,600 feet. Many hiking trails, some with awesome views of the White River Canyon, crisscross the area, but be warned: These are butt-kicking canyon climbs.

Campsites, facilities: There are five sites for tents only. The road to the campground is not good for trailers. Picnic tables and fire grills are provided. Vault toilets are available. There is no drinking water, and garbage must be packed out. Leashed pets are permitted.

Reservations, fees: Reservations are not accepted. Sites are $10 per night. Open May–September, weather permitting.

Directions: From Portland, drive east on U.S. 26 for 55 miles to Government Camp. Continue three miles to a junction, turn right on U.S. 26, and drive south for 12 miles to Highway 216. Turn left (east) on Highway 216 and drive three miles to Forest Road 2120. Turn left (north) on Forest Road 2120 and drive three miles to the campground.

Contact: Mount Hood National Forest, Barlow Ranger District, 541/467-2291, fax 541/467-2271, www.fs.fed.us.

66 BEAR SPRINGS

Scenic rating: 6

on Indian Creek in Mount Hood National Forest

This campground is set along the banks of Indian Creek on the border of the Warm Springs Indian Reservation and features both secluded and open sites set in old-growth forest. The elevation is 3,000 feet.

Campsites, facilities: There are 21 sites for tents or RVs up to 32 feet long. Picnic tables and fire grills are provided. Drinking water, garbage bins, vault toilets, and firewood are available. Leashed pets are permitted.

Reservations, fees: Reservations are not accepted. Sites are $12 per night and $6 per night for each additional vehicle. Open June–September, weather permitting.

Directions: From Portland, drive east on U.S. 26 for 55 miles to Government Camp. Continue three miles to a junction and bear right, staying on U.S. 26, and drive south for 12 miles to Highway 216. Turn left (east) on Highway 216 and drive four miles to Reservation Road. Turn right (east) on Reservation Road and look for the campground on the right.

Contact: Mount Hood National Forest, Barlow Ranger District, 541/467-2291, fax 541/467-2271, www.fs.fed.us.

67 McCUBBINS GULCH

Scenic rating: 5

in Mount Hood National Forest

This small, primitive camp sits alongside a small creek at 3,000 feet in elevation and offers decent fishing and OHV (off-highway vehicle) recreation. A 40-mile network of OHV trails runs through the surrounding forest, with access right from camp. So, though out of the way, this camp gets heavy use; claim a spot early in the day. To the south is the Warm Springs Indian Reservation; do not trespass, as large fines are assessed to those prosecuted. Bear Springs provides a nearby camping alternative.

Campsites, facilities: There are 15 sites for tents and RVs up to 25 feet long. Picnic tables and fire grills are provided. Vault toilets are available. There is no drinking water, and garbage must be packed out. Leashed pets are permitted.

Reservations, fees: Reservations are not accepted. Sites are $10 per night. Open May–September, weather permitting.

Directions: From Portland, drive east on U.S. 26 for 55 miles to Government Camp. Continue three miles to a junction and bear right, staying on U.S. 26, and drive south for 12 miles to Highway 216. Turn left (east) on Highway 216 and drive six miles to Forest Road 2110. Take a sharp left and drive 1.5 miles to the campground entrance on the right.

Contact: Mount Hood National Forest, Barlow Ranger District, 541/467-2291, fax 541/467-2271, www.fs.fed.us.

68 SHELLROCK CREEK

Scenic rating: 6

on Shellrock Creek in Mount Hood National Forest

This quiet little campground (2,200 feet elevation) occupies a nice spot on Shellrock Creek and has been used primarily as an overflow area for Lake Harriet campground. Small trout can be caught here, but remember that on the Clackamas River it's catch-and-release only. Obtain a U.S. Forest Service map for details on the backcountry roads and trails.

Campsites, facilities: There are eight sites for tents or RVs up to 16 feet long. Picnic tables and fire grills are provided. Vault toilets are available. There is no drinking water and garbage must be packed out. Leashed pets are permitted.

Note: In 2010, the Forest Service plans some changes to several campgrounds in the Estacada Ranger District.

Reservations, fees: Reservations are not accepted. Sites are $14 per night, $7 per night per additional vehicle. Open year-round, with limited winter services.

Directions: From Portland, drive south on U.S. 205 to the junction with Highway 24. Take the Highway 224/Estacada exit and turn left (south) onto Highway 224. Drive approximately 13 miles to Estacada. Continue south on Highway 224 for 27 miles in national forest (the road becomes Forest Road 46) to Forest Road 57. Turn left (east) and drive 7.5 miles to Forest Road 58. Turn left and drive north one mile to the campground on the left.

Contact: Mount Hood National Forest, Clackamas River Ranger District, Estacada Ranger Station, 503/630-6861, fax 503/630-2299, www.fs.fed.us.

69 JOE GRAHAM HORSE CAMP

Scenic rating: 8

near Clackamas Lake in Mount Hood National Forest

Named for a forest ranger, this campground sits at 3,250 feet elevation among majestic Douglas fir and hemlock, just north of tiny Clackamas Lake. It's one of two campgrounds in the area that allow horses. Timothy Lake (the setting for the Gone Creek, Hoodview, Meditation Point, Oak Fork, and Pine Point camps) provides a nearby alternative to the northwest. The Pacific Crest Trail is just east of camp.

Campsites, facilities: There are 15 sites for tents, horse trailers, or RVs up to 45 feet long; 11 have corrals, and two have hitching rails. Picnic tables, hitching posts, garbage service, and fire grills are provided. Drinking water and vault toilets are available. Leashed pets are permitted.

Reservations, fees: Reservations are accepted at 877/444-6777 or www.recreation.gov ($10 reservation fee). Sites are $17 per night, $8.50 per night per additional vehicle. Open mid-May–mid-October, weather permitting.

Directions: From Portland, turn east on U.S. 26 and drive 57 miles (just past the town of Government Camp) to the junction with Highway 35. Bear right, continuing southeast on U.S. 26, and drive 15 miles to Forest Road 42 (Skyline Road). Turn right and drive eight miles to the campground on the left.

Contact: Mount Hood National Forest, Zigzag Ranger District, 503/622-3191, fax 503/622-5622, www.fs.fed.us.

70 CLACKAMAS LAKE

Scenic rating: 7

near the Clackamas River in Mount Hood National Forest

This camp, set at 3,400 feet elevation, is a good place to go to escape the hordes of people at the lakeside sites in neighboring camps. The Pacific Crest Trail passes nearby, and Timothy Lake requires little more than a one-mile hike from camp. The Clackamas Lake Historic Ranger Station, a visitors center, is worth a visit and is still using the old, hand crank–style phones once used in lookout towers and guard stations. This is a popular spot for campers with horses, although the facilities could use some updating and repairs.

Campsites, facilities: There are 46 sites for tents, trailers, horse trailers, or RVs up to 45 feet long. Some sites have hitch rails, and horses are permitted at the first 19 sites. Drinking water, garbage service, fire grills, and picnic tables are provided. Vault toilets are available. Boat docks and launching facilities are nearby at Timothy Lake, but only non-motorized boats are allowed. Leashed pets are permitted.

Reservations, fees: Reservations are accepted at 877/444-6777 or www.recreation.gov ($10 reservation fee). Sites are $16 per night, $8 per night per additional vehicle. Open May–mid-September, weather permitting.

Directions: From Portland, turn east on U.S. 26 and drive 57 miles (just past the town of Government Camp) to the junction with Highway 35. Bear southeast, staying on U.S. 26, and drive 15 miles to Forest Road 42 (Skyline Road). Turn right and drive eight miles to Forest Road 57. Continue 500 feet (on Forest Road 42) past the Clackamas Lake Historic Ranger Station to Forest Road 4270. Turn left and drive 0.5 mile to the campground on the left.

Contact: Mount Hood National Forest, Zigzag Ranger District, 503/622-3191, fax 503/622-5622, www.fs.fed.us.

71 DESCHUTES RIVER STATE RECREATION AREA

Scenic rating: 7

on the Deschutes River

This tree-shaded park along the Deschutes River in the Deschutes Canyon offers bicycling and hiking trails and good steelhead fishing in season. The river-level Atiyeh Deschutes River Trail is a favorite jaunt for hikers. A small day-use state park called Heritage Landing, which has a boat ramp and restroom facilities, is located across the river. The U.S. Army Corps of Engineers offers a free train ride and tour of the dam at The Dalles during the summer. Good rafting is a bonus here. For 25 miles upstream, the river is mostly inaccessible by car. Many anglers launch boats here and then go upstream to steelhead fishing grounds. Note that boat fishing is not allowed here; you must wade into the river or fish from shore.

Campsites, facilities: There are 34 sites with partial hookups for tents or RVs up to 50 feet, 25 primitive sites for tents or self-contained RVs up to 30 feet, and four group areas for RVs and tents, which can hold up to 25 people and five RVs each. Picnic tables and fire grills are provided, but campfires are prohibited July 1–September 30. Drinking water, garbage bins, and flush toilets are available. Leashed pets are permitted.

Reservations, fees: Reservations are accepted at 800/452-5687 or www.oregonstateparks.org ($8 reservation fee). Sites with partial-hookup are $12–20 per night, primitive sites are $5–9 per night, $5 per night per additional vehicle. Group sites are $40–71 per night. Some credit cards are accepted. Open year-round, with limited services November–March.

Directions: From Portland, turn east on I-84 and drive about 90 miles to The Dalles. Continue east on I-84 for 12 miles to Exit 97/Deschutes State Recreation Area, turn right, and drive 50 feet to Biggs-Rufus Highway. Turn left and drive about three miles, cross the Deschutes River, and turn right to the campground entrance.

Contact: Deschutes River State Recreation Area, 541/739-2322 or 800/452-5687, www.oregonstateparks.org.

72 LEPAGE PARK

Scenic rating: 6

on the John Day River

Half of the campsites are adjacent to the John Day River and the other half are on the opposite side of the road at this partially shaded campground. The John Day River feeds into the Columbia just 0.12 mile north of the campground. Rattlesnakes are occasionally seen in the area but are not abundant. Anglers come for the smallmouth bass and catfish during the summer. The day-use area has a swimming beach, lawn, boat launch, and boat docks. There are several other campgrounds nearby.

Campsites, facilities: There is a grassy area with 20 walk-in sites for tents and 22 sites with partial hookups for tents or RVs up to 56 feet long; some sites are pull-through. Picnic tables and fire pits are provided. Drinking water, restrooms with flush toilets and showers, and pit toilets are available. A boat ramp, docks, dump station, fish-cleaning station, and garbage containers are also available. Food, gasoline, and coin laundry are available five miles away in the town of Rufus. Leashed pets are permitted.

Reservations, fees: Reservations are accepted at 877/444-6777 or www.recreation.gov ($10 reservation fee). RV sites are $18–20 per night, and tent sites are $12–14 per night. Some credit cards are accepted. Open April–October.

Directions: From Portland on I-84, drive east 120 miles (30 miles past The Dalles) to Exit 114, the John Day River Recreation Area. The campground is just off I-84.

Contact: Army Corps of Engineers, Portland

District, 503/808-5150, fax 503/808-4515; LePage Park, 541/739-2713.

73 BEAVERTAIL

Scenic rating: 6

on the Deschutes River

This isolated campground is set at an elevation of 2,900 feet along the banks of the Deschutes River, one of the classic steelhead streams in the Pacific Northwest. The camp provides fishing and rafting options. The open landscape affords canyon views. This is my favorite put-in spot for a drift boat for fishing float trips on the Deschutes. I've made the trip from Beavertail to the mouth of the Deschutes, ideal in four days, camping at BLM boat-in sites along the river and fly-fishing for steelhead. A boating pass is required to float the river. There are 12 other BLM campgrounds along upper and lower Deschutes River Road. The hardest part is getting used to the freight trains that rumble through the canyon at night.

Campsites, facilities: There are 17 sites for tents or RVs up to 30 feet long and two group sites for up to 16 people. Picnic tables, garbage bins, and fire grills are provided. No campfires are allowed June 1–October 15. Drinking water and vault toilets are available. Boat-launching facilities are nearby. Some facilities are wheelchair accessible. Leashed pets are permitted.

Reservations, fees: Reservations are not accepted. Sites are $8–12 per night, with a 14-day stay limit. Group sites are $25–35 per night. Open year-round.

Directions: From Portland, drive east on U.S. 84 to The Dalles and Highway 197. Turn south and drive to Maupin. Continue through Maupin, cross the bridge, and within a mile look for Deschutes River Road on your left. Turn left on Deschutes River Road and drive 21 miles northeast to the campground.

Contact: Bureau of Land Management, Prineville District, 541/416-6700, fax 541/416-6798, www.blm.gov.

74 SHADY COVE

Scenic rating: 7

on the Little North Santiam River in Willamette National Forest

Shady Cove campground is on the Little North Santiam River in the recently designated Opal Creek Scenic Recreation Area. The Little North Santiam Trail runs adjacent to the campground.

Campsites, facilities: There are 12 sites for tents or RVs up to 16 feet long. Picnic tables, garbage service (summer only), fire grills, and vault toilets are available. There is no drinking water. Leashed pets are permitted.

Reservations, fees: Reservations are not accepted. Sites are $8–10 per night, $5 per night per additional vehicle. Open year-round, weather permitting.

Directions: From Salem on I-5, take Exit 253 to Highway 22. Turn east and drive 23 miles to Mehama and North Fork Road (Marion County Road). Turn left and drive 17 miles northeast to the fork. Bear right on Forest Road 2207 and continue for two miles to the campground on the right.

Contact: Willamette National Forest, Detroit Ranger District, 503/854-3366, fax 503/854-4239, www.fs.fed.us.

75 ELK LAKE

Scenic rating: 9

near Bull of the Woods Wilderness

This remote and primitive campground (3,700 feet elevation) borders the shore of Elk Lake, where boating, fishing, and swimming can be quite good in the summer. Wildflower blooms can be beautiful in the nearby meadows. Several trails in the area provide access to the Bull of the Woods Wilderness (operated by Mount Hood National Forest) and the newly designated Opal Creek Wilderness. The campground also offers beautiful views of Battle Ax Mountain.

Campsites, facilities: There are 12 primitive tent sites. Pit toilets are available. There is no drinking water, and garbage must be packed out. Primitive boat-launching facilities are available. Leashed pets are permitted.

Reservations, fees: Reservations are not accepted. There is no fee for camping. Open June–October, weather permitting.

Directions: From Salem on I-5, take Exit 253, turn east on Highway 22, and drive 52 miles to Detroit. Turn left on Forest Road 46/Breitenbush Road and drive 4.5 miles to Forest Road 4696/Elk Lake Road. Turn left and drive less than one mile to Forest Road 4697. Turn left and drive 9.5 miles to the campground on the left. The road is extremely rough for the last five miles; high-clearance vehicles are recommended.

Contact: Willamette National Forest, Detroit Ranger District, 503/854-3366, fax 503/854-4239, www.fs.fed.us.

76 HUMBUG

Scenic rating: 9

on the Breitenbush River in Willamette National Forest

Fishing and hiking are popular at this campground along the banks of the Breitenbush River, about four miles from where it empties into Detroit Lake. The lake offers many other recreation opportunities. The Humbug Flat Trailhead is behind Sites 9 and 10, and a scenic stroll through an old-growth forest follows the Breitenbush River. The rhododendrons put on a spectacular show May–July.

Campsites, facilities: There are 22 sites for tents or RVs up to 30 feet long. Picnic tables and fire grills are provided. Garbage service (summer only), drinking water, firewood, and vault toilets are available. Leashed pets are permitted.

Reservations, fees: Reservations are not accepted. Sites are $12 per night, $5 per night per additional vehicle. Open year-round, weather permitting, with limited winter facilities.

Directions: From Salem on I-5, take Exit 253, turn east on Highway 22, and drive 52 miles to Detroit. Turn left on Forest Road 46/Breitenbush Road and drive five miles northeast to the campground on the right.

Contact: Willamette National Forest, Detroit Ranger District, 503/854-3366, fax 503/854-4239, www.fs.fed.us.

77 DETROIT LAKE STATE RECREATION AREA

Scenic rating: 7

on Detroit Lake

This campground is set at 1,600 feet elevation along the shore of Detroit Lake, which is 400 feet deep, nine miles long, and has more than 32 miles of shoreline. The park offers a fishing dock and a moorage area, and a boat ramp and bathhouse are available nearby at the Mongold Day Use Area. The heavily stocked lake is crowded on the opening day of trout season in late April.

Campsites, facilities: There are 178 sites with full or partial hookups for RVs up to 60 feet long, 133 tent sites, and 82 boat slips. Drinking water, garbage bins, fire grills, and picnic tables are provided. Firewood and restrooms with flush toilets and showers are available. Recreation facilities include two playgrounds, swimming areas, horseshoe pits, basketball and volleyball courts, an amphitheater, a gift shop, and a visitors center. A camp host is on-site. Two boat docks and launching facilities are nearby. Some facilities are wheelchair accessible. Leashed pets are permitted.

Reservations, fees: Reservations are accepted at 800/452-5687 or www.oregonstateparks.org ($8 reservation fee). RV sites are $16–24 per night, tent sites are $12–19 per night, $5 per night per additional vehicle. Boating moorage is $7 per night. Some credit cards are accepted. Open mid-March–September, weather permitting.

Directions: From Salem, drive east on Highway 22 for 50 miles to the park entrance on the right (located two miles west of Detroit).

Contact: Detroit Lake State Recreation Area, 503/854-3406 or 503/854-3346, www.oregonstateparks.org.

78 PIETY ISLAND BOAT-IN

Scenic rating: 10

on Detroit Lake in Willamette National Forest

BEST

This island gets crowded and has a reputation for sometimes attracting rowdy groups. Other campgrounds along the shore have drinking water. Piety Island Trail climbs 1.5 miles to the top of the island. You'll find great vistas on this island, which sits at 1,600 feet in elevation.

Campsites, facilities: This is an island campground with 22 tent sites accessible only by boat. Picnic tables and fire grills are provided. Pit toilets are available. There is no drinking water. Boat docks, launching facilities, and rentals are nearby. Leashed pets are permitted.

Reservations, fees: Reservations are not accepted. Single sites are $10 per night; double sites are $20 per night. Open year-round, weather permitting.

Directions: From Salem, drive east on Highway 22 for 45 miles to Detroit Lake. Continue east on Highway 22 along the north side of the lake to the boat ramp (three miles west of the town of Detroit). Launch your boat and head southeast to the island in the middle of the lake. The campground is on the east side of the island.

Contact: Willamette National Forest, Detroit Ranger District, 503/854-3366, fax 503/854-4239, www.fs.fed.us.

79 SOUTHSHORE

Scenic rating: 9

on Detroit Lake in Willamette National Forest

This popular camp hugs the south shore of Detroit Lake, where fishing, swimming, and waterskiing are some of the recreation options. The Stahlman Point Trailhead is about half a mile from camp. There's a day-use area for picnicking and swimming. The views of the lake and surrounding mountains are outstanding.

Campsites, facilities: There are eight walk-in tent sites and 22 sites for tents or RVs up to 30 feet long. Fire grills, garbage service, and picnic tables are provided. Vault toilets, drinking water, and firewood are available. Boat-launching facilities are nearby at a day-use area. Some facilities are wheelchair accessible. Leashed pets are permitted.

Reservations, fees: Reservations are not accepted. Sites are $16 for a single site, $32 for double site, and $5 per night per additional vehicle. Open May–late September, with a gate preventing access during the off-season.

Directions: From Salem, drive east on Highway 22 for 52 miles to Detroit. Continue southeast on Highway 22 for 2.5 miles to Forest Road 10 (Blowout Road). Turn right and drive four miles to the campground on the right.

Contact: Willamette National Forest, Detroit Ranger District, 503/854-3366, fax 503/854-4239, www.fs.fed.us.

80 COVE CREEK

Scenic rating: 10

on Detroit Lake in Willamette National Forest

BEST

Cove Creek is a popular campground, and it gets high use in the summer. Situated in a forest, the campground is located on the south side of the lake, about one mile from both Hoover and Southshore campgrounds. Water sports are popular, and both waterskiing and personal watercraft are allowed.

Campsites, facilities: There are 63 sites for tents or RVs of any length and one group site for up to 70 people. Picnic tables and fire rings are provided. Drinking water, restrooms with flush toilets and coin showers, garbage bins, firewood, and a boat ramp are available. Some facilities are wheelchair accessible. Leashed pets are permitted.

Reservations, fees: Reservations are accepted only for the group site at 877/444-6777 or www.recreation.gov ($10 reservation fee). Single sites are $18 per night, double sites are $36 per night, $5 per night per additional vehicle. Group sites are $150 per night and require a two-night minimum stay on weekends. Open May–September, with a gate preventing access in the off-season.

Directions: From Salem, drive east on Highway 22 for 52 miles to Detroit. Continue southeast on Highway 22 for 2.5 miles to Forest Road 10 (Blowout Road). Turn right and drive three miles to the campground on the right.

Contact: Willamette National Forest, Detroit Ranger District, 503/854-3366, fax 503/854-4239, www.fs.fed.us; park information, 503/854-3251.

81 HOOVER

Scenic rating: 9

on Detroit Lake in Willamette National Forest

Hoover campground is located along the eastern arm of Detroit Lake at an elevation of 1,600 feet, near the mouth of the Santiam River. The camp features a wheelchair-accessible fishing area and interpretive trail; fishing, swimming, and waterskiing are some of the recreation options. You're likely to see osprey fishing during the day, a truly special sight.

Campsites, facilities: There are 37 sites for tents or RVs up to 30 feet long. Picnic tables, garbage service, and fire grills are provided. Flush toilets and drinking water are available. Boat docks and launching facilities are nearby. Some facilities are wheelchair accessible. Leashed pets are permitted.

Reservations, fees: Reservations are not accepted. Single sites are $16 per night, double sites are $32 per night, $5 per night per additional vehicle. Open mid-May–mid-September; a gate prevents access in the off-season.

Directions: From Salem, drive east on Highway 22 for 52 miles to Detroit. Continue southeast on Highway 22 for 2.5 miles to Forest Road 10 (Blowout Road). Turn right and drive one mile to the campground on the right.

Contact: Willamette National Forest, Detroit Ranger District, 503/854-3366, fax 503/854-4239, www.fs.fed.us.

82 HOOVER GROUP CAMP

Scenic rating: 9

on Detroit Lake in Willamette National Forest

BEST

This is a perfect spot for a family reunion or club trip. Detroit Lake offers a myriad of activities, including boating, fishing, hiking, and swimming, just to name a few. The campground has nice, open sites and direct access to the lake.

Campsites, facilities: There is one group camp for tents or RVs up to 30 feet long, for up to 70 people and 20 vehicles. Drinking water, fire rings, and picnic tables are provided. Flush toilets, garbage bins, firewood, and a group picnic shelter are available. Boat docks, launching facilities, and rentals are nearby. Some facilities are wheelchair accessible. Leashed pets are permitted.

Reservations, fees: Reservations are accepted at 877/444-6777 or www.recreation.gov ($10 reservation fee). The site is $150 per night, with a two-night minimum for weekend reservations. Open mid-April–late September; a gate prevents access during the off-season.

Directions: From Salem, drive east on Highway 22 for 52 miles to Detroit. Continue southeast on Highway 22 for 2.5 miles to Forest Road 10 (Blowout Road). Turn right and drive 0.5 mile to the campground on the right.

Contact: Willamette National Forest, Detroit Ranger District, 503/854-3366, fax 503/854-4239, www.fs.fed.us; park information, 503/854-3251.

83 SUMMIT LAKE

Scenic rating: 6

on Summit Lake in Mount Hood National Forest

This idyllic camp is set in a remote area along the western slopes of the Cascade Range at an elevation of 4,200 feet. On the shore of little Summit Lake, the camp is primitive but a jewel. It's a perfect alternative to the more crowded camps at Timothy Lake, and you have access to all the same recreation options by driving just a short distance north. Nonmotorized boats are allowed.

Campsites, facilities: There are five tent sites. Fire grills, garbage service, and picnic tables are provided. Vault toilets are available. There is no drinking water. Leashed pets are permitted.

Reservations, fees: Reservations are not accepted. Sites are $12 per night. Open mid-July–September, weather permitting.

Directions: From Portland, turn east on U.S. 26 and drive 57 miles (just past the town of Government Camp) to the junction with Highway 35. Bear southeast, staying on U.S. 26, and drive 15 miles to Forest Road 42 (Skyline Road). Turn right and drive 12 miles south to Forest Road 141 (a dirt road). Turn right and drive west two miles to the campground on the left.

Contact: Mount Hood National Forest, Zigzag Ranger District, 503/622-3191, fax 503/622-5622, www.fs.fed.us.

84 CLEATER BEND

Scenic rating: 8

near the Breitenbush River in Willamette National Forest

Creek views and pretty, shaded sites are the highlights of Cleater Bend, situated on the banks of the Breitenbush River at 2,200 feet elevation. This camp is 0.25 mile from Breitenbush and is a good option if that campground is full. Nearby recreation options include fishing access along the Breitenbush River, the South Breitenbush Gorge National Recreation Trail (three miles away), and Breitenbush Hot Springs (just over a mile away).

Campsites, facilities: There are nine sites for tents or RVs up to 24 feet long. Picnic tables and fire grills are provided. Garbage service, drinking water, vault toilets, and firewood are available. Some facilities are wheelchair accessible. Leashed pets are permitted.

Reservations, fees: Reservations are not accepted. Sites are $12 per night, $5 per night per additional vehicle. Open May–September, with a gate preventing access during the off-season.

Directions: From Salem on I-5, take Exit 253, turn east on Highway 22, and drive 50 miles to Detroit. Turn left on Forest Road 46/Breitenbush Road and drive nine miles to the campground on the right.

Contact: Willamette National Forest, Detroit Ranger District, 503/854-3366, fax 503/854-4239, www.fs.fed.us.

85 BREITENBUSH

Scenic rating: 8

on the Breitenbush River in Willamette National Forest

There is fishing access at this campground along the Breitenbush River. Nearby recreation options include the South Breitenbush Gorge National Recreation Trail, three miles away, and Breitenbush Hot Springs, just over a mile away. If this campground is crowded, try nearby Cleater Bend.

Campsites, facilities: There are 30 sites for tents or RVs up to 24 feet long (longer trailers may be difficult to park and turn). Picnic tables and fire grills are provided. Drinking water, vault toilets, garbage service, and firewood are available. Some facilities are wheelchair accessible. Leashed pets are permitted.

Reservations, fees: Reservations are not accepted. Sites are $12 per night for a single site, $24 per night for a double site, and $5 per night per additional vehicle. Open May–September; a gate prevents access during the off-season.

Directions: From Salem on I-5, take Exit 253, turn east on Highway 22, and drive 50 miles to Detroit. Turn left (north) on Forest Road 46/Breitenbush Road and drive 10 miles to the campground on the right.

Contact: Willamette National Forest, Detroit Ranger District, 503/854-3366, fax 503/854-4239, www.fs.fed.us.

86 LOWER LAKE

Scenic rating: 7

near Olallie Lake in Mount Hood National Forest

This sunny, open campground is set at an elevation of 4,600 feet, about 0.75 mile from Lower Lake, a small but deep lake that's perfect for fishing and swimming. It's also less than a mile from Olallie Lake and near a network of trails that provide access to other nearby lakes. It's advisable to obtain a U.S. Forest Service map that details the backcountry roads and trails.

Note: This camp will likely be upgraded in 2010.

Campsites, facilities: There are eight sites for tents or RVs up to 16 feet long. Picnic tables and fire grills are provided. Vault toilets and garbage service are available. There is no drinking water. Leashed pets are permitted.

Reservations, fees: Reservations are not accepted. Sites are $12 per night. Open July–October.

Directions: From Portland, drive south on U.S. 205 to the junction with Highway 24. Take the Highway 224/Estacada exit and turn left (south) onto Highway 224. Drive approximately 13 miles to Estacada. Continue south on Highway 224 and drive 27 miles in national forest (the road becomes Forest Road 46). Continue south on Forest Road 46 for 20 miles to Forest Road 4690. Turn left on Forest Road 4690 and drive southeast for 8.2 miles to Forest Road 4220. Turn right (south) and drive about 4.5 miles of rough road to the campground on the right.

Contact: Mount Hood National Forest, Clackamas River Ranger District, 503/630-6861, fax 503/630-2299, www.fs.fed.us.

87 CAMP TEN

Scenic rating: 9

on Olallie Lake in Mount Hood National Forest

Here's a camp along the shore of Olallie Lake, a popular area. Camp Ten sits at an elevation of 5,000 feet, on the lake's western shore in the midst of the Olallie Lake Scenic Area, which is home to a number of pristine mountain lakes and a network of hiking trails. (See a U.S. Forest Service map for trail locations.) Boats without motors—including canoes, kayaks, and rafts—are permitted on the lake.

Campsites, facilities: There are 10 sites for tents or RVs up to 16 feet long. Picnic tables, garbage service, and fire grills are provided. Vault toilets are available. There is no drinking water. Leashed pets are permitted.

Reservations, fees: Reservations are not accepted. Sites are $12 per night. Open July–October, weather permitting.

Directions: From Portland, drive south on U.S. 205 to the junction with Highway 24. Take the Highway 224/Estacada exit and turn left (south) onto Highway 224. Drive approximately 13 miles to Estacada. Continue south on Highway 224 and drive 27 miles in national forest (the road becomes Forest Road 46). Continue south on Forest Road 46 for 20 miles to Forest Road 4690. Turn left on Forest Road 4690 and drive southeast for 8.2 miles to Forest Road 4220. Turn right (south) and drive about six miles of rough road to the campground.

Contact: Mount Hood National Forest, Clackamas River Ranger District, 503/630-6861, fax 503/630-2299, www.fs.fed.us.

88 PAUL DENNIS

Scenic rating: 10

on Olallie Lake in Mount Hood National Forest

BEST

This campground, set at an elevation of 5,000 feet, borders the north shore of Olallie Lake. From here, you can see the reflection of Mount Jefferson (10,497 feet). Boats with motors are not permitted on the lake. A trail from camp leads to Long Lake (just east of the border of the Warm Springs Indian Reservation), Monon Lake, and Nep-Te-Pa Lake. It's advisable to obtain a U.S. Forest Service map.

Campsites, facilities: There are 17 sites for tents or RVs up to 16 feet long (trailers not recommended) and three hike-in tent sites. Picnic tables, garbage service, and fire grills are provided. Pit toilets are available. There is no drinking water. A store and ice are nearby. Leashed pets are permitted.

Reservations, fees: Reservations are not accepted. Sites are $12 per night. Open July–October, weather permitting.

Directions: From Portland, drive south on U.S. 205 to the junction with Highway 24. Take the Highway 224/Estacada exit and turn left (south) onto Highway 224. Drive approximately 13 miles to Estacada. Continue south on Highway 224 and drive 27 miles in national forest (the road becomes Forest Road 46). Continue south on Forest Road 46 for 20 miles to Forest Road 4690. Turn left and drive southeast for 8.2 miles to Forest Road 4220. Turn right (south) and drive 6.2 miles to Forest Road 4220-170. Turn left and drive 0.12 mile to the campground.

Contact: Mount Hood National Forest, Clackamas River Ranger District, 503/630-6861, fax 503/630-2299, www.fs.fed.us.

89 PENINSULA

Scenic rating: 10

on Olallie Lake in Mount Hood National Forest

Peninsula, the largest of several campgrounds along Olallie Lake, is set at an elevation of 5,000 feet on the south shore. An amphitheater is located near the campground, and rangers present campfire programs during the summer. Nonmotorized boats are permitted on the lake, and nearby trails lead to a number of smaller lakes in the area, such as Long Lake, Monon Lake, and Nep-Te-Pa Lake.

Campsites, facilities: There are 35 sites for tents or RVs up to 24 feet long and six walk-in tent sites. Picnic tables, garbage service, and fire grills are provided. Vault toilets are available. There is no drinking water. Leashed pets are permitted.

Reservations, fees: Reservations are not accepted. Sites are $12 per night, $6 per night per additional vehicle, and $6 per night for walk-in sites. Open July–October, weather permitting.

Directions: From Portland, drive south on U.S. 205 to the junction with Highway 24. Take the Highway 224/Estacada exit and turn left (south) onto Highway 224. Drive approximately 13 miles to Estacada. Continue south on Highway 224 and drive 27 miles in national forest (the road becomes Forest Road 46). Continue south on Forest Road 46 for 20 miles to Forest Road 4690. Turn left and drive southeast for 8.2 miles to Forest Road 4220. Turn right (south) and drive 6.5 miles of rough road to the campground on the left.

Contact: Mount Hood National Forest, Clackamas River Ranger District, 503/630-6861, fax 503/630-2299, www.fs.fed.us.

90 OLALLIE MEADOWS

Scenic rating: 8

near Olallie Lake in Mount Hood National Forest

Olallie Meadows is set at 4,500 feet elevation along a large and peaceful alpine meadow about three miles from Olallie Lake. Nonmotorized boats are allowed on Olallie Lake. The Pacific Crest Trail passes very close to the campground.

Campsites, facilities: There are seven sites for tents or RVs up to 16 feet long. Picnic tables, garbage service, and fire grills are provided. Vault toilets are available. There is no drinking water. Leashed pets are permitted.

Reservations, fees: Reservations are not accepted. Sites are $12 per night. Open July–October, weather permitting.

Directions: From Portland, drive south on U.S. 205 to the junction with Highway 24. Take the Highway 224/Estacada exit and turn left (south) onto Highway 224. Drive approximately 13 miles to Estacada. Continue south on Highway 224 and drive 27 miles in national forest (the road becomes Forest Road 46). Continue south on Forest Road 46 for 20 miles to Forest Road 4690. Turn left and drive southeast for 8.2 miles to Forest Road 4220. Turn right (south) and drive 1.5 miles to the campground on the left.

Contact: Mount Hood National Forest, Clackamas River Ranger District, 503/630-6861, fax 503/630-2299, www.fs.fed.us.

91 KAH-NEE-TA RESORT

Scenic rating: 7

on the Warm Springs Indian Reservation

This resort features a stellar-rated, full-concept spa, with the bonus of a nearby casino. It is also the only public camp on the east side of the Warm Springs Indian Reservation; there are no other camps within 30 miles. The Warm Springs River runs nearby. Recreation options in the area include an 18-hole golf course, miniature golf, biking and hiking trails, a riding stable, and tennis courts.

Campsites, facilities: There are 55 pull-through sites with full hookups for RVs of any length. A motel and cottage are also available. Cable TV, restrooms with flush toilets and coin showers, propane gas, a dump station, concession stand, coin laundry, ice, a playground, a spa, mineral baths, and an Olympic-sized, spring-fed swimming pool with a 140-foot water slide are available. Some facilities are wheelchair accessible. Leashed pets are permitted, but some areas are restricted.

Reservations, fees: Reservations are accepted at 800/554-4786. Sites are $45 per night for three people. There is a two-night minimum on weekends, and a three-night minimum on holiday weekends. Some credit cards are accepted. Open year-round.

Directions: From Portland, turn east on U.S. 26 and drive about 105 miles to Warm Springs and Agency Hot Springs Road on the left. Turn left and drive 11 miles northeast to Kah-Nee-Ta and the resort on the right.

Contact: Kah-Nee-Ta Resort, 541/553-1112, http://kahneetaresort.com.

92 WHISPERING FALLS

Scenic rating: 10

on the North Santiam River near Detroit Lake in Willamette National Forest

This popular campground sits on the banks of the North Santiam River, where you can fish. If the campsites at Detroit Lake are crowded, this camp provides a more secluded option, and it's only about a 10-minute drive from the lake. Ospreys sometimes nest near the campground.

Campsites, facilities: There are 16 sites for tents or RVs up to 30 feet long. Picnic tables, garbage service, and fire grills are provided. Drinking water and flush toilets are available. Bring your own firewood. Leashed pets are permitted.

Reservations, fees: Reservations are not accepted. Sites are $12 per night, $5 per night per additional vehicle. Open late April–mid-September; a gate prevents access in the off-season.

Directions: From Salem, drive east on Highway 22 for 50 miles to Detroit. Continue east on Highway 22 for eight miles to the campground on the right.

Contact: Willamette National Forest, Detroit Ranger District, 503/854-3366, fax 503/854-4239, www.fs.fed.us.

93 RIVERSIDE

Scenic rating: 7

on the North Santiam River in Willamette National Forest

This campground is set at an elevation of 2,400 feet along the banks of the North Santiam River, where the fishing can be good. A point of interest, the Marion Forks Fish Hatchery and interpretive site lies just 2.5 miles south. Other day-trip options include the Mount Jefferson Wilderness, directly to the east in Willamette National Forest, and Minto Mountain Trail, three miles east.

Campsites, facilities: There are 37 sites for tents or RVs up to 24 feet long. Picnic tables and fire grills are provided. Drinking water and vault toilets are available. Leashed pets are permitted.

Reservations, fees: Reservations are not accepted. Sites are $12 per night, $5 per night per additional vehicle. Open late May–September; a gate prevents access during the off-season.

Directions: From Salem, drive east on Highway 22 for 50 miles to Detroit. Continue southeast on Highway 22 for 14 miles to the campground on the right.

Contact: Willamette National Forest, Detroit

Ranger District, 503/854-3366, fax 503/854-4239, www.fs.fed.us.

94 MARION FORKS

Scenic rating: 8

on the Santiam River in Willamette National Forest

Situated along Marion Creek at 2,500 feet in elevation, this campground is adjacent to the Marion Forks Fish Hatchery. A U.S. Forest Service guard station and a restaurant are across Highway 22. The area boasts some quality hiking trails; the nearest is Independence Rock Trail, 0.25 mile north of the campground.

Campsites, facilities: There are 15 sites for tents or RVs up to 24 feet long. Picnic tables, fire grills, and garbage containers are provided. Vault toilets are available. There is no drinking water. Leashed pets are permitted.

Reservations, fees: Reservations are not accepted. Sites are $10 per night, $5 per night per additional vehicle. Open year-round, weather permitting, with no winter services.

Directions: From Salem, drive east on Highway 22 for 50 miles to Detroit. Continue southeast on Highway 22 for 16 miles to the campground on the left.

Contact: Willamette National Forest, Detroit Ranger District, 503/854-3366, fax 503/854-4239, www.fs.fed.us.

95 BIG MEADOWS HORSE CAMP

Scenic rating: 10

near Mount Jefferson Wilderness in Willamette National Forest

Built by the U.S. Forest Service with the support of a horse club, this camp is used heavily by equestrians riding into the Big Meadows area and the adjacent Mount Jefferson Wilderness. If you're not a horse lover, you may want to stick with Riverside or Marion Forks.

Campsites, facilities: There are nine sites for tents or RVs up to 36 feet long. Picnic tables, garbage service, fire grills, and enclosed four-horse corrals are provided at each site. Drinking water, vault toilets, firewood, and stock water troughs are available. Some facilities are wheelchair accessible. Leashed pets are permitted.

Reservations, fees: Reservations are not accepted. Sites are $14 per night, $5 per night per additional vehicle. Open June–October, weather permitting.

Directions: From Salem, drive east on Highway 22 for 50 miles to Detroit. Continue southeast on Highway 22 for 27 miles to Big Meadows Road (Forest Road 2267). Turn left and drive one mile to Forest Road 2257. Turn left and drive 0.5 mile to the campground on the left.

Contact: Willamette National Forest, Detroit Ranger District, 503/854-3366, fax 503/854-4239, www.fs.fed.us.

96 SHEEP SPRINGS HORSE CAMP

Scenic rating: 7

near the Mount Jefferson Wilderness in Deschutes National Forest

This well-shaded equestrian camp with privacy screening between sites is near the trailhead for the Metolius-Windigo Horse Trail, which heads northeast into the Mount Jefferson Wilderness and south to Black Butte. Contact the U.S. Forest Service for details and maps of the backcountry. The camp is set at an elevation of 3,200 feet.

Campsites, facilities: There are 11 sites for tents or RVs up to 45 feet long. Fire grills are provided. Drinking water, vault toilets, garbage bins, and corrals and box stalls for horses are available.

Reservations, fees: Reservations are accepted at 877/444-6777 or www.recreation.gov ($10 reservation fee). Sites are $14–16 per night, $8 per night per additional vehicle. Open early May–mid-September, weather permitting.

Directions: From Albany, drive east on U.S. 20 for 87 miles to the sign for Jack Lake (located one mile east of Suttle Lake) and Suttle-Sherman Road. Turn left on Forest Road 12 and drive eight miles to Forest Road 1260. Turn left and drive 1.5 miles to Forest Road 1260-200. Turn right and drive 1.5 miles to the campground on the right.

Contact: Deschutes National Forest, Sisters Ranger District, 541/549-7700, fax 541/549-7746; Hoodoo District, 541/822-3799, www.fs.fed.us.

97 JACK CREEK

Scenic rating: 5

near Mount Jefferson Wilderness in Deschutes National Forest

A more primitive alternative to the other camps in the area, this campground sits along the banks of Jack Creek in an open setting among ponderosa pine. The elevation is 3,100 feet. To protect the bull trout habitat, no fishing is permitted here.

Campsites, facilities: There are 20 sites for tents or RVs up to 40 feet long. Picnic tables and fire grills are provided. Vault toilets and garbage bins are available. There is no drinking water. Leashed pets are permitted.

Reservations, fees: Reservations are not accepted. Sites are $12 per night, $6 per night per additional vehicle. Open mid-April–mid-October.

Directions: From Albany, drive east on U.S. 20 for 87 miles to the sign for Jack Lake (located one mile east of Suttle Lake) and Suttle-Sherman Road. Turn left on Forest Road 12 and drive five miles to Forest Road 1230. Turn left and drive 0.75 mile to Forest Road 1232. Turn left and drive 0.25 mile to the campground on the left.

Contact: Deschutes National Forest, Sisters Ranger District, 541/549-7700, fax 541/549-7746, www.fs.fed.us.

98 PELTON

Scenic rating: 8

on Lake Simtustus in Deschutes National Forest

BEST

This campground claims 0.5 mile of shoreline along the north side of Lake Simtustus. Campsites here are shaded with juniper in an area of rolling hills and sagebrush. One section of the lake is accessible for water skis and personal watercraft. Simtustus is a trophy fishing lake for kokanee and brown, bull, and rainbow trout. Just north of the park is the Pelton Wildlife Overlook, where you can view a variety of waterfowl, such as great blue herons, ducks, geese, and shorebirds, as well as eagles and other raptors. Cove Palisades State Park, about 15 miles south, provides additional recreational opportunities.

Campsites, facilities: There are 69 sites, some with partial hookups, for tents or RVs up to 56 feet long, three group sites for up to 12–35 people, and 10 yomes (which are a cross between a yurt and a dome). Drinking water, picnic tables, garbage service, and fire grills are provided. Restrooms with flush toilets and showers, a restaurant, snack bar, general store, ice, fishing supplies, gasoline, and a picnic shelter are available. Also, a full-service marina with boat rentals, marine fuel, a boat launch, boat dock, fishing pier, moorage, swimming beach, volleyball courts, horseshoe pits, and a playground are available. Some facilities are wheelchair accessible. Leashed pets are permitted, and a dog run area is available.

CAMPING

Reservations, fees: Reservations are accepted at 541/475-0517 or www.portlandgeneral.com. Sites are $16–21 per night; the group site is $42–65 per night; yomes are $25 per night. Some credit cards are accepted. Open mid-April–September.
Directions: From Portland, drive south on U.S. 26 for 108 miles to the town of Warm Springs. Continue south two miles to Pelton Dam Road. Turn right and drive three miles to the campground on the right.
Contact: Portland General Electric, 503/464-8515 or 541/475-0516 (store and marina), fax 503/464-2944, www.portlandgeneral.com/parks; campground, 541/475-0517.

99 PERRY SOUTH

Scenic rating: 6

on Lake Billy Chinook in Deschutes National Forest

Perry South campground is located near the shore of the Metolius arm of Lake Billy Chinook. The lake borders the Warm Springs Indian Reservation and can get very crowded and noisy, as it attracts powerboat/water-ski enthusiasts. Recreation options include waterskiing and fishing for bass and panfish, and one of Oregon's nicest golf courses is nearby.
Campsites, facilities: There are 63 sites for tents or RVs up to 95 feet long. Picnic tables, garbage service, and fire grills are provided. Drinking water, vault toilets, firewood, a fish-cleaning station, boat docks, and launching facilities are available. A camp host is on-site. Some facilities are wheelchair accessible. Leashed pets are permitted.
Reservations, fees: Reservations are accepted at 877/444-6777 or www.recreation.gov ($10 reservation fee). Sites are $16–18 per night, $8 per night per additional vehicle. Open May–September, weather permitting.
Directions: From Bend, drive north on U.S. 97 to Redmond, then continue north for 15 miles to the Culver Highway. Take the Culver Highway north to Culver, and continue two miles to Gem Lane. Turn left and drive two miles to Frazier Drive. Turn left and drive a short distance to Peck Road. Turn right and drive through Cove Palisades State Park to Jordan Road at the shore of Lake Billy Chinook. Turn left on Jordan Road and drive about 10 miles (over the bridge) to County Road 64. Continue (bearing left) and drive about eight miles to the campground entrance on the left (on the upper end of the Metolius Fork of Lake Billy Chinook).
Contact: Deschutes National Forest, Sisters Ranger District, 541/549-7700, fax 541/549-7746, www.fs.fed.us.

100 MONTY

Scenic rating: 5

on the Metolius River in Deschutes National Forest

Remote Monty campground is set at 2,000 feet elevation and gets light use. Trout fishing can be good along the banks of the Metolius River, near where it empties into Lake Billy Chinook. Warm Springs Indian Reservation is across the river.
Campsites, facilities: There are 20 sites for tents or RVs up to 20 feet long. Picnic tables, garbage service, and fire grills are provided. Firewood and pit toilets are available. There is no drinking water. Boat docks and launching facilities are nearby at Perry South. Leashed pets are permitted.
Reservations, fees: Reservations are not accepted. Sites are $14 per night, $7 per night per additional vehicle. Open June–mid-September, weather permitting.
Directions: From Bend, drive north on U.S. 97 to Redmond and continue north for 15 miles

to the Culver Highway. Take the Culver Highway north to Culver and continue two miles to Gem Lane. Turn left and drive two miles to Frazier Drive. Turn left and drive a short distance to Peck Road. Turn right and drive through Cove Palisades State Park to Jordan Road at the shore of Lake Billy Chinook. Turn left on Jordan Road and drive about 10 miles (over the bridge) to County Road 64. Turn left and drive about 13 miles to the campground entrance (on the Metolius River above the headwaters of Lake Billy Chinook). The last five miles are very rough.

Contact: Deschutes National Forest, Sisters Ranger District, 541/549-7700, fax 541/549-7746, www.fs.fed.us.

101 COVE PALISADES STATE PARK

Scenic rating: 7

on Lake Billy Chinook

This park is a mile away from the shore of Lake Billy Chinook, where some lakeshore cabins are available. Here in Oregon's high-desert region, summers are warm and sunny with fairly mild but cold winters. Lofty cliffs surround the lake, and about 10 miles of hiking trails crisscross the area. Two popular special events are held here annually: Lake Billy Chinook Day in September and the Eagle Watch in February.

Campsites, facilities: There are two campgrounds: Crooked River Campground offers 91 sites with partial hookups for tents or RVs and three deluxe cabins; Deschutes Campground has 92 tent sites, 82 sites with full hookups for RVs up to 60 feet long, and three group tent areas for up to 25 people each. Picnic tables and fire grills are provided. Drinking water, garbage bins, restrooms with flush toilets and showers, a dump station, firewood, a convenience store, amphitheater, horseshoe pit, playground, and ice are available. Boat docks, launching facilities, a marina, boat rentals, fish-cleaning station, and a restaurant are nearby. Some facilities are wheelchair accessible. Leashed pets are permitted, and there is a designated pet exercise area.

Reservations, fees: Reservations are accepted at 800/452-5687 or www.oregonstateparks.org ($8 reservation fee). RV sites are $17–26 per night, tent sites are $13–20 per night, cabins are $48–80 per night, the group areas are $43–75 per night, $5 per night per additional vehicle. Some credit cards are accepted. Crooked River Campground is open year-round; Deschutes Campground is open May–mid-September.

Directions: From Bend, drive north on U.S. 97 for 13 miles to Redmond and continue north for 15 miles to the Culver Highway. Take the Culver Highway north to Culver and continue two miles to Gem Lane. Turn left and drive two miles to Frazier Drive. Turn left and drive a short distance to Peck Road. Turn right and drive to the park entrance.

Contact: Cove Palisades State Park, 541/546-3412 or 800/551-6949, www.oregonstateparks.org.

102 KOA MADRAS/CULVER

Scenic rating: 6

near Lake Billy Chinook

This KOA has a relaxing atmosphere, with some mountain views. It is set about three miles from Lake Billy Chinook, a steep-sided reservoir formed where the Crooked River, Deschutes River, Metolius River, and Squaw Creek all merge. Like much of the country east of the Cascades, this is a high-desert area.

Campsites, facilities: There are 22 tent sites and 58 pull-through sites with full or partial hookups for RVs of any length; most sites are pull-through. There are also three cabins. Drinking water, fire pits, and picnic tables are provided. Restrooms with flush toilets and showers, propane gas, a dump station, firewood, a convenience store, coin laundry, ice, and a playground are available. Recreational activities include a recreation hall, seasonal heated pool, bicycle rentals, volleyball, horseshoe pits, and tetherball. Boat docks and launching facilities are nearby. Leashed pets are permitted.

Reservations, fees: Reservations are accepted at 800/562-1992. Sites are $21–30 per night, $2–4 per person per night for more than two people. Some credit cards are accepted. Open year-round.

Directions: From Madras, drive south on U.S. 97 for nine miles to Jericho Lane. Turn left (east) and drive 0.5 mile to the campground on the right.

Contact: KOA Madras/Culver, 541/546-3046, fax 541/546-7972, www.koa.com.

OREGON'S COLUMBIA RIVER GORGE HIKING

© SEAN PATRICK HILL

BEST HIKES

Desert Hiking
Cove Palisades State Park, **page 141.**

Hikes for Kids
Latourell Falls, **page 84.**
Oxbow Park, **page 87.**
Wildwood Recreation Site, **page 111.**
Timothy Lake, **page 124.**

Hikes for Views
Larch Mountain Crater, **page 88.**
McNeil Point, **page 106.**
Zigzag Canyon and Paradise Park, **page 113.**
Jefferson Park, **page 138.**

Hikes Through Old-Growth Forests
Opal Creek, **page 131.**

Self-Guided Nature Walks
Lewis and Clark Nature Trail, **page 84.**

Short Backpacking Trips
Eagle Creek, **page 95.**
Mazama Trail to Cairn Basin, **page 107.**

Waterfall Hikes
Wahkeena Falls Loop, **page 85.**
Multnomah Falls, **page 86.**
Oneonta Gorge and Horsetail Falls, **page 86.**
Ramona Falls, **page 105.**

Wheelchair-Accessible Hikes
Mosier Twin Tunnels, **page 100.**
Timothy Lake, **page 124.**

At 11,249, feet Mount Hood is the tallest mountain in Oregon and towers over the city of Portland. Circled by the Timberline Trail – built by the Civilian Conservation Corps in the 1930s – the mountain provides easy access to some of the best alpine country in the state. Wildflower-covered meadows, tumbling creeks, massive glaciers, and a series of stone huts make for exciting hiking. It's as if the whole area rises up to meet the mountain, and all trails lead to Hood, including the Pacific Crest Trail, which skirts just behind the famous Timberline Lodge and spans the Columbia River Gorge and the entire Cascade Range.

Then there is the massive Columbia River, which pounded its way through the Cascade Range in a series of prehistoric floods, the grandest canyon by far. What the deluges left behind is not one gorge, but many; the Oregon side of the Columbia is awash with side gorges, waterfalls, and salmon-filled creeks extending deep into the mountains. Because of the sheer walls here, some of the most challenging climbs in Oregon begin from the shores of the Columbia, including the prominent Mount Defiance, a nearly 5,000-foot ascent with stunning views from the Gorge to the Cascades.

Looming above the Gorge, Mount Hood broods with its glacier-clad slopes. But it's not only the mountain that dominates here; the surrounding area is just as stunning. The Sandy, Hood, and Salmon Rivers flow close by, carving out their own canyons. And ridge upon ridge of other glacier-carved mountains provide spectacular vistas and challenging hiking. With a number of wilderness areas in the area, you'll find some pristine outback lands in northwestern Oregon. Lake upon lake dots the basins, where huckleberries bloom on the shores and deer and elk come down to drink.

With the proximity of these mountains and gorges to a major urban area, it's not hard to see why people flock to Oregon to live, work, and play.

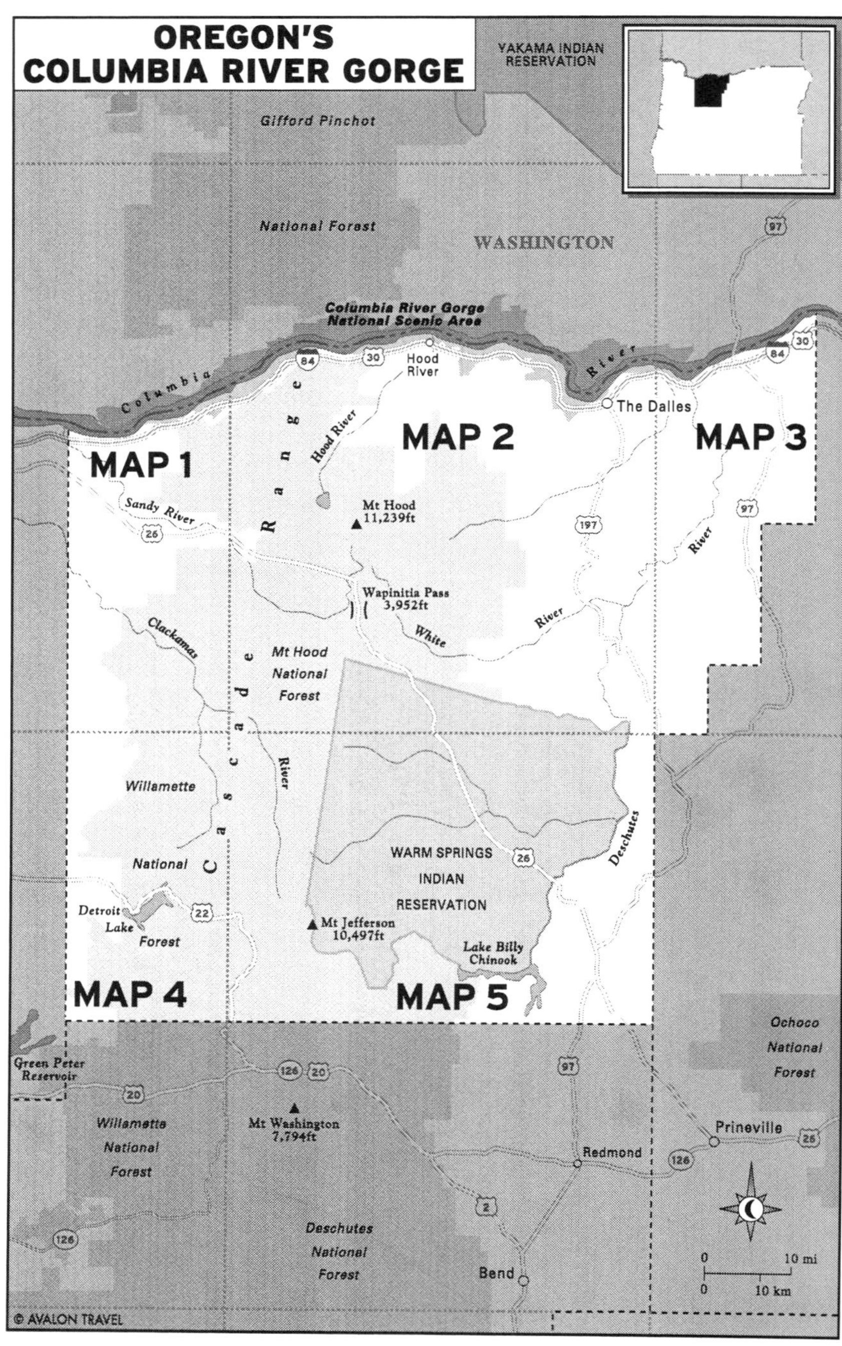

OREGON'S COLUMBIA RIVER GORGE
YAKAMA INDIAN RESERVATION
Gifford Pinchot
National Forest
WASHINGTON
Columbia River Gorge National Scenic Area
Columbia
River
Hood River
The Dalles
MAP 1
MAP 2
MAP 3
Hood River
Sandy River
Mt Hood 11,239ft
Cascade Range
Wapinitia Pass 3,952ft
White
River
River
Clackamas
Mt Hood National Forest
River
Willamette
National
Forest
Detroit Lake
WARM SPRINGS INDIAN RESERVATION
Deschutes
Mt Jefferson 10,497ft
Lake Billy Chinook
MAP 4
MAP 5
Green Peter Reservoir
Ochoco National Forest
Willamette National Forest
Mt Washington 7,794ft
Prineville
Redmond
Deschutes National Forest
Bend
0 10 mi
0 10 km
© AVALON TRAVEL

Map 1

Hikes 1-15

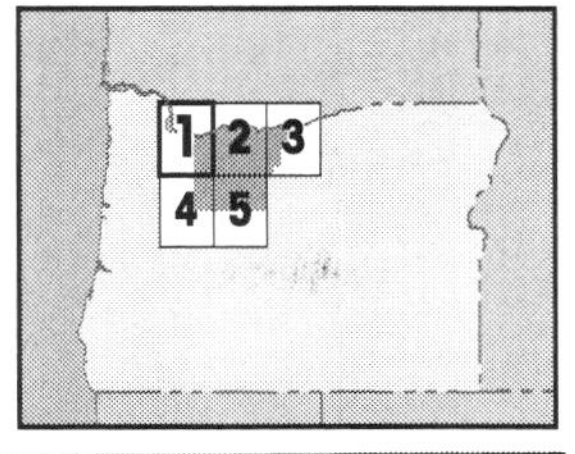

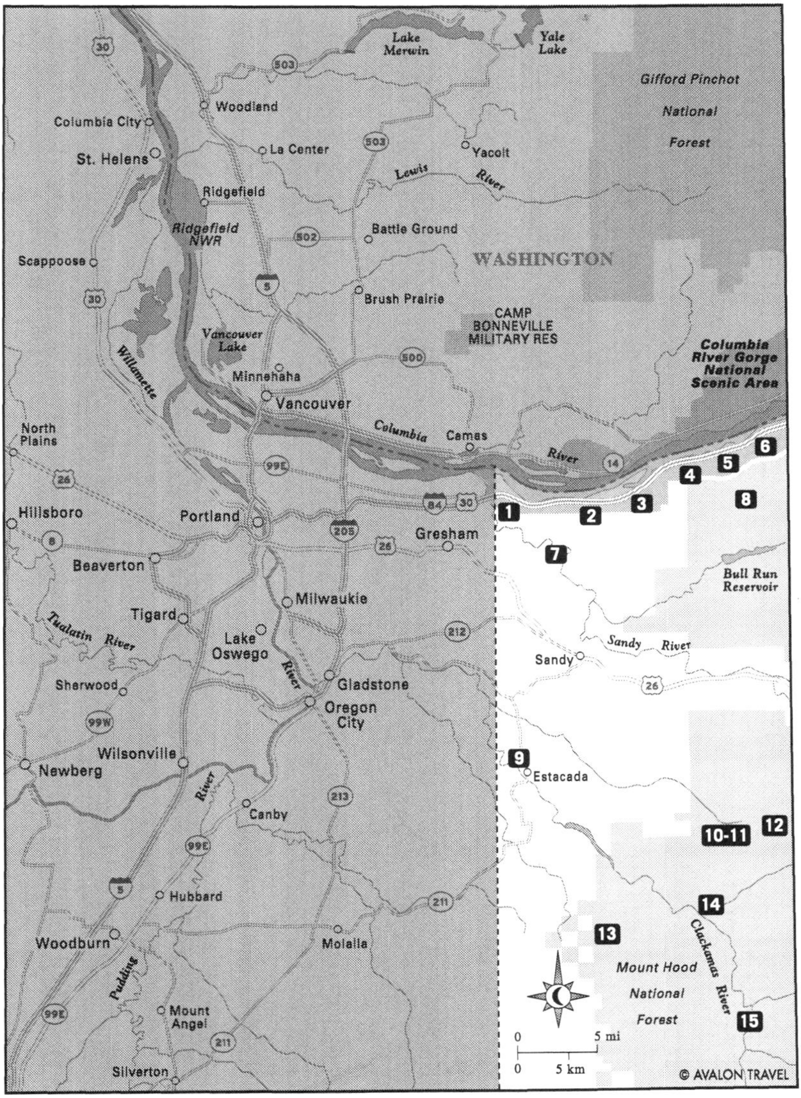

Map 2

Hikes 16-68

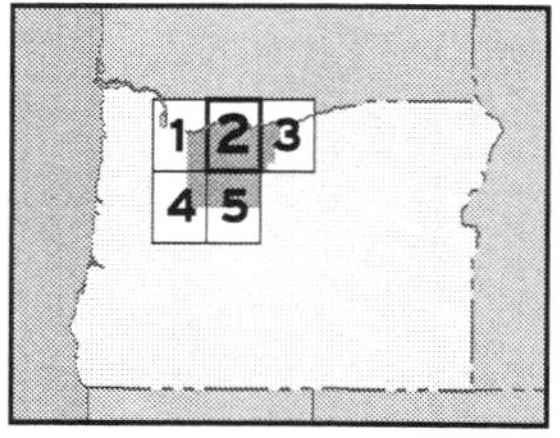

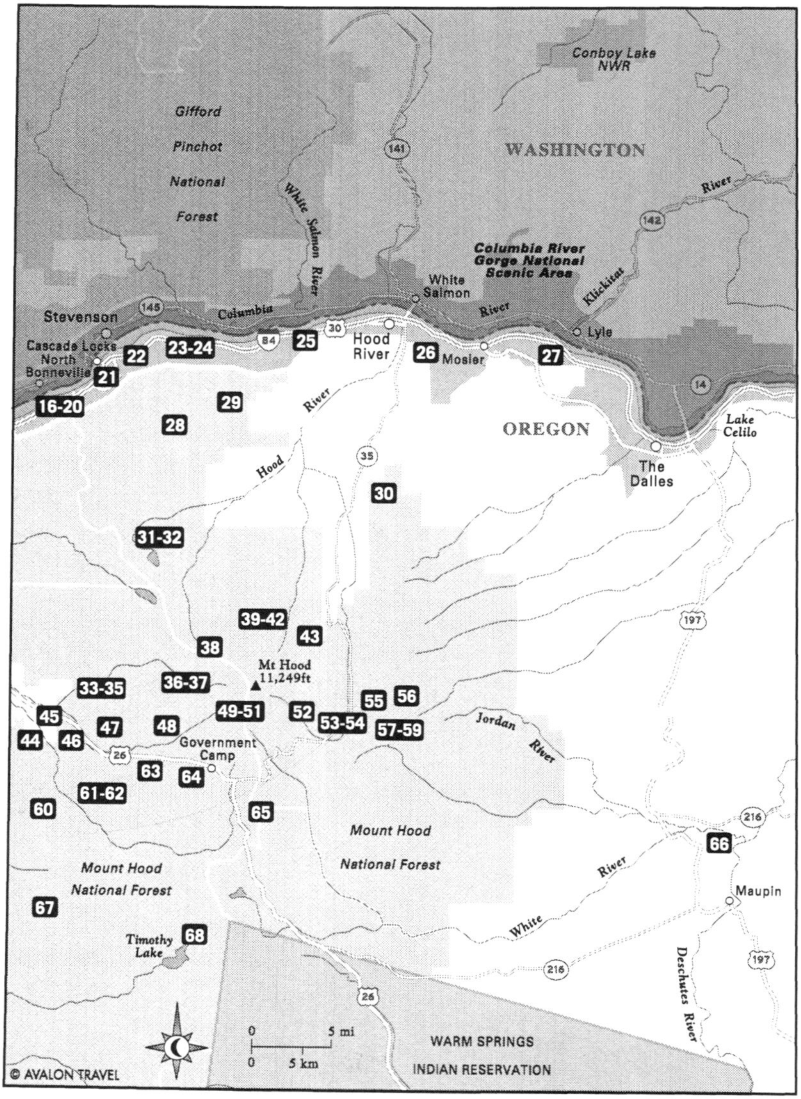

Gifford Pinchot National Forest
WASHINGTON
Conboy Lake NWR
141
White Salmon River
Columbia River Gorge National Scenic Area
142
River
Klickitat
White Salmon
Stevenson
14
Columbia
River
Lyle
Cascade Locks
North Bonneville
22
23-24
84
25
30
Hood River
26
Mosier
27
21
16-20
29
28
River
Hood
14
Lake Celilo
OREGON
The Dalles
35
30
31-32
197
39-42
43
38
Mt Hood 11,249ft
33-35
36-37
55
56
45
49-51
52
53-54
57-59
Jordan River
44
47
48
46
Government Camp
26
63
64
61-62
60
65
216
66
Mount Hood National Forest
Mount Hood National Forest
River
White
Maupin
67
Timothy Lake
68
216
197
Deschutes River
26
0 5 mi
0 5 km
WARM SPRINGS INDIAN RESERVATION

HIKING

Map 3

Hike 69

1
2
3
4
5

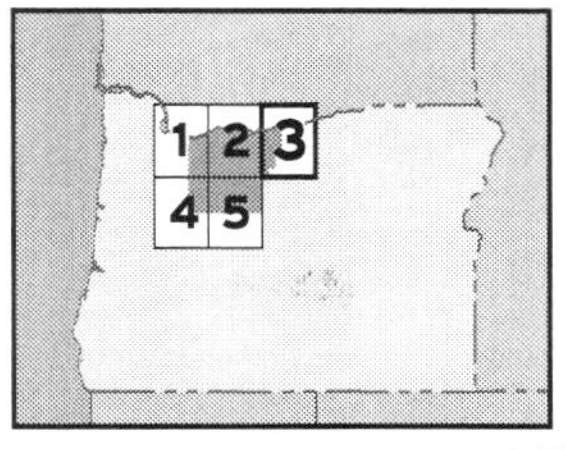

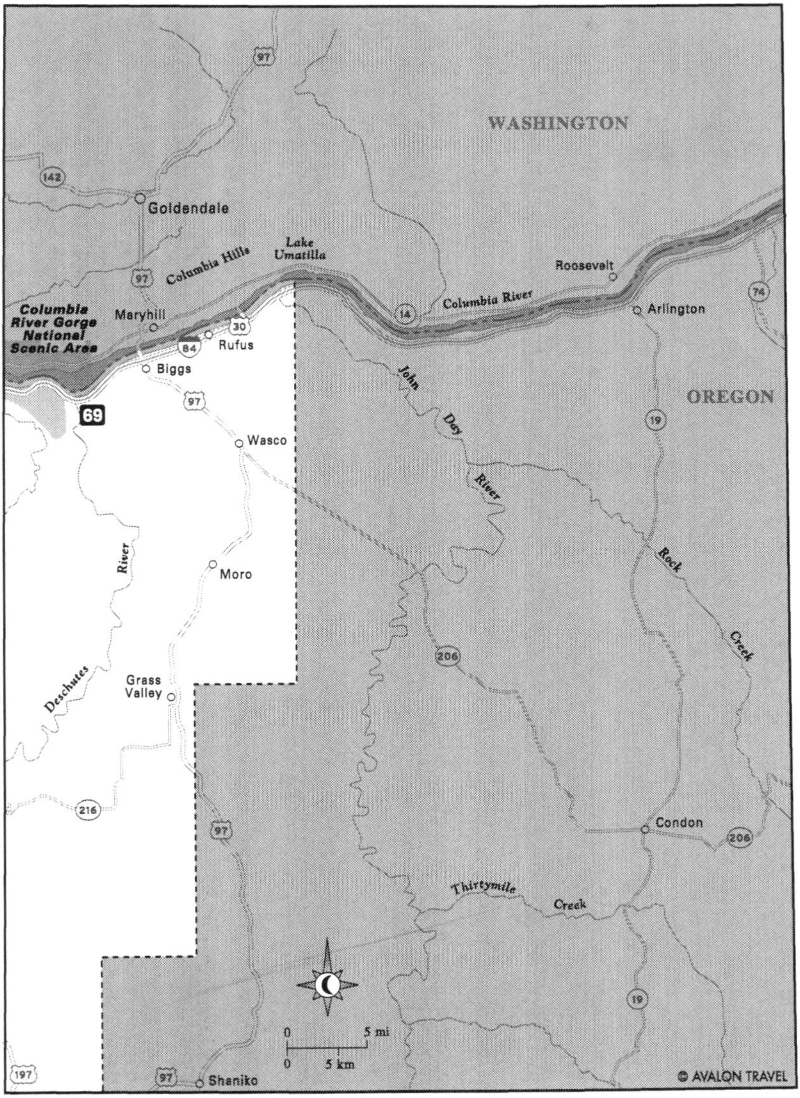

WASHINGTON
OREGON
Goldendale
Columbia Hills
Lake Umatilla
Columbia River
Roosevelt
Arlington
Columbia River Gorge National Scenic Area
Maryhill
Rufus
Biggs
69
Wasco
John Day River
Rock Creek
River
Deschutes
Moro
Grass Valley
Condon
Thirtymile Creek
Shaniko
142
97
14
74
30
84
19
206
216
197
0
5 mi
0
5 km
© AVALON TRAVEL

HIKING

Map 4

Hikes 70-86

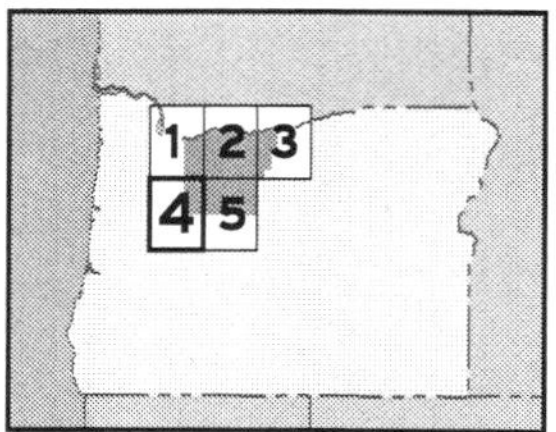

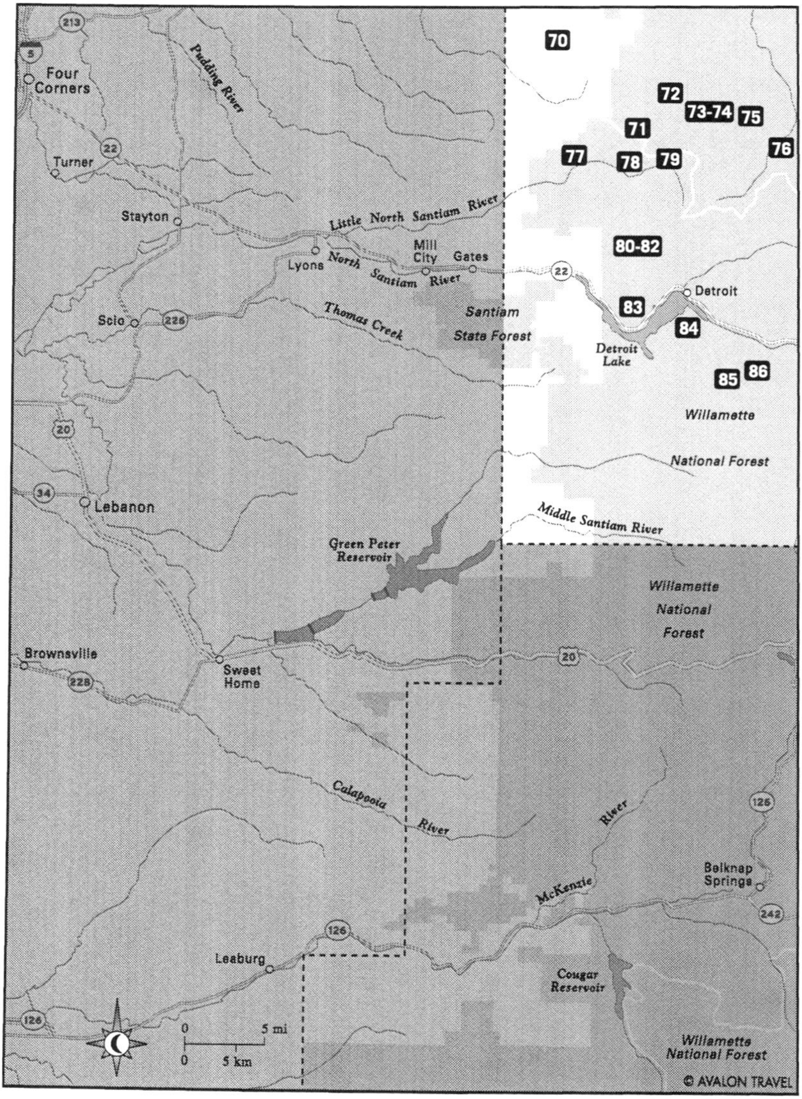

213
5
Four Corners
Pudding River
22
Turner
Stayton
Little North Santiam River
Lyons
North Santiam River
Mill City
Gates
Scio
226
Thomas Creek
Santiam State Forest
20
34
Lebanon
Green Peter Reservoir
Brownsville
228
Sweet Home
Calapooia River
Leaburg
126
0 5 mi
0 5 km
70
72
73-74
75
71
76
77
78
79
80-82
22
Detroit
83
84
Detroit Lake
85
86
Willamette National Forest
Middle Santiam River
Willamette National Forest
20
126
McKenzie River
Belknap Springs
242
Cougar Reservoir
Willamette National Forest

Map 5

Hikes 87-98

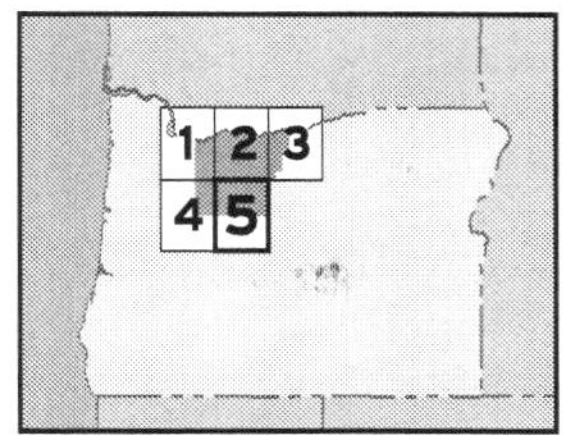

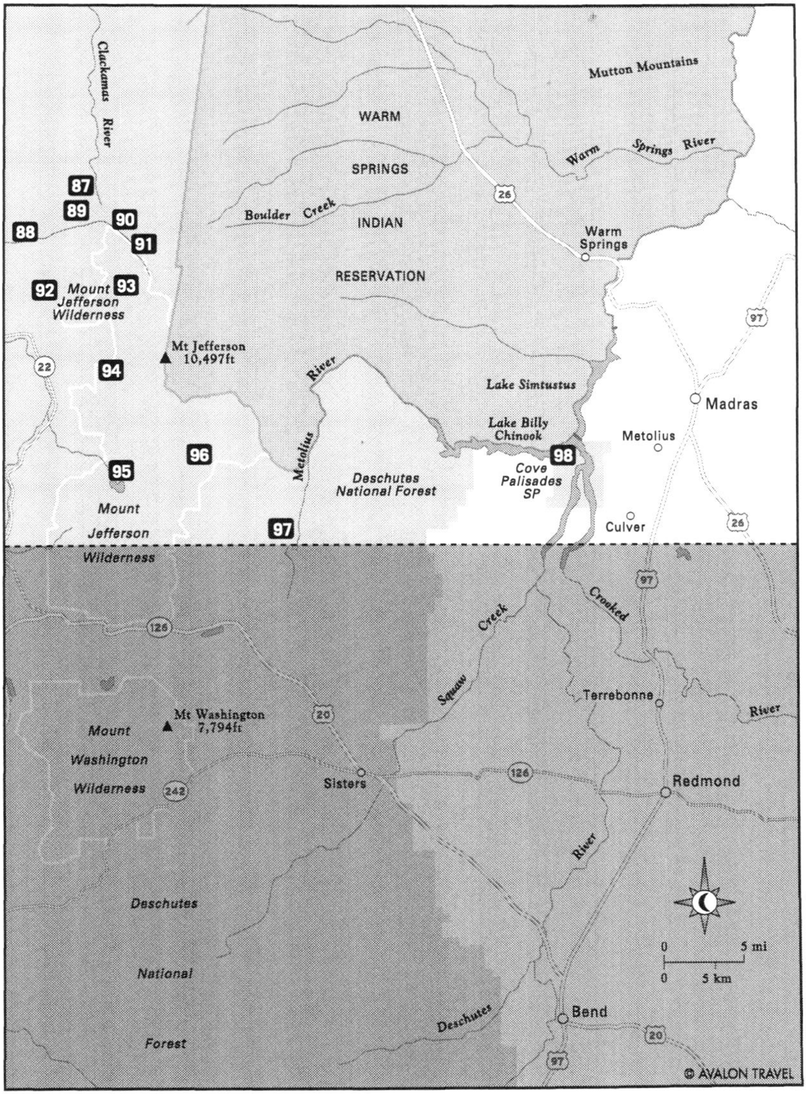

HIKING

1 LEWIS AND CLARK NATURE TRAIL

4.0 mi/2.0 hr

in the Columbia Gorge in Lewis and Clark State Park

BEST

In 1805, Lewis and Clark, nearly to their exploration's goal of the Pacific Ocean and the mouth of the Columbia River, arrived at the banks of Sandy River. They tried to cross it and found themselves sinking, and thus named it the Quicksand River. The name didn't stick, and neither did they—they eventually made it to the Oregon coast and sighted the destination President Jefferson had sent them to. Today you can explore this boundary area between the Cascade Mountains and the Willamette Valley on an easy nature trail that tours white oak, Oregon crabapple, and bigleaf maple woods dotted with flowers like Oregon grape root. A second trail leads to Broughton's Bluff, a popular climbing area, but it's a rocky trail best done on dry days.

The Lewis and Clark Nature Trail begins in the main entrance area. The unnamed, unmaintained Broughton's Bluff climber's trailhead is south from the lot on a gravel path. It switchbacks up to the base of the cliffs.

User Groups: Hikers and dogs. No horses or mountain bikes allowed. No wheelchair facilities.

Permits: Permits are not required. Parking and access are free.

Maps: You can purchase a Trails of the Columbia Gorge Map from Geo-Graphics. For a topographic map, ask the USGS for Camas.

Directions: From Portland, drive east on I-84 to Exit 18 and follow signs less than 0.1 mile to Lewis and Clark State Park.

Contact: Oregon Parks and Recreation Department, 1115 Commercial Street NE, Salem, OR, 97301, 800/551-6949, www.oregonstateparks.org.

2 LATOURELL FALLS

2.3 mi/1.0 hr

east of Gresham in the Columbia River Gorge

BEST

For an introduction to the Columbia Gorge, look no further than Guy W. Talbot State Park, a summer estate for the Talbot family until it was donated to the state. What the state—and by extension, you—got was two waterfalls in a beautiful side canyon and a wonderfully green trail along a splashing creek. Of all the waterfalls in the Gorge, this one is closest to Portland and hence the most accessible. And the drive to get there follows the 1922 Columbia River Highway, a historic road that twists and curves along the Columbia. Not to mention it's one of the easiest, and most level hikes of the bunch—bring the whole family.

From the parking area, take the 0.2-mile paved path down for a quick look at 250-foot Latourell Falls, dropping over lichen-encrusted lava cliffs, then go back to the lot and head uphill on the Latourell Falls Trail to the left. This trail climbs 0.3 mile to a viewpoint over the lower falls and continues steadily and easily 0.5 mile to the twisting 100-foot Upper Latourell Falls and a creek crossing. From here, the path follows the opposite shore 0.5 mile, passing a dizzying overlook of the lower falls that is not for the squeamish, and then switchbacks down one final mile to the picnic area of Guy Talbot Park, circling back to the parking area.

User Groups: Hikers and dogs. No horses or mountain bikes allowed. There is a short wheelchair-accessible path to the lower falls.

Permits: Permits are not required. Parking and access are free.

Maps: You can purchase a Trails of the Columbia Gorge Map from Geo-Graphics. For a topographic map, ask the USGS for Bridal Veil.

Directions: From Portland, drive I-84 east to Exit 28 and turn right on the Columbia River Highway, driving 2.8 miles to a lot on the left.

Contact: Oregon Parks and Recreation Department, 1115 Commercial Street NE, Salem, OR, 97301, 800/551-6949, www.oregonstateparks.org.

3 ANGELS REST

4.4 mi/2.5 hr

east of Gresham in the Columbia River Gorge

If there's one thing the Columbia Gorge is famous for it's wind. Just driving into the Gorge on a blustery day can be an exercise in wheel-gripping anxiety. Trees, though, have a way of deadening that wind, but not so on the burned slopes leading to the Angels Rest, a magnificent view over the Gorge and a spot that truly buffets with wind. On the hardest-blowing days, you can stand on this lava tongue and lean into the wind. Believe me, it will hold you.

From the parking area, climb on the Angels Rest Trail 0.6 mile on the Bridal Veil Trail to Coopey Falls, hidden somewhat in the underbrush. From there the trail climbs 1.6 miles to the edge of the Angels Rest; follow the cliff out for stunning views. From here, return the way you came for an easy 4.4-mile round-trip.

User Groups: Hikers and dogs. No horses or mountain bikes allowed. No wheelchair facilities.

Permits: Permits are not required. Parking and access are free.

Maps: You can purchase a Trails of the Columbia Gorge Map from Geo-Graphics. For a topographic map, ask the USGS for Bridal Veil.

Directions: From Portland, drive I-84 east to Exit 28 and park a few hundred yards past the exit at the junction with the Columbia River Highway.

Contact: Oregon Parks and Recreation Department, 1115 Commercial Street NE, Salem, OR, 97301, 800/551-6949, www.oregonstateparks.org.

4 WAHKEENA FALLS LOOP

5.0 mi/2.5 hr

2 9

east of Gresham in the Columbia River Gorge

BEST

The Columbia Gorge offers an amazing network of trails off the beaten path—though it is true that some of those paths are well beaten, particularly on weekends. This trail is one of them, but don't let that dismay you. With fortitude, and an early start, you can beat the crowds and visit five waterfalls, a massive spring, and deep woods with towering Douglas firs and tiny calypso orchids. Wahkeena Creek is almost a continual waterfall itself, and Multnomah Creek hosts not only the famous Multnomah Falls, but two others besides that higher up on the trail.

From the lot, head up the paved Wahkeena Trail 0.2 mile to a stone bridge beneath 242-foot Wahkeena Falls, a triple cascade in a lava slot that comes crashing down with a vengeance. The next 1.4 miles climbs the canyon, passing the base of Fairy Falls and a left-hand spur trail, the 419, continuing to a junction with Trail 415 to Angels Rest. For a short side trip, head right on the 415 trail a short distance to see the massive spring that gives birth to Wahkeena Creek, then head back to the junction. Continue uphill on the Wahkeena Trail 0.3 mile to a four-way junction and stay straight on the Wahkeena Trail. In 0.9 mile, the trail reaches a junction at Multnomah Creek; go left along the creek 1.8 miles to the base of Multnomah Falls and the historic lodge. From here, go to the left on the Gorge Trail paralleling the Columbia Highway for the 0.8-mile return to your car.

User Groups: Hikers and dogs. No horses or mountain bikes allowed. The steep but paved path to Wahkeena Falls provides wheelchair access.

Permits: Permits are not required. Parking and access are free.

Maps: You can purchase a Trails of the Columbia Gorge Map from Geo-Graphics. For a topographic map, ask the USGS for Bridal Veil.

Directions: From Portland, drive I-84 east to Exit 28 and turn left on the Columbia River Highway for 2.6 miles to the Wahkeena Falls Picnic Ground pullout on the left.

Contact: Columbia Gorge National Scenic Area, 902 Wasco Avenue, Suite 200, Hood River, OR, 97031, 541/308-1700.

5 MULTNOMAH FALLS

2.2-3.6 mi/1.0-2.0 hr 1 8

east of Gresham in the Columbia River Gorge

BEST

Most famous of all the falls in Oregon is perhaps Multnomah—it's not only the tallest, at 542 feet, but nothing rivals its unparalleled beauty. The stone bridge just below the first tier is one of the most photographed places in the state. It's also one of the most heavily visited areas in the state; it's not uncommon to find hundreds of people here at a time, many of them making the steep switchback climb to the top of the falls and the observation deck at the water's edge. To escape the crowds, all you need to do is go higher and farther than that for even more waterfalls along the creek.

From the lot, duck under the highway and train tracks through a tunnel and under a bridge to the Multnomah Lodge. Continue past the viewpoint up the paved Multnomah Falls Trail to the stone bridge at the base of the upper falls. By now you've gone 0.5 mile. To continue to the top, follow the paved path up a long series of switchbacks 0.6 mile to a junction; head right and down along the creek on this paved path to the viewpoint high above the lodge. To add another 1.4 miles and two waterfalls to your hike, continue upstream to the junction with the Wahkeena Trail (see *Wahkeena Falls Loop* listing in this chapter).

User Groups: Hikers and dogs. No horses or mountain bikes allowed. The paved path to the stone bridge provides wheelchair access.

the bridge at Multnomah Falls

Permits: Permits are not required. Parking and access are free.

Maps: You can purchase a Trails of the Columbia Gorge Map from Geo-Graphics. For a topographic map, ask the USGS for Bridal Veil.

Directions: From Portland, drive I-84 east to the Multnomah Falls turnoff at Exit 31 into the lot.

Contact: Columbia Gorge National Scenic Area, 902 Wasco Avenue, Suite 200, Hood River, OR, 97031, 541/308-1700.

6 ONEONTA GORGE AND HORSETAIL FALLS

2.7 mi/1.5 hr 2 9

east of Gresham in the Columbia River Gorge

BEST

The Columbia Gorge, as impressive as it is, isn't the only gorge around here. Take the Oneonta Gorge, for instance, a narrow slot sliced into sheer volcanic rock extending back more than a mile into the cliffs. On a summer day, with the right clothes and footwear, it's possible to wade back into the gorge to a secret waterfall. The more common way to see this gorge is to climb up and around it, passing numerous falls and crossing a crazily high bridge on your way to a triple waterfall falling on Oneonta Creek.

The hike begins at 176-foot Horsetail Falls, climbing the cliffs to the Gorge Trail. Turn right on the Gorge Trail and continue up to 80-foot Ponytail Falls, which the trail ducks behind, and a viewpoint over the Columbia River. The trail follows the creek and switchbacks down to a steel bridge over two falls, the lower one careening into the Oneonta Gorge. All this takes place in the first 1.3 miles.

At a junction on the far side of the bridge, go left on the Oneonta Trail, climbing steadily up 0.9 mile to 120-foot Triple Falls, pouring over a basalt lip. Just beyond lies a bridge and an area to stop and explore. To make a loop of the trail, head back down to the junction by the high bridge, this time going left to stay on the Oneonta Trail. In the next 0.9 mile, the trail descends to another viewpoint, then gradually returns to the highway. Keep right at a junction with the Gorge Trail, going 0.2 mile back to the highway, then following the highway east toward the mouth of the Oneonta Gorge—a designated botanical area—and a partially renovated tunnel through which the old highway once passed. The walk along the highway is a short 0.5 mile back to the Horsetail lot.

User Groups: Hikers and dogs. No mountain bikes or horses allowed. No wheelchair facilities.

Permits: Permits are not required. Parking and access are free.

Maps: You can purchase a Trails of the Columbia Gorge Map from Geo-Graphics. For a topographic map, ask the USGS for Multnomah Falls.

Directions: From Portland, drive I-84 east to Exit 35 for Ainsworth Park and follow the Columbia Highway to the right 1.5 miles to the Horsetail Falls Trailhead parking area.

Contact: Columbia Gorge National Scenic Area, 902 Wasco Avenue, Suite 200, Hood River, OR, 97031, 541/308-1700.

7 OXBOW PARK

3.5 mi/2.0 hr

southeast of Gresham on the Sandy River

BEST

Just a short ways past the bustle of highways and shopping centers that is Gresham lies this jewel of a park along an oxbow on the Sandy River. There are 1,200 acres of quiet woods, browsing deer, an ancient forest, and cobbled beaches on the river curving around Alder Ridge—all awaiting exploration. Along the way, you'll see anglers, campgrounds, and likely an osprey or two hunting fish in the river. A few stretches of trail may be wiped out when you visit due to winter storms; they don't seriously disrupt these hikes, since the network of trails and a few paved roads gives easy portage around the destruction. On top of that, you'll see firsthand what effect massive rains have on this ever-changing landscape. Kids will love it here, as the trails are easy and fun.

There are so many options for hiking, it's hard to say where to begin. The lot at Area C makes as good a spot as any, so start there and follow the trail out of the lot into the woods toward the river. At a junction, head right 0.5 mile through the woods, staying left at all junctions, until you reach the large lot and group picnic area. From here, you'll be able to see the huge washout the river slope suffered, taking many large trees and a half-mile length of trail with it. Head for the road, crossing it and heading up a gravel road. Go uphill to a junction on the left and head down into the woods for 0.8 mile. At the next junction, go right 0.2 mile, then left 0.2 mile toward the river. At a trail junction near a group camping site, and if the trail is mended, you can follow

HIKING

the river 0.6 mile around the oxbow, passing a stone beach and some impressive washouts (if not, pay attention to your map, adjusting as you go). From the junction marked "M," continue along the river 0.4 mile to the boat ramp. At this point, you'll have to use the road for 0.8 mile along the campsites, heading downstream. When you return to the picnic area "A," you can head back into the woods to return to your car.

User Groups: Hikers and dogs. Horses and mountain bikes on designated trails only. Paved portions of the park are wheelchair accessible.

Permits: Permits are not required. A fee of $4 per car is collected at the entrance. An annual pass is $40.

Maps: A brochure and map is available at the entrance gate or online at www.oregonmetro.gov. For a topographic map, ask the USGS for Sandy.

Directions: From I-205, take Exit 19 and go east on Division Street. Cross Burnside Street in Gresham and continue as the road becomes Oxbow Parkway. After 13 miles turn left at a four-way junction and follow park signs 1.4 miles to the entrance. Continue along the river to the first trail parking area, marked "C," on the left.

Contact: Metro Regional Center, 600 NE Grand Avenue, Portland OR, 97232, 503/797-1700.

8 LARCH MOUNTAIN CRATER

6.0 mi/3.0 hr 3 8

above Multnomah Falls in the Columbia River Gorge

BEST

Sherrard Point, at 4,055 feet, has a commanding view of the Columbia River Gorge, several Cascade peaks, and the distant city of Portland. It also looks down into the remnants of its volcanic crater, ground out by glaciers and the headwaters of Multnomah Creek. For a firsthand look at the crater, including its marshy core where bog orchids thrive, you'll have to climb down and into the heart of this ancient mountain.

Sherrard Point from Larch Mountain Crater

From the parking lot, the trail to Sherrard Point begins to the left of a signpost. Follow this obvious paved path to a junction and head right and steeply uphill, finally climbing a row of stairs to the impressive overlook. Then head back down, but this time follow the right-hand junction that heads into a picnic area, then head downhill on the Larch Mountain Trail to the right down a cathedral-like wooded ridge. After 1.5 miles, the trail crosses a dirt road, and in another 0.4 mile connects with a spur trail, Multnomah Creek Way. Take this trail to the right for 0.2 mile, then at a junction with the Multnomah Way Trail, go to the right again, following the young Multnomah Creek into the crater. This 2.5-mile section skirts the boggy meadows with views to Sherrard Point's massive volcanic plug. The trail makes use of an old logging road then joins the Oneonta Trail. Go right up the ridge 0.9 mile, where avalanche lilies bloom in spring right out of the snow. When the trail reaches the Larch Mountain Road, head to the right on the paved road 0.3 mile back to the lot.

User Groups: Hikers, dogs, horses, and mountain bikes. No wheelchair facilities.

Permits: Permits are not required. A federal Northwest Forest Pass is required to park here; the cost is $5 a day or $30 for an annual pass. You can buy a day pass at the trailhead, at ranger stations, or through private vendors.

Maps: You can purchase a Trails of the Columbia Gorge Map from Geo-Graphics. For a topographic map, ask the USGS for Multnomah Falls.

Directions: From Portland, drive I-84 east to the Corbett exit (Exit 22), and drive one mile uphill to Corbett. Turn left on the Columbia River Highway for two miles and fork right on Larch Mountain Road for 12 miles to its end.

Contact: Columbia Gorge National Scenic Area, 902 Wasco Avenue, Suite 200, Hood River, OR, 97031, 541/308-1700.

9 MILO MCIVER STATE PARK

6.0 mi/2.0 hr 1 7

northwest of Estacada off Highway 211

There's more to this state park than Frisbee golf, a fish hatchery, and an annual Civil War re-enactment. A woodsy loop trail sets out from the fish hatchery in the southern day-use area and follows a path along the Clackamas River, shared by equestrians. Because this park receives the national average for rainfall, winter is not the best time to go, unless you like hiking in the mud. The Nature Trail continues past views of the Clackamas River to the northern day-use area, connecting to loops with the Maple Ridge Trail and Cedar Knoll Trail.

User Groups: Hikers, dogs, and horses. No mountain bikes allowed. Paved portions of the trail are wheelchair accessible.

Permits: Permits are not required. A $3 day-use fee is collected at the camping entrance, or you can get an annual Oregon Parks and Recreation pass for $25; contact Oregon Parks and Recreation, 800/551-6949.

Maps: For a free park brochure, call Oregon Parks and Recreation, 800/551-6949, or download a free map at www.oregonstateparks.org. For a topographic map, ask the USGS for Estacada.

Directions: From Estacada, drive OR 211 south toward Molalla one mile, following signs to McIver Park and the fish hatchery. The trail heads around the hatchery to the right.

Contact: Oregon Parks and Recreation Department, 1115 Commercial Street NE, Salem, OR, 97301, 800/551-6949, www.oregonstateparks.org.

10 OLD BALDY

7.7 mi/4.0 hr 3 8

east of Estacada in Mount Hood National Forest

In 1999, a group of environmental activists barricaded the access road to Old Baldy, protesting the cutting of old-growth trees here. After a standoff with the Forest Service, the timber sale buyers decided to back out, and all is at peace again. Now you can visit Old Baldy along an ancient route predating the Forest Service through groves of noble fir. Though the peak itself, once the site of a fire lookout, is now largely overgrown and viewless, there is a cliff-edge viewpoint along the way with views to Mount Hood and Mount Adams.

From the Baldy Trailhead, go left on the Baldy Trail and follow it 2.9 miles, rounding Githens Mountain. At a crest, near a rock cairn, head to the right 30 yards to the cliff viewpoint. Returning to the trail, continue 0.9 mile to 4,200-foot Old Baldy.

User Groups: Hikers, dogs, horses, and mountain bikes. No wheelchair facilities.

Permits: Permits are not required. Parking and access are free.

Maps: For a map of the Mount Hood National Forest, contact the Mount Hood National Forest Headquarters, 16400 Champion Way, Sandy, OR, 97055, 503/668-1700. For a topographic map, ask the USGS for Wildcat Mountain.

Directions: From I-205 near Oregon City, take Exit 12 and drive east toward Estacada 18 miles. Drive through town and continue 1.6 miles on Highway 224. Just beyond milepost 25, turn left on Surface Road for 1.1 mile and turn right on Squaw Mountain Road. Follow this paved road, which becomes Road 4614, for 14.4 miles. Park on a pullout on the right, and at the end of a short path find the Old Baldy Trailhead.

Contact: Mount Hood National Forest, Clackamas River Ranger District, 595 NW Industrial Way, Estacada, OR, 97023, 503/630-6861.

11 TUMALA MOUNTAIN

4.4 mi/2.5 hr  2 8

east of Estacada in Mount Hood National Forest

Near the headwaters of both the North Fork Clackamas River and the South Fork Eagle Creek, the mountain formerly known as Squaw Mountain rises 4,770 feet above the Salmon-Huckleberry Wilderness. This is the site of an old fire watchtower, of which only an old concrete staircase remains, and the view of Mount Hood and Mount Jefferson is unimpeded, as is the view down to the Tumala Lakes Basin. As of 2001, the Oregon State Legislature called for the removal of the word "Squaw" from all place names, and the Oregon Geographic Names Board has worked to replace that antiquated and derogatory name with the word "Tumala," a Chinook word meaning "tomorrow" or "afterlife."

From the Fanton Trailhead, located in an old clear-cut, climb 0.7 mile through an old-growth forest, passing a marsh and primitive campsite. At the Old Baldy Trail, turn right for 0.6 mile, then right again at the next junction. Climb to the peak up 0.4 mile of trail and finally along an old service road, going to the left on this rutted track.

User Groups: Hikers, dogs, horses, and mountain bikes. No wheelchair facilities.

Permits: Permits are not required. Parking and access are free.

Maps: For a map of the Mount Hood National Forest, contact the Mount Hood National Forest Headquarters, 16400 Champion Way, Sandy, OR, 97055, 503/668-1700. For a topographic map, ask the USGS for Estacada.

Directions: From I-205 near Oregon City, take Exit 12 and drive east toward Estacada 18 miles. Drive through town and continue 1.6 miles on Highway 224. Just beyond milepost 25, turn left on Surface Road for 1.1 miles and turn right on Squaw Mountain Road. Follow this paved road, which becomes Road 4614, for 13.4 miles. Turn right on a gravel road to the Fanton Trailhead.

Contact: Mount Hood National Forest, Clackamas River Ranger District, 595 NW Industrial Way, Estacada, OR, 97023, 503/630-6861.

12 SHEEPSHEAD ROCK

2.8 mi/1.5 hr  1  7

east of Estacada in Mount Hood National Forest

If it wasn't timber thieves and sheepherders threatening these forests in the early 1900s, it was fire. The Forest Service built a guard station atop The Plaza, a wide plateau, in order to thwart the people, and a fire watchtower atop nearby Salmon Mountain to thwart the flames. Now the whole area is within the Salmon-Huckleberry Wilderness, all accessible by the Plaza Trail. An easy destination is Sheepshead Rock, a barren stony outcrop atop mighty cliffs.

From the trailhead, go right for 1.4 miles along the Plaza Trail, which joins an old road at the guard station site, then continues. The trail descends from the plateau, and just before it switchbacks back up, a side trail to the right leads to a scramble up Sheepshead Rock.

User Groups: Hikers, dogs, and horses. No mountain bikes allowed. No wheelchair facilities.

Permits: A free self-issue Wilderness Permit is required and is available at the trailhead. Parking and access are free.

Maps: For a map of the Mount Hood National Forest and the Salmon-Huckleberry Wilderness, contact the Mount Hood National Forest Headquarters, 16400 Champion Way, Sandy, OR, 97055, 503/668-1700. For a topographic map, ask the USGS for Three Lynx.

Directions: From I-205 near Oregon City, take Exit 12 and drive east toward Estacada 18 miles. Drive through town and continue 6.5 miles on Highway 224. Across from Promontory Park, turn left at a sign for Silver Fox RV Park and go left onto Road 4610. Follow this road 18.4 miles, forking left at 7.1 miles, right at eight miles, and left at 17 miles. Watch for a trailhead sign on the left and park at the Twin Springs Campground a hundred yards beyond on the right. Walk back to the trailhead.

Contact: Mount Hood National Forest, Zigzag Ranger District, 70220 East Highway 26, Zigzag, OR, 97049, 503/622-3191.

13 MEMALOOSE LAKE AND SOUTH FORK MOUNTAIN

4.6 mi/2.5 hr  2 8

southeast of Estacada in Mount Hood National Forest

Less than an hour from Portland, you'll feel as if you're deep in the mountains. Memaloose Lake sits beneath South Fork Mountain in what remains of an ancient cirque from the Ice Age, and now plays home to salamanders and huckleberries. The lake is as family-friendly as it gets, but for a challenge you can continue on to the top of the mountain with views of nine Cascade peaks—a rarity, for sure.

From the trailhead, the Memaloose Lake Trail climbs modestly over 1.3 miles, switchbacking at its end down to the lake. To climb South Fork Mountain on an unmaintained trail, don't confuse it with the spur trails leading to the shores and campsites around the lake, but continue to the left up 700 feet in 1.0 mile.

User Groups: Hikers, dogs, horses, and mountain bikes. No wheelchair facilities.

Permits: Permits are not required. Parking and access are free.

Maps: For a map of the Mount Hood National Forest, contact the Mount Hood National Forest Headquarters, 16400 Champion Way, Sandy, OR, 97055, 503/668-1700. For a topographic map, ask the USGS for Wanderers Peak.

Directions: From I-205 near Oregon City, take Exit 12 and drive east toward Estacada 18 miles. Drive through town and continue 9.2 miles on Highway 224. Between mileposts 33 and 34, go right across a bridge onto Memaloose Road 45 and drive 11.2 miles. Keep right on a gravel road for one more mile to a trailhead on the left.

Contact: Mount Hood National Forest, Clackamas River Ranger District, 595 NW Industrial Way, Estacada, OR, 97023, 503/630-6861.

HIKING

14 CLACKAMAS RIVER

7.8 mi one-way/4.0 hr  2  8

southeast of Estacada in Mount Hood National Forest

This breezy trail follows the rough and tumbling Clackamas River on a great day's journey. Along the way, you'll pass a couple of waterfalls, including Pup Creek Falls in a side canyon, and The Narrows, where the river squeezes through a gorge between two pieces of a lava flow, narrowing the river to a thin whitewater rush. Though the trail parallels the highway, the road is on the far shore.

The trailside has some great up-and-down hauls through dense woods and even passes a couple beaches.

From the Fish Creek Trailhead, follow the trail along the river, rounding a bend, for 3.6 miles. At that point, there is a side trail to the right leading in 200 yards to a viewpoint of Pup Creek Falls. Continue on the main trail 1.3 miles to The Narrows. From there, the trail continues on for three miles to an upper trailhead at Indian Henry Campground.

User Groups: Hikers and dogs. Horses and mountain bikes not allowed. No wheelchair facilities.

Permits: Permits are not required. A federal Northwest Forest Pass is required to park here; the cost is $5 a day or $30 for an annual pass. You can buy a day pass at the trailhead, at ranger stations, or through private vendors.

Maps: For a map of the Mount Hood National Forest, contact the Mount Hood National Forest Headquarters, 16400 Champion Way, Sandy, OR, 97055, 503/668-1700. For a topographic map, ask the USGS for Three Lynx.

Directions: From I-205 near Oregon City, take Exit 12 and drive east toward Estacada 18 miles. Drive through town and continue 14.4 miles on Highway 224. Past milepost 39, after crossing the second green bridge, turn right on Fish Creek Road 54. Follow this road 0.2 mile, cross the Clackamas River, then park at a big lot on the right. To reach Indian Henry Campground, stay left on OR 224, following the river seven miles. Follow signs for Indian Henry Campground straight on Road 4620 for 0.6 mile and park in a lot on the right across from the campground entrance.

Contact: Mount Hood National Forest, Clackamas River Ranger District, 595 NW Industrial Way, Estacada, OR, 97023, 503/630-6861.

15 RIVERSIDE NATIONAL RECREATION TRAIL

8.0 mi/3.0 hr — 2 — 8

southeast of Estacada in Mount Hood National Forest

The Riverside Trail is only one of three in the Mount Hood Forest to be designated a National Recreation Trail. It's outstanding natural beauty is due to thick forests of Douglas fir and red cedar, and the fact that the river provides companionship for the trail's whole length. It's worth it to hike the whole thing in one burst.

From the trailhead, the trail goes in two directions. To the left, it ambles down 1.4 miles to a beach and its terminus at the Riverside Campground. To the right, it extends out 2.6 miles along cliffs, over creeks, down to a beach, down to a nice pool, and to a fine viewpoint over the river, before continuing along the Oak Grove Fork to its end at the Rainbow Campground.

User Groups: Hikers, dogs, and mountain bikes. Horses not allowed. No wheelchair facilities.

Permits: Permits are not required. A federal Northwest Forest Pass is required to park here; the cost is $5 a day or $30 for an annual pass. You can buy a day pass at the trailhead, at ranger stations, or through private vendors.

Maps: For a map of the Mount Hood National Forest, contact the Mount Hood National Forest Headquarters, 16400 Champion Way, Sandy, OR, 97055, 503/668-1700. For a topographic map, ask the USGS for Fish Creek Mountain.

Directions: From I-205 near Oregon City, take Exit 12 and drive east toward Estacada 18 miles. Drive through town and continue 26 miles on Highway 224 to the Ripplebrook Bridge. Turn right onto Road 46 for 1.8 miles to a Riverside Trailhead sign and a parking lot on the right.

Contact: Mount Hood National Forest, Clackamas River Ranger District, 595

NW Industrial Way, Estacada, OR, 97023, 503/630-6861.

16 NESMITH POINT AND ELOWAH FALLS

3.0-9.8 mi/1.5-5.0 hr 3 8

west of Cascade Locks in the Columbia River Gorge

© SEAN PATRICK HILL

Columbia River Gorge from Nesmith Point

Two very different hikes launch from Yeon State Park, named for one of the principal architects of the historic Columbia River Highway. The first views 289-foot Elowah Falls from both the bottom and the top, making use of a unnerving but fenced cliff-ledge trail to climb over Elowah to Upper McCord Creek Falls. The second climbs steeply up a dry gorge to Nesmith Point, almost 4,000 feet above the trailhead, and provides absolutely stunning views to the mountains on the far side of the Columbia River.

To hike to the falls, take the left-hand Trail 400 from the parking lot 0.4 mile to a junction. Two trails lead from here: The first goes 0.4 mile to the left to a footbridge at the base of Elowah Falls; the second heads up the cliff face 0.7 miles to 60-foot Upper McCord Falls, with sweeping views from the dynamite-blasted ledge along the cliff.

To climb to Nesmith Point, take the right-hand junction from Yeon Park on Trail 428. The first 0.9 mile climbs steadily through the forest. At a junction with the Gorge Trail by a creek, head left. From here, the trail climbs 2,300 feet in only 2.4 miles, reaching its crest at a saddle with excellent views. Continue on this ridgeline trail 1.3 miles, passing a spring along the way, turning uphill through a forest of towering trees not unlike being in a massive cathedral. The trail joins an old road, so go right up 0.3 mile to a cliff-edge view and the site of an old watchtower, with one building's ruins still collapsing into the ground.

User Groups: Hikers and dogs. No mountain bikes or horses allowed. No wheelchair facilities.

Permits: Permits are not required. Parking and access are free.

Maps: You can purchase a Trails of the Columbia Gorge Map from Geo-Graphics. For a topographic map, ask the USGS for Tanner Butte.

Directions: From Portland, drive I-84 east and take Exit 35 for Ainsworth Park, and turn left toward Dodson for 200 feet, then turn right onto Frontage Road. Follow Frontage Road 2.1 miles to a pullout on the right.

Contact: Oregon Parks and Recreation Department, 1115 Commercial Street NE, Salem, OR, 97301, 800/551-6949, www.oregonstateparks.org.

17 WAHCLELLA FALLS

1.8 mi/1.0 hr 1 8

west of Cascade Locks in the Columbia River Gorge

Once the stretch of Columbia River Highway ends, it's easy to miss off-the-beaten-path spots like Wahclella Falls. It's unfortunate, because this double-plunge waterfall tumbling into the canyon where massive boulders line Tanner Creek is unique and worth a visit. The Wahclella Falls Trail sets out on an old road that becomes a trail beyond an old dam, heading into the canyon 0.9 mile along Tanner Creek. Watch for a side falls along the way. The trail comes to a junction, the beginning of a short loop. Go left to reach the base of the falls, a pounding cataract, then cross the creek on a footbridge, passing a small cave and the giant boulders left from a landslide decades ago. The trail crosses the creek again on a footbridge and climbs to rejoin the original trail. Head left to return to the lot.

User Groups: Hikers and dogs. No horses or mountain bikes allowed. No wheelchair facilities.

Permits: Permits are not required. A federal Northwest Forest Pass is required to park; the cost is $5 a day or $30 for an annual pass. You can buy a day pass at the trailhead, at ranger stations, or through private vendors.

Maps: You can purchase a Trails of the Columbia Gorge Map from Geo-Graphics. For a topographic map, ask the USGS for Tanner Butte.

Directions: From Portland, drive I-84 east and take Exit 40 for the Bonneville Dam. At the intersection, keep right and then stay to the right again for the parking area.

Contact: Columbia Gorge National Scenic Area, 902 Wasco Avenue, Suite 200, Hood River, OR, 97031, 541/308-1700.

18 WAUNA VIEWPOINT

3.8 mi/2.0 hr 2 8

west of Cascade Locks in the Columbia River Gorge

Two sections of the Columbia River Highway are abandoned but open as a State Trail. Paralleling the interstate that eventually made this highway obsolete, the old highway is open to hikers and bikers, and provides access to other trails, including a viewpoint of Wauna Point, a challenging climb. For an easy day, you can hike out the old highway and back, a two-mile walk that hugs Tooth Rock on a parapet-like section of the road. Either way, this stretch of old road accesses the Wauna Viewpoint nicely.

Beginning at the Tooth Rock Trailhead, follow the paved path 0.2 mile to a junction. Stay straight on the old highway another 0.8 mile to the road's end at a stone stairway.

For a different hike from the same trailhead, try Wauna Viewpoint. Follow the old highway from the Tooth Rock Trailhead to the junction and go right 0.4 mile on a poorly marked spur trail toward Wauna. Take the next trail to the right, heading uphill 0.1 mile to an old roadbed that marks the Gorge Trail. Stay left, going uphill to find the continuation of the trail. Follow the trail to the left another 0.4 mile. Then go right at a sign for Wauna Viewpoint, plodding up the switchbacks to the 1,050-foot viewpoint near a powerline base. From here you can spot Mount Adams in Washington. Head back the way you came.

User Groups: Hikers and dogs. Mountain bikes allowed on paved trails only. No horses allowed. Paved portions are wheelchair accessible.

Permits: Permits are not required. Parking and access are free.

Maps: You can purchase a Trails of the Columbia Gorge Map from Geo-Graphics. For a topographic map, ask the USGS for Bonneville Dam.

Directions: From Portland, drive I-84 east and

take Exit 40 for the Bonneville Dam. At the intersection, keep right and then turn left for the parking area.

Contact: Oregon Parks and Recreation Department, 1115 Commercial Street NE, Salem, OR, 97301, 800/551-6949, www.oregonstateparks.org, and Columbia Gorge National Scenic Area, 902 Wasco Avenue, Suite 200, Hood River, OR, 97031, 541/308-1700.

19 EAGLE CREEK

12.0 mi/7.0 hr 3 9

west of Cascade Locks in the Columbia River Gorge

BEST

Eagle Creek is surely one of the best hikes in Oregon—and it's one of the oldest, built in the 1910s as part of the Columbia River Highway project. You'll pass six waterfalls in all, and for the finale you'll walk behind Tunnel Falls through a little cave carved out of the cliff wall. The whole route is nothing short of spectacular, and there's ample opportunity to backpack as well, with several woodsy group camping areas along the way. Of course, parts of the trail are perilous, walking alongside sheer cliffs with naught but a cable handrail to ease the anxiety. Almost every year, it seems, someone falls into the canyon and needs to be rescued, or worse. Keep an eye on kids and dogs, and the trip will be one for posterity.

From the trailhead, head upstream on the Eagle Creek Trail. At 1.5 miles, a side trail leads to a viewpoint of Metlako Falls, and at 2.1 miles a side trail leads down to Punchbowl Falls, a great place to spot water ouzels, little grey birds that spend much of their time underwater and darting in and out of waterfalls looking for insects. Returning to the trail, the next 1.2 miles brings you to the first high bridge, crossing not only a creek but a faultline. From here, it's 0.4 mile farther to Tenas Camp, then another mile to Wy-East Camp, and finally another 0.6 mile to Blue Grouse Camp. Once you've passed Blue Grouse Camp, it's only 0.7 mile to Tunnel Falls, and if you're not yet tired out, head around the bend a short distance to reach another falls and a good lunch spot. Return as you came.

User Groups: Hikers and dogs. No horses or mountain bikes allowed. No wheelchair facilities.

Permits: Permits are not required. A federal Northwest Forest Pass is required to park here; the cost is $5 a day or $30 for an annual pass. You can buy a day pass at the trailhead, at ranger stations, or through private vendors.

Maps: You can purchase a Trails of the Columbia Gorge Map from Geo-Graphics. For a topographic map, ask the USGS for Bonneville Dam.

Directions: From Portland, drive I-84 east and take Exit 41 for Eagle Creek. At the intersection, keep right for one mile to the parking area.

Contact: Columbia Gorge National Scenic Area, 902 Wasco Avenue, Suite 200, Hood River, OR, 97031, 541/308-1700.

20 RUCKEL RIDGE

9.6 mi/5.0 hr 4 8

west of Cascade Locks in the Columbia River Gorge

Ruckel Creek Trail may not be appropriately named, since it provides only two glimpses of Ruckel Creek. But what this trail accomplishes is far more ambitious: a demanding climb to the Benson Plateau, where trails go off in all directions like the strands of a spider's web. Along the way, you'll pass mysterious pits that could be 1,000 years old, most likely vision quest sites for young Native American men. The rest is what my friend used to call a "death march" up the rugged ridge into the Hatfield Wilderness area with views to Table Mountain and Mount Adams.

From the trailhead in the Eagle Creek Campground, follow the Gorge Trail east 0.7 mile east, following the paved old Columbia River Highway for a spell. Cross Ruckel Creek on a picturesque stone bridge and head to the right on the Ruckel Creek Trail, which quickly becomes a thigh-burner. In 0.3 mile, you'll enter a moss-covered rockslide area, where you'll find the pits. Touch nothing and remove nothing; these sites are federally protected. The next 1.5 miles is steep, arriving at a viewpoint at 2,000 feet. After this, the trail affords a break for 1.5 miles through a fairly level, grassy slope before climbing again steeply for the remaining 0.8 mile. Once on top, walk through the woods to a trail fork, and go right to visit Ruckel Creek. Return as you came.

User Groups: Hikers and dogs. No wheelchair facilities.

Permits: Permits are not required. A federal Northwest Forest Pass is required to park here; the cost is $5 a day or $30 for an annual pass. You can buy a day pass at the trailhead, at ranger stations, or through private vendors.

Maps: You can purchase a Trails of the Columbia Gorge Map from Geo-Graphics. For a topographic map, ask the USGS for Bonneville Dam.

Directions: From Portland, drive I-84 east and take Exit 41 for Eagle Creek. At the intersection, keep right and then turn left into the parking area.

Contact: Columbia Gorge National Scenic Area, 902 Wasco Avenue, Suite 200, Hood River, OR, 97031, 541/308-1700.

21 DRY CREEK FALLS

4.8 mi/2.0 hr

 1 7

south of Cascade Locks in Mount Hood National Forest

There's a sign for the Pacific Crest Trail on the Bridge of the Gods, a long steel bridge spanning the Columbia River. How else would through-hikers get over that river? Just off the road here, the beginning of the Oregon stretch of the PCT starts into the forest. Within a few miles is the first footbridge over rushing water, the misnamed Dry Creek. Hikers may not realize that the old road leading off the PCT and upstream comes to a 50-foot waterfall pouring through a slot in lumpy lava flows. Don't let the early stage of the trail fool you; this is actually a quiet walk through some deep fir woods.

From the trailhead, head south on the PCT, away from the Bridge of the Gods, going under I-84 and briefly up a dirt road, following PCT signs typically nailed to trees (and a telephone pole). The trail spurs to the left off the road. After 1.2 miles, cross an old powerline road and continue into the woods. After 0.9 mile, the trail crosses Dry Creek, but take the road to the right up 0.3 mile to the base of the falls and an abandoned diversion dam that, if anything, adds charm to this spot.

User Groups: Hikers, dogs, and horses. No mountain bikes allowed. No wheelchair facilities.

Permits: Permits are not required. A federal Northwest Forest Pass is required to park here; the cost is $5 a day or $30 for an annual pass. You can buy a day pass at the trailhead, at ranger stations, or through private vendors.

Maps: You can purchase a Trails of the Columbia Gorge Map from Geo-Graphics. For a topographic map, ask the USGS for Bonneville Dam and Carson.

Directions: From Portland, drive I-84 east to the Cascade Locks (Exit 44) and follow signs for the Bridge of the Gods. Just before the tollbooth for the bridge, turn right into a parking area. The trail begins across the road.

Contact: Columbia Gorge National Scenic Area, 902 Wasco Avenue, Suite 200, Hood River, OR, 97031, 541/308-1700.

22 HERMAN CREEK TO INDIAN POINT

8.0-8.4 mi/4.0-4.5 hr

 3  8

east of Cascade Locks in the Columbia River Gorge

Herman Creek Trail is a bit of a misnomer, since you'll have to go 4.2 miles just to get to a point on the water. The destination, though, is a truly lovely and untrammeled spot on the confluence of Casey and Herman Creeks. On the way, you'll pass tiger lilies in summer and a side creek with a nice waterfall. This trail is also the access point for a killer climb to Indian Point, a promontory high above the Columbia River and sweeping views.

For the hike above Herman Creek, begin from the campground, climbing through a boulder field on the Herman Creek Trail 0.6 mile to a junction with the Herman Bridge spur. Go left 0.7 mile, staying on the Herman Creek Trail, where the trail eventually joins an old road. At the next junction, site of Herman Camp, go to the right to stay on Herman Creek, keeping right at the next junction as well, for 2.6 miles. After that, you'll reach a second camp and a junction of trails; an unmarked side trail to the right goes down the canyon 0.3 mile to the confluence.

For the Indian Point climb, begin from the campground, climbing through the boulder field 0.6 mile to a junction with the Herman Bridge spur. Go left 0.7 mile, where the trail eventually joins the old road. At the next junction, site of Herman Camp, go left up the Gorton Creek Trail and climb steadily for 2.6 miles to a junction. Continue 50 yards up the Gorton Creek Trail and take an unmarked side trail to the left 0.1 mile to Indian Point. Return to the junction and go left down the Cutoff Trail 0.6 mile to the Nick Eaton Trail, going right on this trail down a steep ridge for two miles. At the junction with the old road, follow it back to Herman Camp, then return to the right down the road as you came to the Herman Creek campground.

User Groups: Hikers, dogs, and horses. No mountain bikes allowed. No wheelchair facilities.

Permits: A free self-issue Wilderness Permit is required and is available on the trail. A federal Northwest Forest Pass is required to park here; the cost is $5 a day or $30 for an annual pass. You can buy a day pass at the trailhead, at ranger stations, or through private vendors.

Maps: You can purchase a Trails of the Columbia Gorge Map from Geo-Graphics. For a topographic map, ask the USGS for Carson.

Directions: From Portland, drive I-84 east to Cascade Locks (Exit 44), driving through town for two miles. At the next on-ramp for I-84, go straight onto a road marked "To Oxbow Fish Hatchery" and follow this road two miles to a Forest Service complex, and turn right into the Herman Creek Campground entrance to a parking area at the end of the road. In the winter, the gate is closed, but you can park off the road near the gate and walk in to the campground.

Contact: Columbia Gorge National Scenic Area, 902 Wasco Avenue, Suite 200, Hood River, OR, 97031, 541/308-1700.

23 STARVATION CREEK FALLS

2.5 mi/1.0 hr

east of Cascade Locks in the Columbia River Gorge

Located just off I-84, nestled in a canyon beneath Starvation Ridge, is a 186-foot waterfall on Starvation Creek. The creek is named for an 1884 disaster; a train was stranded in the snow for weeks here, and the passengers were paid to help dig it out as they waited for food to arrive.

It's easy enough to walk to Starvation Creek Falls from the lot along a paved stretch of the out-of-use section of the Columbia River Highway. But there are more falls back in those hills above the freeway, and a somewhat demanding hike visits them all.

After visiting Starvation Creek Falls, head west on the paved Mount Defiance Trail skirting the highway, following signs for Mount Defiance. At a junction with the Starvation Ridge Cutoff Trail in 0.3 mile, stay to the right for 0.6 mile, passing Cabin Creek Falls and Hole-in-the-Wall Falls. These falls were a bizarre undertaking by highway workers in

1938 to prevent Warren Creek Falls from constantly flooding out the highway. They fixed this by tunneling the creek right through a cliff—quite a feat.

The trail climbs to a junction, and it's worth it to head right on the Mount Defiance Trail a short distance for a peak at Lancaster Falls, which falls right down to the trail. Go back to the junction and head uphill to the right on the Warren Creek Trail. In the course of an unbelievable mile, the trail fords Warren Creek and climbs to high meadows overlooking the Gorge and traces some precarious cliffs. At the Starvation Ridge Cutoff Trail, head to the left and down an incredibly steep 0.3 mile to return to the old highway site, heading to the right to return to the Starvation Creek Falls lot.

User Groups: Hikers and dogs. No mountain bikes or horses allowed. Paved areas of the park are wheelchair accessible.

Permits: Permits are not required. Parking and access are free.

Maps: You can purchase a Trails of the Columbia Gorge Map from Geo-Graphics. For a topographic map, ask the USGS for Mount Defiance.

Directions: From Cascade Locks, drive 10 miles east on I-84 to the Starvation Creek trailhead at Exit 55.

Contact: Oregon Parks and Recreation Department, 1115 Commercial Street NE, Salem, OR, 97301, 800/551-6949, www.oregonstateparks.org, and Columbia Gorge National Scenic Area, 902 Wasco Avenue, Suite 200, Hood River, OR, 97031, 541/308-1700.

24 MOUNT DEFIANCE AND STARVATION RIDGE

11.4 mi/1 day

east of Cascade Locks in the Columbia River Gorge

Mount Defiance is one of the most difficult hikes in the entire state of Oregon, so let's just say that right off the bat. Are you ready for a rough-and-tumble challenge in the highest degree? Then climb this monster of a trail—with a nearly 5,000-foot elevation gain—to the peak rising from the Hatfield Wilderness. Talk about views. This being the highest point in the Columbia Gorge, you'll see Cascade peaks ringing you in. For a real day of it, try an exhausting but ultimately rewarding loop trail down Starvation Ridge. Don't let words like "Defiance" and "Starvation" get you down, but give yourself a full day to tackle this one.

Following signs for Mount Defiance, hike along the highway for the first mile on the Mount Defiance Trail, keeping right at junctions and passing two waterfalls. After the second junction with the Warren Creek Trail, continue to the right toward Mount Defiance, passing Lancaster Falls and charging up the mountain 3.9 miles on switchbacks and through the woods to a junction with the Mitchell Point Trail, which will serve as the return route. Go uphill 0.2 mile to the next junction, and take the Mount Defiance Trail to the right, overlooking Bear Lake and the Hatfield Wilderness. In one mile, you'll arrive at the peak.

To head down, pass the tower and look for an old trail sign. Follow this trail down 0.8 mile, crossing a road twice, then go downhill at the next junction 0.2 mile, then head right 0.8 mile along the Mitchell Trail, reaching Warren Lake. Continue forward, watching for a junction and turning left onto the Starvation Ridge Trail, for a total of 3.7 miles. Near the bottom, take the right-hand Starvation Cutoff Trail, steeply switchbacking 0.3 mile, then going right on the Mount Defiance Trail 0.3 mile back to the lot.

User Groups: Hikers and dogs. No mountain bikes or horses allowed. No wheelchair facilities.

Permits: A free self-issue Wilderness Permit is required and is available on the trail. Parking and access are free.

Maps: You can purchase a Trails of the

Columbia Gorge Map from Geo-Graphics. For a topographic map, ask the USGS for Mount Defiance.

Directions: From Cascade Locks, drive 10 miles east on I-84 to the Starvation Creek trailhead at Exit 55.

Contact: Columbia Gorge National Scenic Area, 902 Wasco Avenue, Suite 200, Hood River, OR, 97031, 541/308-1700.

25 WYGANT PEAK

8.5 mi/5.5 hr 4 8

east of Cascade Locks in the Columbia River Gorge

Two prominent points rise above a small rest area on I-84: 1,200-foot Mitchell Point and 2,144-foot Wygant Peak. The trail up 1.1 miles to Mitchell is relatively easy; it's a hardier hike to get to forested Wygant Peak, but along the way there are great views over the Gorge and a loop-trail option along Perham Creek. What makes it hardy is that, for the most part, this trail is not maintained, meaning that you'll be ducking under fallen trees and hopping over some collapsed trail. Use caution. What's most frustrating is how much longer it takes when you have to bushwhack your way along the route.

From the lot, head back down the road to a gated road, following the clearly marked Wygant Trail one mile along both trail and a stretch of the old Columbia River Highway to a junction. Stay straight on the Wygant Trail for 1.6 miles, crossing Perham Creek and topping a viewpoint before climbing to the Chetwood Trail. To climb Wygant, go right 1.7 miles past a few good viewpoints to the peak.

Returning 1.7 miles to the junction, you can either return as you came or try some adventure by going right on the Chetwood Trail for 1.5 mile, crossing Perham Creek higher up in its canyon, before returning to the Wygant Trail via the Perham Loop Trail.

footbridge on the Wygant Trail

When you hit the Wygant, go right to return to the car. Be aware that this extra loop is every bit as unmaintained as the Wygant, and the creek crossing should be done when the water is low.

User Groups: Hikers and dogs. No mountain bikes or horses allowed. Paved areas of the park are wheelchair accessible.

Permits: Permits are not required. Parking and access are free.

Maps: You can purchase a Hood River map from Geo-Graphics. For a topographic map, ask the USGS for Mount Defiance.

Directions: From Cascade Locks, drive 14 miles east on I-84 to Exit 58 to the Lausman State Park rest area.

Contact: Oregon Parks and Recreation Department, 1115 Commercial Street NE, Salem, OR, 97301, 800/551-6949, www.oregonstateparks.org.

26 MOSIER TWIN TUNNELS

4.5 mi one-way/2.0 hr

east of Hood River in the Columbia River Gorge

BEST

The old Columbia River Highway sat abandoned for decades—until 1995, when stretches of it were restored to become part of the state trail system. The stretch between the city of Hood River and the town of Mosier is perfect for a long bike ride or an easy hike—excepting, perhaps, the wind, which is famous in the Columbia Gorge.

The real treasures here are a couple of tunnels that took two years to build. For an easy visit to the tunnels, start on the Mosier side and go as far as you'd like: to the County Line Overlook, a viewpoint over Koberg Beach State Wayside, or all the way to the Hood River trailhead. By the time you get east of Hood River you're in a new landscape of basalt rock and oak and ponderosa pine, differing dramatically from the more lush western Gorge.

From the Mosier parking area, follow a paved path to the gated road that marks the trail's entrance. From here it's a 0.7-mile walk to the Mosier Twin Tunnels and their sturdy roof, built to withstand massive rockfall. In another 0.9 mile, you'll reach the County Line Overlook on the border of Wasco and Hood River Counties. Yet another 0.8 mile beyond that is a 0.2-mile side trail out on a cliff to the overlook of Koberg Beach. From here, it's another 1.9 miles to the trail's end.

User Groups: Hikers, dogs, and mountain bikes. No horses allowed. The Historic Columbia Highway Trail is entirely wheelchair accessible, and there is a separate parking area for wheelchair users.

Permits: Permits are not required. A $3 day-use fee is collected at the park entrance, or you can get an annual Oregon Parks and Recreation pass for $25; contact Oregon Parks and Recreation, 800/551-6949.

Maps: For a map of the Historic Columbia River Highway State Trail, contact Oregon Parks and Recreation Department, 800/551-6949, www.oregonstateparks.org. For a topographic map, ask the USGS for White Salmon and Hood River.

Directions: Drive east of Hood River five miles on I-84 to the Mosier exit (Exit 69). Go south from the exit 0.2 mile to Mosier and turn left on Rock Creek Road for 0.7 mile to the Hatfield Trailhead on the left. For the western trailhead, take I-84, exit 64, and follow Government Camp signs for 0.3 mile. At a stop sign, go left on Old Columbia River Drive for 1.3 miles to road's end.

Contact: Oregon Parks and Recreation Department, 1115 Commercial Street NE, Salem, OR, 97301, 800/551-6949, www.oregonstateparks.org.

27 TOM MCCALL PRESERVE

5.6 mi/3.0 hr

2 7

east of Hood River in the Columbia River Gorge

More than 300 varieties of plants grow on the dramatic oak grasslands above the Columbia River and Rowena Dell. Thanks to The Nature Conservancy, this fabulous preserve—named for former Oregon Governor McCall, a conservationist—is open to everyone. Spring and early summer mark some of the showiest wildflower shows anywhere, though poison oak has a grip here, too. Lava flows and ash deposits coupled with massive floods have produced this strange mound-and-swale topography that baffles even the experts on that sort of thing. Here you'll find meadowlarks, the Oregon state bird, as well as canyon wrens, Pacific chorus frogs, and mule deer. Flowers include grass widows, prairie stars, lupine, Indian paintbrush, balsamroot, milk vetch, shooting stars, and waterleaf, several of which are found only in the Gorge.

Two trails lead out from the Rowena Crest Viewpoint. Opposite the highway from the parking area, a sign marks the lower plateau trail, an easy 2.2-mile round-trip that visits two ponds and several viewpoints. The upper trail to Tom McCall Point leads uphill for 1.7 miles to the 1,722-foot knob overlooking the eastern Gorge.

User Groups: Hikers only. No dogs, horses, or mountain bikes allowed. No wheelchair facilities.

Permits: Permits are not required. Parking and access are free.

Maps: Brochures are typically available at the trailhead. For a topographic map, ask the USGS for White Salmon.

Directions: Drive east of Hood River five miles on I-84 to the Mosier exit (Exit 69) and follow "Scenic Loop" signs 6.6 miles to the Rowena Crest Viewpoint.

Contact: The Nature Conservancy, 821 SE 14th Street, Portland, OR, 97214, 503/802-8100.

28 WAHTUM LAKE

4.1 mi/2.5 hr 

south of Hood River in the Hatfield Wilderness

Hiking the entire length of the Eagle Creek Trail (see *Eagle Creek* listing in this chapter) is one way to get to Wahtum Lake, but it requires a backpack and several days. There's an easier way: You can start right from the deep blue lake itself and follow the Pacific Crest Trail to a viewpoint on the rocky bluffs of Chinidere Mountain, looking out to Tanner Butte, the Benson Plateau, and five Cascade peaks.

From the Wahtum Lake Campground, take the Wahtum Express Trail down 0.2 mile to the lake. Turn right on the Pacific Crest Trail, rounding the lake through the Hatfield Wilderness and going 1.6 miles to a junction, going left. Then go right and uphill past a "Chinidere Mountain" sign up a steep 0.4 mile to the former lookout site. To return via the loop, head down to the PCT, go left 100 yards, and continue right 0.9 mile on the Chinidere Mountain Trail. You'll pass campsites and cross a creek, then join the Eagle Creek Trail. Stay to the left at this junction and the PCT junction, going another 0.4 mile and passing more campsites along the lakeshore. At the final junction, go right on the Wahtum Express to return 0.2 mile to the car.

User Groups: Hikers, dogs, and horses. No mountain bikes allowed. No wheelchair facilities.

Permits: A free self-issue Wilderness Permit is required and is available at the trailhead. A federal Northwest Forest Pass is required to park here; the cost is $5 a day or $30 for an annual pass. You can buy a day pass at the trailhead, at ranger stations, or through private vendors.

Maps: You can purchase a Trails of the Columbia Gorge Map from Geo-Graphics. For a topographic map, ask the USGS for Wahtum Lake.

Directions: Drive I-84 east of Portland to West Hood River at Exit 62, driving 1.1 miles into Hood River. Turn right on 13th Street, and follow signs for Odell for 3.4 miles. Cross the Hood River Bridge and turn right on a fork past Tucker Park for 6.3 miles. Fork right again toward Dee, cross the river, and turn left toward Lost Lake for 4.9 miles. Turn right at a "Wahtum Lake" sign and follow Road 13 for 4.3 miles, then go right on Road 1310 for six miles to the Wahtum Lake Campground.

Contact: Columbia Gorge National Scenic Area, 902 Wasco Avenue, Suite 200, Hood River, OR, 97031, 541/308-1700.

29 BEAR LAKE AND MOUNT DEFIANCE

6.4 mi/ 3.5 hr 

south of Hood River in the Hatfield Wilderness

The grueling way up Mount Defiance (see *Mount Defiance and Starvation Ridge* listing in this chapter) isn't for everyone; this is a far easier way to the top, and one that visits pretty little Bear Lake along the way. It's so shallow and warm in summer that it's perfect for a quick swim.

Follow the Mount Defiance Trail to a junction and go right for 0.5 mile. A left-hand trail at the next junction leads 0.8 mile to Bear Lake. Continuing on the Mount Defiance Trail 0.9 mile, the path comes to another junction; go right 0.2 mile to the peak. To make a loop of it, with a view down to Bear Lake, walk past the tower and look for an old trail sign for the Mount Defiance Trail. Follow this trail down 0.8 mile, crossing a road twice, then go left on an unmarked trail one mile, rounding the peak. This will bring you back to the Mount Defiance Trail, which you can follow 1.4 miles back to the road.

User Groups: Hikers, dogs, and horses. No mountain bikes allowed. No wheelchair facilities.

Permits: A free self-issue Wilderness Permit is required and is available on the trail. Parking and access are free.

Maps: You can purchase a Trails of the Columbia Gorge Map from Geo-Graphics. For a topographic map, ask the USGS for Mount Defiance.

Directions: Drive I-84 east of Portland to West Hood River at Exit 62, driving 1.1 miles into Hood River. Turn right on 13th Street, and follow signs for Odell for 3.4 miles. Cross the Hood River Bridge and turn right on a fork past Tucker Park for 6.3 miles. Fork right again toward Dee, cross the river, and turn right toward Rainy Lake. Follow paved Punchbowl Road for 1.4 miles and continue on gravel Road 2820 for 10 miles to a sign for Mount Defiance Trail on the right.

Contact: Columbia Gorge National Scenic Area, 902 Wasco Avenue, Suite 200, Hood River, OR, 97031, 541/308-1700.

30 BALD BUTTE

8.2 mi/5.0 hr

south of Hood River in Mount Hood National Forest

Not to be confused with the plethora of other Bald Buttes out there, this one has the required old lookout site to provide a sweeping view of the Hood River Valley and nearby Mount Hood, then clear out into the Washington Cascades: St. Helens, Rainier, and Adams. Not bad for a hike that'll make you work for it, gaining 2,300 feet in elevation when all is said and done. Making use of the popular horse-and-bike trail on Surveyor's Ridge, this peak still remains fairly off-the-map.

Take the Oakridge Trail 2.5 miles from the grassy meadow into the fir and oak forest and climb the switchbacks. Turn left on the Surveyor's Ridge Trail for 0.9 mile then stay straight on a dirt road another 0.7 mile to the summit.

User Groups: Hikers, dogs, mountain bikes, and horses. No wheelchair facilities.

Permits: Permits are not required. Parking and access are free.

Maps: For a map of the Mount Hood National Forest, contact Mount Hood National Forest Headquarters, 16400 Champion Way, Sandy, OR, 97055, 503/668-1700. For a topographic map, ask the USGS for Parkdale.

Directions: From I-84 at Hood River, take Exit 64 and follow Highway 35 south for 14.8 miles. Turn left on Smullen Road 0.3 mile, then turn left on a gravel road 0.1 mile to the trailhead.

Contact: Mount Hood National Forest, Hood River Ranger District, 6780 Highway 35, Parkdale, OR, 97041, 541/352-6002.

31 LOST LAKE

3.2 mi/1.5 hr

south of Hood River in Mount Hood National Forest

Located on the north slope of Mount Hood, this lake has long been a popular destination for travelers. The Hood River tribe knew about it, naming it "Heart of the Mountains." A resort and campground are there now, and the lakeshore has been restored after years of heavy use. In just over three miles, you can treat yourself to stunning views of Mount Hood and Lost Lake Butte, watching for high-elevation birds along the water. The 3.4-mile shoreline loop trail can be taken in either direction, and a junction near a group camp leads to Lost Lake Butte (see *Lost Lake Butte,* next listing).

User Groups: Hikers and dogs. Mountain bikes and horses not allowed. Parts of the trail are wheelchair accessible.

Permits: Permits are not required. There is a day-use fee of $7 collected at the entry booth.

Maps: For a map of the Mount Hood National Forest, contact Mount Hood National Forest Headquarters, 16400 Champion Way, Sandy, OR, 97055, 503/668-1700. For a topographic map, ask the USGS for Bull Run Lake.

Directions: From Exit 62 in Hood River, drive 1.1 miles into town, turn right on 13th Street and follow signs for Odell for five miles. Cross a bridge and fork right past Tucker Park for 6.3 miles, then fork right again toward Dee and follow signs 14 miles to Lost Lake. Drive past the Lost Lake entry booth, go toward the store, and follow the lake to the right to a picnic area at the end of the road.

Contact: Mount Hood National Forest, Hood River Ranger District, 6780 Highway 35, Parkdale, OR, 97041, 541/352-6002.

32 LOST LAKE BUTTE

3.8 mi/2.0 hr 2 8

south of Hood River in Mount Hood National Forest

Rising over a thousand feet above picturesque Lost Lake, this butte of the same name has a character all its own. Hiking its viewless forested slopes will eventually lead to an unimpeded view of Mount Rainier, Mount Adams, and Mount Hood. Along the way, you'll find beargrass blooms in summer and rhododendron blossoms in spring.

This hike begins from Campground Loop B, climbing 1.9 miles up the forested slope to some easy switchbacks at the top. The best views are from the remains of an old watchtower.

User Groups: Hikers and dogs. Mountain bikes and horses not allowed. Parts of the trail are wheelchair accessible.

Permits: Permits are not required. There is a day-use fee of $7 collected at the entry booth.

Maps: For a map of the Mount Hood National Forest, contact Mount Hood National Forest Headquarters, 16400 Champion Way, Sandy, OR, 97055, 503/668-1700. For a topographic map, ask the USGS for Bull Run Lake.

Directions: From Exit 62 in Hood River, drive 1.1 miles into town, turn right on 13th Street and follow signs for Odell for five miles. Cross a bridge, and fork right past Tucker Park for 6.3 miles, then fork right again toward Dee and follow signs 14 miles to Lost Lake. Drive past the Lost Lake entry booth, go toward the store, and follow the lake to the right to a picnic area at the end of the road.

Contact: Mount Hood National Forest, Hood River Ranger District, 6780 Highway 35, Parkdale, OR, 97041, 541/352-6002.

33 WEST ZIGZAG MOUNTAIN

11.0 mi/8.0 hr 4 9

north of Zigzag in the Mount Hood Wilderness

Just above the town of Zigzag, the border of the Mount Hood Wilderness begins at the base of Zigzag Mountain, so big it becomes two peaks: East and West. Tackling West Zigzag is no mean feat, as the trail climbs nearly 3,000 feet in only 2.3 miles, then heads out over the ridge to a lookout site. Still, this well-graded trail won't totally break you; it'll just strengthen your calves a bit.

The first 1.3 miles of the Zigzag Mountain Trail switchback up steeply. The next 2.3 miles climbs as well, to a high point of 4,300 feet. After that, the next 1.9 miles provides some views over the mountains, coming to the old lookout site atop some rocky cliffs.

User Groups: Hikers, dogs, and horses. No mountain bikes allowed. No wheelchair facilities.

Permits: A free self-issue Wilderness Permit is required and is available at the trailhead. Parking and access are free.

Maps: For a map of the Mount Hood National Forest, contact Mount Hood National Forest Headquarters, 16400 Champion Way, Sandy, OR, 97055, 503/668-1700. A map of the Mount Hood Wilderness is available from Geo-Graphics. For a topographic map, ask the USGS for Rhododendron.

Directions: Drive east of Portland 42 miles on U.S. 26 to Zigzag, turning left onto East Lolo Pass Road for 0.4 mile. Turn right on East Mountain Drive for 0.2 mile, keeping right at a fork. After 0.5 mile, watch for a sign on the left for the Zigzag Mountain Trail and park on the shoulder.

Contact: Mount Hood National Forest, Zigzag Ranger District, 70220 East Highway 26, Zigzag, OR, 97049, 503/622-3191.

34 EAST ZIGZAG MOUNTAIN

8.0 mi/5.0 hr 3 9

north of Zigzag in the Mount Hood Wilderness

Like West Zigzag Mountain, East Zigzag Mountain provides some immense views over the surrounding country. The difference, though, is that this trail isn't quite as difficult. It's still difficult, just not bone-crushingly so. What you'll find is a ramble through Devil's Meadow, a side trail to Cast Lake, and high-alpine country looking out over the Mount Hood Wilderness.

From the Burnt Lake Trailhead, follow signs for Devil's Meadow. The Burnt Lake Trail follows an old road into this abandoned campground, going 2.6 miles to a junction, the start of the loop. Follow "Burnt Lake" signs to the right, going 1.4 miles to a junction atop a ridge. Go left one mile, passing the East Zigzag summit at 4,971 feet and arriving at a junction with the Cast Creek Trail, heading to the left. The next junction leads to Cast Lake on the right, which will add 1.2 miles to your round-trip mileage. Continuing on the Zigzag Mountain Trail, you'll reach a junction with the Devil's Tie Trail; take this left-hand turn for 0.4 mile to return to Devil's Meadow, then go right the remaining 2.6 miles back to the trailhead.

User Groups: Hikers and dogs. No horses or mountain bikes. No wheelchair facilities.

Permits: A free self-issue Wilderness Permit is required and is available at the trailhead. Parking and access are free.

Maps: For a map of the Mount Hood National Forest, contact Mount Hood National Forest Headquarters, 16400 Champion Way, Sandy, OR, 97055, 503/668-1700. A map of the Mount Hood Wilderness is available from Geo-Graphics. For a topographic map, ask the USGS for Government Camp.

Directions: Drive east of Portland 47 miles on U.S. 26 to the village of Rhododendron. Turn left on Road 27 for 0.6 mile. Turn left on gravel Road 207 for 4.5 miles until it ends; this road is rough, so cars should take it slow.

Contact: Mount Hood National Forest, Zigzag Ranger District, 70220 East Highway 26, Zigzag, OR, 97049, 503/622-3191.

35 BURNT LAKE

6.8 mi/3.5 hr 2 8

northeast of Zigzag in the Mount Hood Wilderness

The area around Burnt Lake burned once and left massive hollowed-out cedar stumps. It's a heavily visited spot in the Mount Hood Forest, and rightfully so: It reflects nearby Mount Hood and is ringed in by big trees and a half-mile loop trail. Along the way, the nearly hidden Lost Creek Falls lie a bit off the trail and East Zigzag Mountain looms overhead like a great wall.

From the Burnt Lake Trailhead, follow the trail between two creeks—Burnt Lake Creek and Lost Creek—for 2.4 miles, crossing Burnt Lake Creek and arriving at a side trail to the left leading down to Lost Creek Falls. Continue on the main trail another mile to arrive at the shore of Burnt Lake.

User Groups: Hikers and dogs. No horses or mountain bikes allowed. No wheelchair facilities.

Permits: A free self-issue Wilderness Permit is required and is available at the trailhead. A federal Northwest Forest Pass is required to park here; the cost is $5 a day or $30 for an annual pass. You can buy a day pass at the trailhead, at ranger stations, or through private vendors.

Maps: For a map of the Mount Hood National Forest, contact Mount Hood National Forest Headquarters, 16400 Champion Way, Sandy, OR, 97055, 503/668-1700. A map of the Mount Hood Wilderness is available from Geo-Graphics. For a topographic map, ask the USGS for Government Camp.

Directions: Drive east of Portland 42 miles on U.S. 26 to Zigzag. Turn left on East Lolo Pass Road, following this route 4.2 miles and turn right on Road 1825 for 0.7 mile. Turn right across the Sandy River Bridge and continue on Road 1825 another 2.1 miles to the entrance for Lost Creek Campground. Go left on a gravel road 1.4 miles to its end at a parking area.

Contact: Mount Hood National Forest, Zigzag Ranger District, 70220 East Highway 26, Zigzag, OR, 97049, 503/622-3191.

36 RAMONA FALLS

7.1 mi/3.5 hr

northeast of Zigzag in the Mount Hood Wilderness

BEST

The Sandy River flows from Mount Hood and tumbles down a rocky bed. It's not filled with sand, though early pioneers thought it was. Actually, the milky color of many young mountain rivers is due to glacial silt.

This fine loop travels upstream to Ramona Falls, a 120-foot drop in a lovely fern-draped glen of columnar basalt. If the bridge is out when you visit (as it has been in the past), you will have to ford the Sandy River; this is easiest and safest late in the summer, when the water drops and exposes stones to cross over.

From the trailhead, head up the Sandy River 1.4 miles to a crossing. After fording the river, turn right on the PCT Horse Trail for 1.5 miles to a junction with the Pacific Crest Trail, and go left 0.5 mile to reach the falls on Ramona Creek. At the next junction just beyond the waterfall, continue left for 1.8 miles on the PCT, then take a left turn for 0.5 mile to return to the Sandy River crossing, fording it then going right the remaining 1.4 miles to the lot.

User Groups: Hikers, dogs, and horses. No mountain bikes allowed. No wheelchair facilities.

Permits: A free self-issue Wilderness Permit is required and is available at the trailhead. A federal Northwest Forest Pass is required to park here; the cost is $5 a day or $30 for an annual pass. You can buy a day pass at the trailhead, at ranger stations, or through private vendors.

Maps: For a map of the Mount Hood National Forest, contact Mount Hood National Forest Headquarters, 16400 Champion Way, Sandy, OR, 97055, 503/668-1700. A map of the Mount Hood Wilderness is available from Geo-Graphics. For a topographic map, ask the USGS for Bull Run Lake.

Directions: From Portland, drive U.S. 26 east toward Mount Hood 42 miles. At Zigzag, turn left onto East Lolo Pass Road and go 4.2 miles, then turn right on Road 1825. Drive 0.7 mile and turn right across the Sandy River. Continue 1.8 miles on Road 1825 and go left on Road 100 for 0.5 mile to a parking area at the end of the road.

Contact: Mount Hood National Forest, Zigzag Ranger District, 70220 East Highway 26, Zigzag, OR, 97049, 503/622-3191.

37 YOCUM RIDGE

16.2 mi/10.0 hr 5 10

northeast of Zigzag in the Mount Hood Wilderness

The meadows on Yocum Ridge are the definition of "alpine country." Set beside the Sandy Glacier on the slopes of Mount Hood, the source of the Sandy River, this makes for one of the most spectacular views on the mountain. The ascent is as arduous as the scenery is spectacular: You'll need to climb 3,800 feet from the Sandy River to get to this lush viewpoint.

From the trailhead, head up the Sandy River 1.4 miles to a crossing. After fording the river, turn right on the PCT Horse Trail for 1.5 miles to a junction with the Pacific Crest Trail, and go left 0.5 mile to reach the falls on Ramona Creek. At the next junction just beyond the waterfall, turn right on the Timberline Trail. Follow this trail 0.6 mile to a right-hand junction up the Yocum Ridge for 4.7 miles.

User Groups: Hikers, dogs, and horses. No mountain bikes allowed. No wheelchair facilities.

Permits: A free self-issue Wilderness Permit is required and is available at the trailhead. A federal Northwest Forest Pass is required to park here; the cost is $5 a day or $30 for an annual pass. You can buy a day pass at the trailhead, at ranger stations, or through private vendors.

Maps: For a map of the Mount Hood National Forest, contact Mount Hood National Forest Headquarters, 16400 Champion Way, Sandy, OR, 97055, 503/668-1700. A map of the Mount Hood Wilderness is available from Geo-Graphics. For a topographic map, ask the USGS for Mount Hood North.

Directions: From Portland, drive U.S. 26 east toward Mount Hood 42 miles. At Zigzag, turn left onto East Lolo Pass Road and go 4.2 miles, then turn right on Road 1825. Drive 0.7 mile and turn right across the Sandy River. Continue 1.8 miles on Road 1825 and go left on Road 100 for 0.5 mile to a parking area at the end of the road.

Contact: Mount Hood National Forest, Zigzag Ranger District, 70220 East Highway 26, Zigzag, OR, 97049, 503/622-3191.

38 MCNEIL POINT

8.8 mi/5.0 hr 4 10

northeast of Zigzag in the Mount Hood Wilderness

In the 1930s, the Civilian Conservation Corps built a series of beautiful stone shelters encircling Mount Hood along the Timberline Trail. Only three remain, and the loftiest must surely be the one on McNeil Point, named for Portland newspaperman Fred McNeil. The climb to the towering plateau is every bit as amazing, circling Bald Mountain, ascending through thick huckleberry fields, and finally following a towering ridge to some alpine ponds and the 6,100-foot plateau edge. But be careful: The scenery here is so spectacular that you may want to move into the cabin like a modern-day Thoreau and never leave again.

Start by climbing on the Top Spur Trail up 0.5 mile to the Pacific Crest Trail, going right at a junction, then left at the next aside a big map board. Follow the Timberline Trail 2.3 miles, staying to the right on Timberline and hiking the ridge high above the roaring Muddy Fork. At 5,300 feet, you'll pass a faint side trail, but stay on the main Timberline Trail another 0.6 mile, passing a couple of ponds and the end of the Mazama Trail to a junction. Head up this trail to the right, following a ridge up a mile to the stone shelter high atop McNeil Point. Return the way you came.

User Groups: Hikers, dogs, and horses. No mountain bikes allowed. No wheelchair facilities.

Permits: A free self-issue Wilderness Permit is required and is available at the trailhead.

A federal Northwest Forest Pass is required to park here; the cost is $5 a day or $30 for an annual pass. You can buy a day pass at the trailhead, at ranger stations, or through private vendors.

Maps: For a map of the Mount Hood National Forest, contact Mount Hood National Forest Headquarters, 16400 Champion Way, Sandy, OR, 97055, 503/668-1700. A map of the Mount Hood Wilderness is available from Geo-Graphics. For a topographic map, ask the USGS for Mount Hood North.

Directions: From Portland, drive U.S. 26 east toward Mount Hood 42 miles. At Zigzag, turn left onto East Lolo Pass Road and go 4.2 miles, then turn right on Road 1825. In 0.7 mile, go straight on Road 1828 and follow signs for "Top Spur Trail" for 7.1 miles to a parking pullout on the gravel road.

Contact: Mount Hood National Forest, Zigzag Ranger District, 70220 East Highway 26, Zigzag, OR, 97049, 503/622-3191.

39 MAZAMA TRAIL TO CAIRN BASIN

8.6 mi/5.0 hr

northeast of Zigzag in the Mount Hood Wilderness

BEST

This difficult trail is maintained by the Mazamas, Portland's oldest outdoors club. In 1894, the Mazamas (155 men and 38 women in all) climbed this mountain to its peak to elect their first president. Now you can get a sense of what brought them here. The trail climbs massive Cathedral Ridge to the glassy tarns and wildflower meadows on Mount Hood. The stone shelter in Cairn Basin is a good destination—with views of the forests, meadows, and peak of Mount Hood. You can make this a short backpacking trip, too, by pitching your tent at Cairn Basin.

The path is straightforward, if steep. From the trailhead, climb the Mazama Trail one mile to the Mount Hood Wilderness sign atop a series of switchbacks. Continue 2.7 miles to this trail's terminus with the Timberline Trail. To the right is a short walk to a couple mountain tarns. Continue to the left, where a right-hand junction leads to McNeil Point (see *McNeil Point,* previous listing), or continue on to the left to Cairn Basin, a total of 0.6 mile from the end of the Mazama Trail.

User Groups: Hikers and dogs. No horses or mountain bikes allowed. No wheelchair facilities.

Permits: A free self-issue Wilderness Permit is required and is available at the trailhead. Parking and access are free.

Maps: For a map of the Mount Hood National Forest, contact Mount Hood National Forest Headquarters, 16400 Champion Way, Sandy, OR, 97055, 503/668-1700. A map of the Mount Hood Wilderness is available from Geo-Graphics. For a topographic map, ask the USGS for Mount Hood North.

Directions: From Portland, drive U.S. 26 east toward Mount Hood 42 miles. At Zigzag, turn left onto East Lolo Pass Road and go 10.5 miles to Lolo Pass. Turn right on McGee Creek Road 1810 for 5.5 miles and turn right on gravel Road 1811 for 2.5 miles to a parking pullout.

Contact: Mount Hood National Forest, Hood River Ranger District, 6780 Highway 35, Parkdale, OR, 97041, 541/352-6002.

40 CAIRN BASIN VIA VISTA RIDGE

7.9 mi/4.0 hr

north of Hood River in the Mount Hood Wilderness

The stone shelter at Cairn Basin is set among some towering old-growth trees, near meadows and picturesque views of Mount Hood's enormous peak and the Ladd Glacier. This loop trail also leads through two other mountain meadows: Wy'East Basin (an ancient Native American name for this iconic mountain)

© SEAN PATRICK HILL

view of Mount Hood from Eden Park

and Eden Park. You can easily get water from nearby Ladd Creek, making this a good destination for backpacking. Vista Ridge Trail is easier than the nearby Mazama Trail and has views to distant peaks to boot.

Start up the Vista Ridge Trail 0.4 mile, and keep right at a junction, climbing Vista Ridge for 2.1 miles. At the next junction, head to the left 0.3 mile to arrive at the edge of Wy'East Basin. Then go right on the Timberline Trail 1.1 rambling miles with excellent views to Cairn Basin. Just past the stone shelter, take a right-hand trail down a steep slope to Eden Park, continuing to the Vista Ridge Trail, a total of 1.5 miles. Then go left to return the way you came.

User Groups: Hikers and dogs. No horses or mountain bikes allowed. No wheelchair facilities.

Permits: A free self-issue Wilderness Permit is required and is available at the trailhead. Parking and access are free.

Maps: For a map of the Mount Hood National Forest, contact Mount Hood National Forest Headquarters, 16400 Champion Way, Sandy, OR, 97055, 503/668-1700. A map of the Mount Hood Wilderness is available from Geo-Graphics. For a topographic map, ask the USGS for Mount Hood North.

Directions: From Portland, drive U.S. 26 east toward Mount Hood 42 miles. At Zigzag, turn left onto East Lolo Pass Road and go 10.5 miles to Lolo Pass. Turn right on McGee Creek Road 1810 for 7.7 miles to Road 18. Continue on this paved road 3.2 miles and turn right on Road 16, then follow "Vista Ridge Trail" signs nine miles up Road 16 and Road 1650 to the trailhead.

Contact: Mount Hood National Forest, Hood River Ranger District, 6780 Highway 35, Parkdale, OR, 97041, 541/352-6002.

41 ELK COVE

8.0 mi/5.0 hr 3 9

north of Hood River in the Mount Hood Wilderness

Elk Cove, a magnificent meadow on the slopes of Mount Hood, is not only an amazing destination for a day trip but a great spot to camp. Indeed, many people do spend the night here—such as ambitious backpackers who tackle the entire length of the Timberline Trail, which circles Mount Hood, visiting an array of unforgettable spots. The trail to Elk Cove starts fairly high up the mountain, making it one of the easier destinations on Mount Hood.

The popular hike to Elk Cove from the Cloud Cap Campground is officially closed due to massive flooding on the Timberline Trail. Check with the US Forest Service before attempting this route. The following description is another way to get to Elk Cove from the Vista Ridge Trail.

Start up the Vista Ridge Trail 0.4 mile, and keep right at a junction, climbing Vista Ridge for 2.1 miles. At the next junction, head to the left 0.3 mile to arrive at the edge of Wy'East Basin. Then go left on the Timberline Trail; in just under a mile, you'll reach Elk Cove's meadows and the junction with the Elk Cove Trail.

User Groups: Hikers and dogs. No horses or mountain bikes allowed. No wheelchair facilities.

Permits: A free self-issue Wilderness Permit is required and is available at the trailhead. A federal Northwest Forest Pass is required to park here; the cost is $5 a day or $30 for an annual pass. You can buy a day pass at the trailhead, at ranger stations, or through private vendors.

Maps: For a map of the Mount Hood National Forest, contact Mount Hood National Forest Headquarters, 16400 Champion Way, Sandy, OR, 97055, 503/668-1700. A map of the Mount Hood Wilderness is available from Geo-Graphics. For a topographic map, ask the USGS for Mount Hood North.

Directions: From Portland, drive U.S. 26 east toward Mount Hood 42 miles. At Zigzag, turn left onto East Lolo Pass Road and go 10.5 miles to Lolo Pass. Turn right on McGee Creek Road 1810 for 7.7 miles to Road 18. Continue on this paved road 3.2 miles and turn right on Road 16, then follow "Vista Ridge Trail" signs nine miles up Road 16 and Road 1650 to the trailhead.

Contact: Mount Hood National Forest, Hood River Ranger District, 6780 Highway 35, Parkdale, OR, 97041, 541/352-6002.

42 COOPER SPUR

6.8 mi/4.0 hr

north of Hood River in the Mount Hood Wilderness

From Cloud Cap Campground, this trail climbs to one of three CCC-built stone shelters on the flanks of Mount Hood, this one on a windswept ridge populated by a few whitebark pines, the highest-growing tree in Oregon. But the fun has only started. A steady climb over the gravely ridge of the Cooper Spur leads to an impressive view of Mount Hood and the Eliot Glacier, which on a good summer day can be heard cracking and shifting under its own massive weight. Views extend far out to Mount Jefferson and north to the peaks of the Washington Cascades. Be sure to bring sunblock and a wide-brimmed hat; there's no protection up here from the relentless sun.

From the Cloud Cap Campground, head to the Timberline Trail and go left, following it up some small gorges 1.2 miles to a four-way junction. Go right onto the Cooper Spur Trail 0.1 mile to the Cooper Spur stone shelter. Continue on this trail 2.6 miles to get up the Cooper Spur to a saddle, where a rock is carved with a 1910 commemoration for a Japanese climbing party.

User Groups: Hikers and dogs. No horses or mountain bikes allowed. No wheelchair facilities.

Permits: A free self-issue Wilderness Permit is required and is available at the trailhead. A federal Northwest Forest Pass is required to park here; the cost is $5 a day or $30 for an annual pass. You can buy a day pass at the trailhead, at ranger stations, or through private vendors.

Maps: For a map of the Mount Hood National Forest, contact Mount Hood National Forest Headquarters, 16400 Champion Way, Sandy, OR, 97055, 503/668-1700. A map of the Mount Hood Wilderness is available from Geo-Graphics. For a topographic map, ask the USGS for Mount Hood North.

Directions: From Highway 35 on the east side of Mount Hood, between mileposts 73 and 74, go west on Cooper Spur Road for 3.3 miles to Tilly Jane Junction, and turn left on Road 3512 to go 10.3 miles to the Cloud Cap Campground.

Contact: Mount Hood National Forest, Hood River Ranger District, 6780 Highway 35, Parkdale, OR, 97041, 541/352-6002.

43 CLOUD CAP VIA POLALLIE RIDGE

6.0 mi/3.5 hr 3 7

on the northeast slope of Mount Hood

Atop a timbered knoll high on the flanks of Mount Hood is the Cloud Cap Inn, built in 1889 and listed on the National Register of Historic Places. Though the historic chalet is accessible by road, there's an old ski trail that leads there—making it that much more of a destination. Along the way, the trail passes the deep and scoured Polallie Canyon, with side trail options to the Cooper Spur and the stone shelter on its flanks (see *Cooper Spur,* previous listing). You'll also pass just behind the Tilly Jane Campground and its 1924 cookhouse and old amphitheater.

From the trailhead, hike 2.6 miles up Tilly Jane Ski Trail and along the Polallie Canyon to Tilly Jane Campground, then head to the right on a 0.5-mile spur trail to Cloud Cap Campground. From here, go to the road and follow it up a short distance to views from the old inn. Head back to Tilly Jane and follow the sign for "Tilly Jane #600A" to the Polallie Ridge Trail for a return loop.

User Groups: Hikers and dogs. No horses or mountain bikes allowed. No wheelchair facilities.

Permits: Permits are not required. Parking and access are free.

Maps: For a map of the Mount Hood National Forest, contact Mount Hood National Forest Headquarters, 16400 Champion Way, Sandy, OR, 97055, 503/668-1700. For a topographic map, ask the USGS for Mount Hood North.

Directions: From Highway 35 on the east side of Mount Hood, between mileposts 73 and 74, go west on Cooper Spur Road for 3.3 miles to Tilly Jane Junction, and turn left on Road 3512 to go 1.4 miles to a trail sign on the left.

Contact: Mount Hood National Forest, Hood River Ranger District, 6780 Highway 35, Parkdale, OR, 97041, 541/352-6002.

44 WILDCAT MOUNTAIN AND MCINTYRE RIDGE

10.0 mi/5.5 hr 4 8

southeast of Sandy in Mount Hood National Forest

The long McIntyre Ridge, alternately easy and steep, climbs to Wildcat Mountain and its overgrown former watchtower site. But the ridge has great views of the Mount Hood country from its meadows, looking over the Salmon-Huckleberry Wilderness and out to nearby Huckleberry Mountain.

From the McIntyre Ridge Trailhead, the path begins its climb through acres of huckleberry fields and forest 2.1 miles to the first clear viewpoint. Another 0.8 mile leads to a fine mountain meadow with awesome views, though the trails meander every which way here. The next 1.6 miles heads out into another large meadow to a junction with the Douglas Trail. Go left and up for 0.5 mile to the 4,480-foot summit of Wildcat Mountain.

User Groups: Hikers, dogs, and horses. No mountain bikes allowed. No wheelchair facilities.

Permits: A free self-issue Wilderness Permit is required and is available at the trailhead. Parking and access are free.

Maps: For a map of the Mount Hood National Forest and the Salmon-Huckleberry Wilderness, contact Mount Hood National Forest Headquarters, 16400 Champion Way, Sandy, OR, 97055, 503/668-1700. For a topographic map, ask the USGS for Wildcat Mountain.

Directions: From Portland, drive U.S. 26 toward Mount Hood. At 11 miles past Sandy, turn right onto East Wildcat Creek Road for 1.5 miles. Note that the BLM has closed the road to McIntyre Ridge from this point for the time being; contact the Forest Service for updates and for information on other access points. To hike into the trailhead from here, stay on the larger road at all forks for three miles. The McIntyre Ridge Trailhead is after the last stretch of deeply rutted road.

Contact: Mount Hood National Forest, Zigzag Ranger District, 70220 East Highway 26, Zigzag, OR, 97049, 503/622-3191.

45 WILDWOOD RECREATION SITE/BOULDER RIDGE/ HUCKLEBERRY MOUNTAIN

1.5-11.6 mi/1.0-6.0 hr 

southeast of Sandy off U.S. 26

BEST

A network of trails here spans the Wildwood Recreation Site and the Salmon-Huckleberry Wilderness, located along the Wild and Scenic Salmon River. There's plenty to do here, including fishing, swimming, wildlife-watching, and a number of short loop trails. It's also the gateway to a challenging loop up Boulder Ridge to the summit of Huckleberry Mountain and back down again. If you're camping with a group of people and you have two cars, I recommend a shuttle to tackle Boulder Ridge; otherwise, the loop requires you to hike a long ways down roads and highways. If you try this loop, you'll follow the deep Cheeney Creek canyon and pass the abandoned shaft of the Bonanza Mine. If you have the kids, you can make it an easy day and stick to the easier Wildwood Trails.

The Wildwood loops are an easy 1.5 mile altogether and are all-accessible. To try the loops, or part of them, follow either the 0.7-mile Wetland Trail or the 0.8-mile Streamwatch Loop, which both begin at the trailhead parking area.

For a more challenging day, take the Wetland Trail loop 0.3 mile to the right to the Boulder Ridge Trail. This path climbs steeply up Boulder Ridge, passing two viewpoints 4.3 miles to a junction with the Plaza Trail. Turn right and go up another mile to a crest on Huckleberry Mountain. Another 0.5 mile follows the ridge to the Bonanza Trail. This, or any point before, would be a fine turnaround point.

If you've arranged for a shuttle, go left on the Bonanza Trail, following it down the mountain 2.4 miles to the mine shaft near a creek, and the remaining 2.7 miles to the end of the trail, fording a creek at the end.

User Groups: Hikers and dogs. No horses or mountain bikes allowed. Wildwood Trails are wheelchair accessible.

Permits: Permits are not required. The BLM charges a $5 parking fee at the site.

Maps: For a map of the Mount Hood National Forest and the Salmon-Huckleberry Wilderness, contact Mount Hood National Forest Headquarters, 16400 Champion Way, Sandy, OR, 97055, 503/668-1700. For a topographic map, ask the USGS for Rhododendron and Wildcat Mountain.

Directions: Follow U.S. 26 past Sandy 15.4 miles, and turn south into the Wildwood Recreation Site. To shuttle a car for the Bonanza Trail, drive U.S. 26 another mile east of Wildwood to a stoplight at Welches and turn right on Welches Road for 1.3 miles, staying left at a fork, and driving 0.7 mile to another junction, heading straight across a one-lane bridge. Take the second gravel street to the left and follow East Grove Lane to a fork. The road closed by a cable is the start of the Bonanza Trail. The Wildwood Trails begin in the Recreation Area.

Contact: Bureau of Land Management, Salem District Office, 1717 Fabry Road SE, Salem, OR, 97306, 503/375-5646, and Mount Hood National Forest, Zigzag Ranger District, 70220 East Highway 26, Zigzag, OR, 97049, 503/622-3191.

46 HUNCHBACK MOUNTAIN

4.2-9.0 mi/2.0-4.5 hr 

at Zigzag in the Salmon-Huckleberry Wilderness

How did Hunchback Mountain get its name? I have two guesses: one is the general hunching shape of the mountain itself, easily discernable from the highway, and the other is the way you feel when you're going up this beast. Yes, Hunchback Mountain is steep, steep, steep, and coming down is no easier. The nine-mile round-trip out to the Great Pyramid is an ample day's journey. There are good viewpoints along the way, and once you're on top of the ridge things get a bit easier. A bit.

From the trailhead, climb on Hunchback Mountain Trail, a steep path, for 2.1 harsh, switchbacking miles to a viewpoint on some sheer rimrock just inside the wilderness boundary. In another 0.3 mile, a side trail leads to the big, jumbled "Viewpoint Rockpile"—another great view. Another 1.1 miles leads to the "Viewpoint Helispot 260," though as far as I know no helicopter has landed here in a long time. Another mile past that leads to a side trail by a junction leading out to a viewpoint on the 4,030-foot Great Pyramid, overlooking the Salmon River canyon. Though Devil's Peak is farther on, this is a good spot to turn around; the trail sharply drops in elevation after this, only to rise again later.

User Groups: Hikers and dogs. No mountain bikes or horses allowed. No wheelchair facilities.

Permits: A free self-issue Wilderness Permit is required and is available at the trailhead. Parking and access are free.

Maps: For a map of the Mount Hood National Forest and the Salmon-Huckleberry Wilderness, contact Mount Hood National Forest Headquarters, 16400 Champion Way, Sandy, OR, 97055, 503/668-1700. For a topographic map, ask the USGS for Rhododendron.

Directions: From Portland, drive 42 miles east on U.S. 26 to the Zigzag Ranger Station in Zigzag. Turn left into a large parking lot by the trailhead.

Contact: Mount Hood National Forest, Zigzag Ranger District, 70220 East Highway 26, Zigzag, OR, 97049, 503/622-3191.

47 CASTLE CANYON

1.8 mi/1.0 hr

2 7

north of Rhododendron in the Mount Hood Wilderness

This fun trail leads to some colossal rock formations. You'll climb up about 800 feet in 0.9 mile to reach the jagged spires of Castle Canyon, and you'll have the opportunity to scramble up and play around on the peaks and ridges looking out far over the valleys below. But be careful: These cliffs are high. If you bring pets or children, be sure to keep them close.

User Groups: Hikers and dogs. No horses or mountain bikes. No wheelchair facilities.

Permits: Permits are not required. Parking and access are free.

Maps: For a map of the Mount Hood National Forest, contact Mount Hood National Forest Headquarters, 16400 Champion Way, Sandy, OR, 97055, 503/668-1700. A map of the Mount Hood Wilderness is available from Geo-Graphics. For a topographic map, ask the USGS for Rhododendron.

Directions: Drive east of Portland 44 miles on U.S. 26 to the village of Rhododendron, and turn left on East Littlebrook Lane. Keep left on the paved road 0.3 mile and turn left on the gravel road, following Barlow Road Route for 0.4 mile to a trailhead sign on the right. Park on the shoulder.

Contact: Mount Hood National Forest, Zigzag Ranger District, 70220 East Highway 26, Zigzag, OR, 97049, 503/622-3191.

48 HIDDEN LAKE

4.0 mi/2.0 hr

2

7

north of Government Camp in Mount Hood National Forest

The name is appropriate enough, as this mountain lake is secreted on an access trail to the Mount Hood Wilderness. Though the lake has no views to speak of, it's circled with pink rhododendrons. Think of this easy-in, easy-out four-mile loop trail as a destination in and of itself, or as a way into the Zigzag Canyon and Paradise Park areas of the Mount Hood Wilderness. From the trailhead, follow the Hidden Lake Trail.

User Groups: Hikers, dogs, and horses. No mountain bikes allowed. No wheelchair facilities.

Permits: A free self-issue Wilderness Permit is required and is available at the trailhead. A federal Northwest Forest Pass is required to park here; the cost is $5 a day or $30 for an annual pass. You can buy a day pass at the trailhead, at ranger stations, or through private vendors.

Maps: For a map of the Mount Hood National Forest, contact Mount Hood National Forest Headquarters, 16400 Champion Way, Sandy, OR, 97055, 503/668-1700. A map of the Mount Hood Wilderness is available from Geo-Graphics. For a topographic map, ask the USGS for Mount Hood South and Government Camp.

Directions: From Portland, drive U.S. 26 toward Mount Hood. At 4.1 miles east of the town of Rhododendron, turn left on Road 2639 for two miles to the trailhead.

Contact: Mount Hood National Forest, Zigzag Ranger District, 70220 East Highway 26, Zigzag, OR, 97049, 503/622-3191.

49 ZIGZAG CANYON AND PARADISE PARK

4.4–12.3 mi/2.5–8.0 hr 

from Timberline Lodge in the Mount Hood Wilderness

BEST

Some of the most dramatic alpine territory in the Pacific Northwest is easily accessible from the classic Timberline Lodge, a gem of a building on the slopes of Mount Hood. The Pacific Crest Trail passes by the lodge on its way around the mountain and on toward the

Paradise Park on Mount Hood

Columbia Gorge, and it is this access that opens up the high meadows of Paradise Park and the deep, glacier-carved gorge of Zigzag Canyon. This is some serious hiking: Take lots of water and stamina and be prepared for unforgettable mountain country. You can take the trail in bits or as a 12-plus mile-escapade; either way you'll be circling the mountain on one of the most famous trails in the country. Bring a camera.

From Timberline Lodge, you can either walk the road past the lodge, which turns to trail, or follow the PCT, which runs behind the lodge; either way, in 0.7 mile both paths meet beyond the last ski lift. From here, hike 1.5 miles down and out of the gravelly Little Zigzag Canyon and on to the lip of massive Zigzag Canyon, a good turnaround point for the less ambitious.

From here, it's a 1.5-mile crossing down and back up from the 700-foot-deep canyon, but it's a pleasure along the way—with wildflowers, shady woods, and a waterfall upstream from the crossing of the Zigzag River. Once out of the canyon, the loop begins through the meadows of Paradise Park. Go right on an uphill climb leading to the boulder-strewn meadows of this unparalleled scenic area, a 2.4-mile walk through heaven. After the trail slopes back down to the PCT, go left for 2.4 miles, passing lovely waterfalls along the way, to return to the beginning of the loop and the return trail.

User Groups: Hikers, dogs, and horses. No mountain bikes allowed. No wheelchair facilities.

Permits: A free self-issue Wilderness Permit is required and is available at the trailhead. Parking and access are free.

Maps: For a map of the Mount Hood National Forest, contact Mount Hood National Forest Headquarters, 16400 Champion Way, Sandy, OR, 97055, 503/668-1700. A map of the Mount Hood Wilderness is available from Geo-Graphics. For a topographic map, ask the USGS for Government Camp and Mount Hood South.

Directions: From Portland, drive U.S. 26 toward Mount Hood for 54 miles. Past Government Camp, turn left for six miles at the sign for Timberline Lodge. Park in the lot.

Contact: Mount Hood National Forest, Zigzag Ranger District, 70220 East Highway 26, Zigzag, OR, 97049, 503/622-3191.

50 SILCOX HUT

2.2 mi/2.0 hr

at Timberline Lodge on Mount Hood

President Franklin D. Roosevelt showed up in 1937 for the dedication of Timberline Lodge, an incredible work of art that made use of some of the best Northwest artists and artisans. The building was a Works Progress Administration project during the Great Depression; it's received much care and attention over the years, leaving a legacy of beauty. These days you can visit, eat here, or even stay overnight. Just above the lodge is the Silcox Hut, which was at the top of the Magic Mile Chairlift from 1939 to 1962, until it sat idle for 30 years. Today it operates in the style of a classic European chalet, and you can hike here for views extending south to Mount Jefferson and the Three Sisters.

Start by following the paved path along the right-hand side of Timberline Lodge and turn right on the Pacific Crest Trail, crossing a gully, then heading uphill 1,100 feet on the Mountaineer Trail to Silcox Hut—a total of one mile. Descend a different way by heading over to the top of the Magic Mile Chairlift and following the service road down 1.2 miles back to the lodge.

User Groups: Hikers and dogs. No horses or mountain bikes allowed. No wheelchair facilities.

Permits: Permits are not required. Parking and access are free.

Maps: For a map of the Mount Hood National Forest, contact Mount Hood National Forest Headquarters, 16400 Champion Way, Sandy, OR, 97055, 503/668-1700. For a topographic map, ask the USGS for Mount Hood South.

Directions: From Portland, drive U.S. 26 toward Mount Hood for 54 miles. Past Government Camp, turn left for six miles at the sign for Timberline Lodge. Park in the lot.

Contact: Mount Hood National Forest, Zigzag Ranger District, 70220 East Highway 26, Zigzag, OR, 97049, 503/622-3191.

51 TIMBERLINE TRAIL

40.7 mi/4-5 days 5 10

in the Mount Hood Wilderness

Up for a backpacking adventure? Want to see the best that Mount Hood has to offer, including Zigzag Canyon, Paradise Park, Ramona Falls, Bald Mountain, Cairn Basin, Wy'East Basin, Elk Cove, and the Cooper Spur? The Timberline Trail circles Mount

Hood, almost completely in a wilderness area, with easy access from historic Timberline Lodge. Crossing meadows rich with wildflowers, gorges carved by prehistoric glaciers, mountain hemlock forests—and passing snowfields, waterfalls, and views in every direction—this is one of the most breathtaking trails in Oregon.

Due to a flood and landslide in 2006, a major crossing was swept away at the Eliot Branch of the Hood River, leaving behind an insurmountable gorge where the trail once was. The Forest Service has closed this portion of the trail and expressly forbids trying to cross it, though for the determined it is possible to circumvent the disaster by detouring on a number of trails between Elk Cove and Cloud Cap. Please use care, avoid the dangerous washout, and contact the Forest Service for updates on the condition of the trail.

There are numerous access points, the most popular being Timberline Lodge, Cairn Basin, the Mazama Trail, and Cloud Cap (see listings in this chapter).

User Groups: Hikers, dogs, and horses. No mountain bikes allowed. No wheelchair facilities.

Permits: A free self-issue Wilderness Permit is required and is available at the trailhead. Parking and access are free.

Maps: For a map of the Mount Hood National Forest, contact Mount Hood National Forest Headquarters, 16400 Champion Way, Sandy, OR, 97055, 503/668-1700. A map of the Mount Hood Wilderness is available from Geo-Graphics. For a topographic map, ask the USGS for Mount Hood North.

Directions: From Portland, drive U.S. 26 toward Mount Hood for 54 miles. Past Government Camp, turn left for six miles at the sign for Timberline Lodge. Park in the lot.

Contact: Mount Hood National Forest, Zigzag Ranger District, 70220 East Highway 26, Zigzag, OR, 97049, 503/622-3191, or Hood River Ranger District, 6780 Highway 35, Parkdale, OR, 97041, 541/352-6002.

52 ELK MEADOWS

6.8 mi/3.0 hr

north of Hood River in the Mount Hood Wilderness

This unassuming entrance to the Mount Hood Wilderness leads to two of its most famous spots: the sweeping Elk Meadow, rimmed in by trees and shadowed by Mount Hood itself; and Gnarl Ridge, a deep canyon carved from the mountain's flanks. Though camping is prohibited within Elk Meadow in order to protect vegetation, there are camping spots back in the trees along a 1.2-mile perimeter trail, and there's a shelter used by cross-country skiers in the winter season.

From the trailhead, walk one mile on the Elk Meadows Trail to a junction, going to the right for 0.6 mile and entering the Mount Hood Wilderness. At a second junction, go straight and cross Newton Creek, then switchback up one mile to a four-way junction. Going to the right leads out to Elk Mountain; to the left, Lamberson Butte and Gnarl Ridge. Go straight a short 0.2 mile to the Elk Meadows perimeter trail, which you can hike clockwise or counterclockwise, avoiding the trails that radiate away from the meadow.

User Groups: Hikers, dogs, and horses. No mountain bikes allowed. No wheelchair facilities.

Permits: A free self-issue Wilderness Permit is required and is available at the trailhead. A federal Northwest Forest Pass is required to park here; the cost is $5 a day or $30 for an annual pass. You can buy a day pass at the trailhead, at ranger stations, or through private vendors.

Maps: For a map of the Mount Hood National Forest, contact Mount Hood National Forest Headquarters, 16400 Champion Way, Sandy, OR, 97055, 503/668-1700. A map of the Mount Hood Wilderness is available from Geo-Graphics. For a topographic map, ask the USGS for Badger Lake.

Directions: From Portland, drive U.S 26 to

Mount Hood and take Highway 35 toward Hood River for 8.3 miles. Go 1.5 miles past the Mount Hood Meadows turnoff and turn left on the Clark Creek Sno-Park loop for 0.3 mile to the second pullout.

Contact: Mount Hood National Forest, Hood River Ranger District, 6780 Highway 35, Parkdale, OR, 97041, 541/352-6002.

53 EAST FORK HOOD RIVER

4.6 mi/2.0 hr 1 7

on the East Fork Hood River

Portions of the East Fork Hood River Trail remain flood damaged from a massive landslide that occurred in November 2006, but this northernmost section is still fine. Just contact the US Forest Service before you go. This stretch of trail is quite popular with mountain bikers, who can make short work of it in only a few hours. But hikers are different, having a bit more length to deal with, but they get to glide along a riverbank that effectively drowns out any highway noise. The main access point is the Pollalie Trailhead; from here, going left leads 1.1 miles to a junction with the Tamanawas Trail, and going 0.6 miles further leads to a river crossing to the East Fork Trailhead, but the bridge was wiped out in a 2006 flood. Should the rest of the East Fork Trail reopen, it will continue to a lower trailhead and a sandy stretch near the defunct Robinhood Campground.

User Groups: Hikers, dogs, and mountain bikes. Horses not allowed. No wheelchair facilities.

Permits: A free self-issue Wilderness Permit is required and is available at the trailhead. A federal Northwest Forest Pass is required to park here; the cost is $5 a day or $30 for an annual pass. You can buy a day pass at the trailhead, at ranger stations, or through private vendors.

Maps: For a map of the Mount Hood National Forest, contact Mount Hood National Forest Headquarters, 16400 Champion Way, Sandy, OR, 97055, 503/668-1700. For a topographic map, ask the USGS for Dog River and Badger Lake.

Directions: Drive Highway 35 on the east side of Mount Hood about 8.5 miles south from the junction with U.S. 26 to the Polallie Trailhead on the left.

Contact: Mount Hood National Forest, Hood River Ranger District, 6780 Highway 35, Parkdale, OR, 97041, 541/352-6002.

54 TAMANAWAS FALLS

5.6 mi/2.0 hr 2 8

in the Mount Hood National Forest

This 100-foot waterfall on the flanks of Mount Hood is named Tamanawas for the Chinook Indian word meaning "spiritual guardian." Cascading in a curtain over a water-carved grotto, these falls certainly are guarding the wilderness beyond. Hiking to this spot is easy and the walk along Cold Spring Creek makes it that much better. Making a loop of it won't add too much time and effort, and you'll be rewarded by the Polallie Overlook, which looks over a vast canyon carved by a 1980 flash flood that took out both the forest and the highway. Such is the power of Mother Nature in these mountains.

To get to the falls, cross the river and head right on the East Fork Trail for 0.6 mile, then left at a junction for 0.9 mile to a junction, which will be the start of the loop. Continue 0.4 mile, crossing the creek and arriving at the falls. Head back to the junction, this time going left if you want to try the loop. You'll go up and over a ridge and down 1.6 miles to a side trail on the left for the Polallie Overlook, then continue on to a junction at the Polallie Trailhead. Stay to the right, following the highway and the river 1.7 miles back to the trailhead.

User Groups: Hikers and dogs. No horses or mountain bikes allowed. No wheelchair facilities.

Permits: Permits are not required. A federal Northwest Forest Pass is required to park here; the cost is $5 a day or $30 for an annual pass. You can buy a day pass at the trailhead, at ranger stations, or through private vendors.
Maps: For a map of the Mount Hood National Forest, contact Mount Hood National Forest Headquarters, 16400 Champion Way, Sandy, OR, 97055, 503/668-1700. For a topographic map, ask the USGS for Dog River.
Directions: Drive Highway 35 on the east side of Mount Hood to the East Fork Trailhead near milepost 72.
Contact: Mount Hood National Forest, Hood River Ranger District, 6780 Highway 35, Parkdale, OR, 97041, 541/352-6002.

55 BADGER LAKE VIA GUMJUWAC SADDLE

5.4-11.5 mi/3.0-7.0 hr 

east of Mount Hood in the Badger Creek Wilderness

First of all, let it be said that not just any old car can make it to the Gumjuwac Saddle; only vehicles with clearance should attempt this. If you're driving one of those little economy cars, start at the Highway 35 trailhead instead, located between mileposts 68 and 69. Either way, the destination here is Badger Lake. But there are a myriad of ways to get here. You could take the easy route on the Divide Trail, which leads 2.5 miles straight from the Gumjuwac Saddle to the Badger Creek Trail; a left and a right on this trail will bring you to the shore and an old campground. And there are plenty more ways than that, including following Gumjuwac Creek and Badger Creek on a 6.7-mile loop, or the Gunsight Trail, passing Gunsight Butte on an 8.5-mile loop with the Divide Trail, or the big 11.5-mile difficult trek from Highway 35.
User Groups: Hikers, dogs, and horses. No mountain bikes allowed. No wheelchair facilities.
Permits: A free self-issue Wilderness Permit is required and is available at the trailhead. Parking and access are free.
Maps: For a map of the Mount Hood National Forest or the Badger Creek Wilderness, contact Mount Hood National Forest Headquarters, 16400 Champion Way, Sandy, OR, 97055, 503/668-1700. For a topographic map, ask the USGS for Badger Lake.
Directions: From Highway 35 on the east side of Mount Hood, between mileposts 70 and 71, go east on Dufur Mill Road 44 for 3.8 miles, then turn right on High Prairie Road 4410. Go 4.7 miles, staying always uphill, to a T-junction where the road goes from gravel to dirt. Go right on Bennett Pass Road 3550 for 1.9 very rugged miles to the trailhead by a large sign.
Contact: Mount Hood National Forest, Barlow Ranger District, 780 NE Court Street, Dufur, OR, 97021, 541/467-2291.

56 LOOKOUT MOUNTAIN

2.4 mi/1.0 hr 

east of Mount Hood in Mount Hood National Forest

Not nearly as well known as the nearby Mount Hood Wilderness, the Badger Creek Wilderness provides the same rugged country and sweeping views, especially from 6,525-foot Lookout Mountain, whose views encompass Mount Rainier to the Three Sisters. For the ambitious, this trail can be extended along the Divide Trail stretching along a row of craggy palisades with a side trail down to scenic Oval Lake.

The Lookout Mountain Trail begins on an old road through the sub-alpine meadows of High Prairie, heading across through wildflowers and up a long switchback to the Divide Trail. Go right to the summit, a 1.2-mile walk in all. To continue on the Divide Trail, go 1.4 mile to a junction. Going left and down 0.2 mile takes you to Oval Lake, but staying on the Divide Trail another 0.3 mile brings you to a viewpoint on Palisade Point.

User Groups: Hikers, dogs, and horses. No mountain bikes allowed. No wheelchair facilities.

Permits: A free self-issue Wilderness Permit is required and is available at the trailhead. A federal Northwest Forest Pass is required to park here; the cost is $5 a day or $30 for an annual pass. You can buy a day pass at the trailhead, at ranger stations, or through private vendors.

Maps: For a map of the Mount Hood National Forest or the Badger Creek Wilderness, contact Mount Hood National Forest Headquarters, 16400 Champion Way, Sandy, OR, 97055, 503/668-1700. For a topographic map, ask the USGS for Badger Lake.

Directions: From Highway 35 on the east side of Mount Hood, between mileposts 70 and 71, go east on Dufur Mill Road 44 for 3.8 miles, then turn right on High Prairie Road 4410. Go 4.7 miles, staying always uphill, to a T-junction where the road goes from gravel to dirt. Go left on High Prairie Road 200 yards and park at the trailhead on the right.

Contact: Mount Hood National Forest, Barlow Ranger District, 780 NE Court Street, Dufur, OR, 97021, 541/467-2291.

57 BALL POINT

2.0-7.0 mi/1.0-3.5 hr

east of Mount Hood in the Badger Creek Wilderness

Heading east into the Badger Creek Wilderness, you begin to cross into another ecosystem and climate. Things here on the eastern slope of the Cascades are a bit drier, and you're more likely to find these pine-oak grasslands, where big showy balsamroots burst in summer. From atop Ball Point, you'll overlook everything from Cascade peaks as far as Mount Jefferson and the Three Sisters to the distant farmlands of Eastern Oregon.

The School Canyon Trail to Ball Point is an easy one-mile climb to a saddle, but it's worth it while you're here to continue on another 2.6 miles to a viewpoint at a helispot with a camping spot nearby and a spring. Views overlook Little Badger Creek, and its namesake trail switchbacks steeply down to it, running four miles to Road 2710—along the way you'll pass an old mine. The School Canyon Trail continues on to Flag Point. If this is too far in its entirety, you can turn back at any time.

User Groups: Hikers, dogs, and horses. No mountain bikes allowed. No wheelchair facilities.

Permits: A free self-issue Wilderness Permit is required and is available at the trailhead. Parking and access are free.

Maps: For a map of the Mount Hood National Forest or the Badger Creek Wilderness, contact Mount Hood National Forest Headquarters, 16400 Champion Way, Sandy, OR, 97055, 503/668-1700. For a topographic map, ask the USGS for Flag Point and Friend.

Directions: From Portland, drive U.S. 26 beyond Mount Hood. After milepost 68, at a sign for Wamic, turn left on Road 43 and drive six miles. Turn right on Road 48 and go 15.2 miles, then turn left on Road 4810 and follow signs to Bonney Crossing Campground. After 0.2 mile, stay right on Road 4810 and go another 1.9 miles, then go right on Road 4811 for 1.2 miles, and turn right on the rough gravel road 2710 for 6.7 miles, going toward Tygh Valley. Turn left on Road 27 for 2.1 miles to a pullout and sign on the left for the School Canyon Trail.

Contact: Mount Hood National Forest, Barlow Ranger District, 780 NE Court Street, Dufur, OR, 97021, 541/467-2291.

58 DOUGLAS CABIN TRAIL

8.0 mi/4.5 hr 3 8

east of Mount Hood in the Badger Creek Wilderness

The Douglas Cabin Trail traverses the Badger Creek Wilderness, offering access to a number of spots. The destination is the Flag Point Lookout, which—unlike other lookouts in this region—is sometimes staffed (when it's not, it's available for rental). You'll have to climb 1,200 feet to get to the lookout, and 60 more feet to get up to the top of the lookout itself, but the views of Mount Hood and the surrounding area are tremendous. Built in 1973, this observation cabin sits atop a timber pole tower that itself sits atop 5,650-foot Flag Point Butte. You can reach the cabin via a straight shot on the Douglas Cabin Trail, hitting 4,820-foot Gordon Butte along the way.

User Groups: Hikers, dogs, and horses. No mountain bikes allowed. No wheelchair facilities.

Permits: A free self-issue Wilderness Permit is required and is available at the trailhead. Parking and access are free.

Maps: For a map of the Mount Hood National Forest or the Badger Creek Wilderness, contact Mount Hood National Forest Headquarters, 16400 Champion Way, Sandy, OR, 97055, 503/668-1700. For a topographic map, ask the USGS for Flag Point.

Directions: From Portland, drive U.S. 26 beyond Mount Hood. After milepost 68, at a sign for Wamic, turn left on Road 43 and drive six miles. Turn right on Road 48 and go 15.2 miles, then turn left on Road 4810 and follow signs to Bonney Crossing Campground. After 0.2 mile, stay right on Road 4810 and go another 1.9 miles, then go right on Road 4811 for 1.2 miles, and turn right on the rough gravel road 2710 for 5.6 miles, and go left for 3.5 miles. (Note: The access road is gated October 1 to May 1.)

Contact: Mount Hood National Forest, Barlow Ranger District, 780 NE Court Street, Dufur, OR, 97021, 541/467-2291.

59 BADGER CREEK

11.4–23.8 mi/6 hr–2 days 

east of Mount Hood in the Badger Creek Wilderness

By the time Badger Creek makes its way from the alpine forests of nearby Mount Hood to the sagebrush deserts of Eastern Oregon, it crosses a diverse array of landscapes with a variety of attendant plant life. At the beginning of the Wilderness area just above Bonney Crossing, the trail along Boulder Creek passes through an area of white oak, ponderosa pine, Western red cedar, and grand fir. Flowers along the way include the rare lady's slipper orchid, trilliums, balsamroot, larkspur, twinflowers, and white prairie stars—all in a gorgeous canyon with opportunities for long hikes all the way to Badger Lake.

The Badger Creek Trail sets out across the road from the Bonney Crossing Campground, heading in 5.7 miles to the confluence with Pine Creek, a good destination for the day. Return the way you came. If you're backpacking, consider going the rest of the way to Badger Lake, an additional 6.2 miles upstream (see *Badger Lake via Gumjuwac Saddle* listing in this chapter).

User Groups: Hikers, dogs, and horses. No mountain bikes allowed. No wheelchair facilities.

Permits: A free self-issue Wilderness Permit is required and is available at the trailhead. A federal Northwest Forest Pass is required to park here; the cost is $5 a day or $30 for an annual pass. You can buy a day pass at the trailhead, at ranger stations, or through private vendors.

Maps: For a map of the Mount Hood National Forest or the Badger Creek Wilderness, contact Mount Hood National Forest Headquarters, 16400 Champion Way, Sandy, OR, 97055,

503/668-1700. For a topographic map, ask the USGS for Flag Point.

Directions: From Portland, drive U.S. 26 beyond Mount Hood. After milepost 68, at a sign for Wamic, turn left on Road 43 and drive six miles. Turn right on Road 48 and go 15.2 miles, then turn left on Road 4810 and follow signs to Bonney Crossing Campground. After 0.2 mile, stay right on Road 4810 and go another 1.9 miles, then go right on Road 4811 for 1.2 miles, and turn right on the rough gravel road 2710 for 1.8 miles. The trail is on the left, but you will need to park in the lot along the entrance road to Bonney Crossing Campground and walk to the trailhead on Road 2710.

Contact: Mount Hood National Forest, Barlow Ranger District, 780 NE Court Street, Dufur, OR, 97021, 541/467-2291.

60 SALMON BUTTE

8.8 mi/5.0 hr 

south of Zigzag in the Salmon-Huckleberry Wilderness

Here's a straightforward trail whose view is anything but. From the peak of Salmon Butte, you'll look far out over the Salmon River Canyon to massive Mount Hood. Not only that, but you'll see Mount Jefferson and the Three Sisters on the Oregon side, and Mount Adams, Mount St. Helens, and Mount Rainier on the Washington side. No wonder they put a lookout here, though all that remains are bits and pieces.

From behind the gate, head up the Salmon Butte Trail 4.4 miles, connecting on the old road at the top and following it uphill to the summit. The trail is a single-shot with no junctions, up to the 4,900-foot peak and back.

User Groups: Hikers, dogs, and horses. No mountain bikes allowed. No wheelchair facilities.

Permits: A free self-issue Wilderness Permit is required and is available at the trailhead. A federal Northwest Forest Pass is required to park here; the cost is $5 a day or $30 for an annual pass. You can buy a day pass at the trailhead, at ranger stations, or through private vendors.

Maps: For a map of the Mount Hood National Forest and the Salmon-Huckleberry Wilderness, contact Mount Hood National Forest Headquarters, 16400 Champion Way, Sandy, OR, 97055, 503/668-1700. For a topographic map, ask the USGS for High Rock.

Directions: Drive east of Portland 42 miles on U.S. 26 to Zigzag. Turn south on Salmon River Road, following the paved road 4.9 miles to a bridge. Crossing the bridge, follow the gravel road 1.7 miles to a pullout on the left.

Contact: Mount Hood National Forest, Zigzag Ranger District, 70220 East Highway 26, Zigzag, OR, 97049, 503/622-3191.

61 SALMON RIVER TO DEVIL'S PEAK

15.7 mi one-way/1-2 days 

south of Zigzag in the Salmon-Huckleberry Wilderness

Just beyond civilization and a busy highway, the Salmon River extends into a deep wilderness area and roars beneath Hunchback Mountain through a canyon of its own making. The river rumbles far below the trail, and the view, once it opens up, is staggering. Atop Devil's Peak, rising off Hunchback, an old fire watchtower provides a good destination, not to mention a rugged climb. Hike the river or turn this one into a loop, but either way the route is good for backpacking.

From the trailhead, head into the old-growth forest following the Salmon River Trail for 3.6 miles, passing the primitive Rolling Riffle Camp, to arrive at a stupendous viewpoint high above the canyon and looking out over the mountains of the Salmon-Huckleberry Wilderness. Return as you came, or continue on another 2.5 miles, passing another campsite on Goat Creek, to a junction. Turn left and uphill for 2.0 miles on the Kinzel Lake Trail to reach a car campground on said lake. Continue to Road 2613, go left on the Hunchback Trail to arrive at Devil's Peak, a total of 1.6 miles. To complete a strenuous loop, continue on the Hunchback Trail another 2.4 miles and go left on the Green Canyon Way Trail, descending 3.3 miles back to the road. Go left 0.3 mile to return to your vehicle via the road.

User Groups: Hikers and dogs. No horses or mountain bikes allowed. No wheelchair facilities.

Permits: A free self-issue Wilderness Permit is required and is available at the trailhead. A federal Northwest Forest Pass is required to park here; the cost is $5 a day or $30 for an annual pass. You can buy a day pass at the trailhead, at ranger stations, or through private vendors.

Maps: For a map of the Mount Hood National Forest and the Salmon-Huckleberry Wilderness, contact Mount Hood National Forest Headquarters, 16400 Champion Way, Sandy, OR, 97055, 503/668-1700. For a topographic map, ask the USGS for Rhododendron, High Rock, and Wolf Peak.

Directions: Drive east of Portland 42 miles on U.S. 26 to Zigzag. Turn south on Salmon River Road, following the paved road 4.9 miles to a pullout on the left before a bridge.

Contact: Mount Hood National Forest, Zigzag Ranger District, 70220 East Highway 26, Zigzag, OR, 97049, 503/622-3191.

62 DEVIL'S PEAK LOOKOUT

8.2 mi/4.5 hr 3 8

south of Zigzag in Mount Hood National Forest

The use of airplanes largely made fire watchtowers irrelevant, so federal agencies removed most of them. Most, but not all. Some remain staffed year after year, and some remain as great rest stops for hikers—or even for camping. The Devil's Peak Lookout is kept unlocked for hikers. Volunteers keep it looking good, and will continue to do so if you do your share. There is no outhouse here, so you'll have to make like you're backpacking, packing out all trash and toilet paper.

The trail is simple: a 4.1-mile climb up the Cool Creek Trail to a junction, meeting up with the Hunchback Trail (go right, then left at the next junction to the tower). Along the way there are some views to Mount Hood. Do this trail as an alternative to hiking in on the Salmon River Trail (previous listing).

User Groups: Hikers and dogs. No horses or mountain bikes allowed. No wheelchair facilities.

Permits: Permits are not required. Parking and access are free.

Maps: For a map of the Mount Hood National Forest, contact Mount Hood National Forest Headquarters, 16400 Champion Way, Sandy, OR, 97055, 503/668-1700. For a topographic map, ask the USGS for Government Camp.

Directions: Drive east of Portland 42 miles on U.S. 26 to Zigzag. Go 1.4 miles east of Zigzag and turn right on Still Creek Road, following this road 2.6 miles to the end of the pavement and an additional 0.3 mile on gravel to the crossing of Cool Creek. About 300 yards farther, watch on the right for a "Cool Creek Trail" sign and park here.

Contact: Mount Hood National Forest, Zigzag Ranger District, 70220 East Highway 26, Zigzag, OR, 97049, 503/622-3191.

63 LAUREL HILL

1.0–9.4 mi/0.5–4.0 hr

west of Government Camp in Mount Hood National Forest

In what seems like a distant past, Oregon Trail pioneers came trundling into Oregon in their covered wagons. For the longest time, all they could do on the last stretch was to raft the Columbia River, which then (before being dammed) was a rugged and dangerous roller-coaster ride. In 1845, Sam Barlow laid out his version of a new trail, which brought pioneers over Mount Hood to a nondescript knoll called Laurel Hill. Actually, it was anything but nondescript to the pioneers; on one cliff-edge, they had to lower their wagons down by a rope winched around the trees. Those trees still bear the burn marks, and you can see them for yourself, along with bits of the old wagon trail, on a series of trails around Laurel Hill. You can also hike an abandoned stretch of the old 1921 Mount Hood Highway, ducking through a tunnel on the way to Little Zigzag Falls.

The "wagon chute" is an easy one-mile round-trip walk from Highway 26 near a big historic marker sign just before milepost 51. Park along the highway and take the path to the top of the cliff, following the old Oregon Trail. You'll see quickly enough why the pioneers were so frustrated.

For a more extensive hike, start from the upper trailhead for the Pioneer Bridle Trail and follow the trail for 1.4 miles to the old tunnel, and turn right on the abandoned road. From here, it's 0.3 mile to the waterfall, following this road to the trail on the right. From the tunnel, you can continue on the Pioneer Bridle Trail another 0.4 mile to a junction that will lead you to the left and over busy Highway 26 to the Wagon Chute trail, and beyond this junction the trail continues another 2.3 miles.

User Groups: Hikers, dogs, and horses. No mountain bikes allowed. No wheelchair facilities.

Permits: Permits are not required. A pass is not required to park at the historic marker on U.S. 26, but for the Pioneer Brindle Trailhead a federal Northwest Forest Pass is required to park; the cost is $5 a day or $30 for an annual pass. You can buy a day pass at the trailhead, at ranger stations, or through private vendors.

Maps: For a map of the Mount Hood National Forest, contact Mount Hood National Forest Headquarters, 16400 Champion Way, Sandy, OR, 97055, 503/668-1700. For a topographic map, ask the USGS for Government Camp.

Directions: To reach the upper trailhead, drive on U.S. 26 from Portland toward Mount Hood. Between mileposts 52 and 53, turn left off the highway onto Road 522 (across from the Mount Hood Ski Bowl entrance) for 0.2 mile to the lot for the Glacier View Sno-Park.

Contact: Mount Hood National Forest, Zigzag Ranger District, 70220 East Highway 26, Zigzag, OR, 97049, 503/622-3191.

64 MIRROR LAKE

3.2 mi/1.5 hr

west of Government Camp in Mount Hood National Forest

It's easy to see how popular this trail is; its parking area is along the highway and it's always bursting at the seam. This trail ascends the oddly named Tom Dick & Harry Mountain to an amazing viewpoint of Mount Hood, the enormous Zigzag Valley, and little Mirror Lake, which you'll pass along the way named Mirror. Use is regulated at Mirror Lake, and only six designated campsites are available. From the peak, you'll be able to visit only one peak out of three; the other two are protected for peregrine falcons.

From the trailhead, cross Camp Creek above Yocum Falls and climb the Mirror Lake Trail 1.4 miles to Mirror Lake. A 0.4-mile loop trail circles the lake. If you're continuing to the 4,920-foot peak, stay right and climb another 1.8 miles to the viewpoint.

User Groups: Hikers and dogs only. No horses or mountain bikes allowed. No wheelchair facilities.

Permits: Permits are not required. A federal Northwest Forest Pass is required to park here; the cost is $5 a day or $30 for an annual pass. You can buy a day pass at the trailhead, at ranger stations, or through private vendors.

Maps: For a map of the Mount Hood National Forest, contact Mount Hood National Forest Headquarters, 16400 Champion Way, Sandy, OR, 97055, 503/668-1700. For a topographic map, ask the USGS for Government Camp.

Directions: From Portland, drive U.S. 26 towards Mount Hood. Between mileposts 51 and 52, park along the south shoulder of the highway at the trailhead.

Contact: Mount Hood National Forest, Zigzag Ranger District, 70220 East Highway 26, Zigzag, OR, 97049, 503/622-3191.

65 TWIN LAKES

5.0-9.1 mi/2.5-5.0 hr 

south of Mount Hood in Mount Hood National Forest

Just off the Wapinitia Pass, the Frog Lake Sno-Park offers wintry access to the Pacific Crest Trail where it curves near the old Barlow Road and a ridge and butte named for old Barlow, too. In a big glacial valley, a modern campground sits in for an old pioneer campground, and is still named Devil's Half Acre today. You can see these sites from Palmateer Point, a good destination on a fun loop that passes the two Twin Lakes, with options for swimming and exploring for all ages.

From the Frog Lake Sno-Park lot, follow the PCT 1.4 miles to a right-hand junction. Go right 0.7 mile to Lower Twin Lake, a good destination for a short walk. A 0.9-mile trail circles the lake. Continue beyond the lake another 1.4 miles on the Palmateer Point Trail, passing the smaller Upper Twin Lake and cliffs with views of Mount Hood. From here, continue 0.6 mile to the right and go right 0.3 mile to the Point. To complete the loop, return to the Palmateer Trail and continue to the right 0.9 mile to the junction with the PCT, and go left 3.5 miles back to the lot.

User Groups: Hikers, dogs, and horses. No mountain bikes allowed. No wheelchair facilities.

Permits: Permits are not required. A federal Northwest Forest Pass is required to park here; the cost is $5 a day or $30 for an annual pass. You can buy a day pass at the trailhead, at ranger stations, or through private vendors.

Maps: For a map of the Mount Hood National Forest, contact Mount Hood National Forest Headquarters, 16400 Champion Way, Sandy, OR, 97055, 503/668-1700. For a topographic map, ask the USGS for Mount Hood South.

Directions: From Government Camp, drive eight miles east on U.S. 26 to milepost 62, turning left into Frog Lake Sno-Park.

Contact: Mount Hood National Forest, Barlow Ranger District, 780 NE Court Street, Dufur, OR, 97021, 541/467-2291.

66 WHITE RIVER FALLS

0.6 mi/0.25 hr 

north of Maupin on the White River

By the time you're out roaming in the dry landscapes east of the Cascade Mountains, things get real distant from one another. You have to travel out quite a ways to get to a place like the small state park on the White River, but once you're there you'll find a lot to investigate. For one thing, you've got a three-tiered waterfall on the White River plunging over a basalt shelf into a canyon on its way to the Deschutes River. You'll also find an abandoned powerhouse that supplied Wasco and Sherman Counties with power from 1910 until 1960. There are also a couple beaches and an oak bench, but some of these areas should only be hunted by the most intrepid of explorers willing to endure poison oak and a rugged canyon mouth.

The trail from the parking lot is a simple 0.3-mile descent to a number of viewpoints and the old powerhouse. From there, you could go farther over the course of a mile through pungent sagebrush to a beach and oak grove. The trail to the mouth, however, is a fainter path yet, another 1.2 miles to a beach on the Deschutes beneath a railroad span.

User Groups: Hikers and dogs only. No mountain bikes or horses. Paved trails are wheelchair accessible.

Permits: Permits are not required. Parking and access are free.
Maps: For a topographic map, ask the USGS for Maupin.
Directions: From Highway 197 near milepost 34 between The Dalles and Maupin, go east on Highway 216 for four miles towards Sherars Bridge to the White River Falls State Park entrance on the right.
Contact: Oregon Parks and Recreation Department, 1115 Commercial Street NE, Salem, OR, 97301, 800/551-6949, www.oregonstateparks.org.

67 ROCK LAKES

7.7 mi/3.0 hr 

southeast of Estacada in Mount Hood National Forest

In the high country between the Roaring and Clackamas Rivers, these Ice Age–carved lakes glisten in the sun. Getting there is the hard part, as you'll have to endure some crummy roads; but once there you'll be privy to meadows, forested lakes, glacier-scoured country, and an impressive rock outcrop called High Rock.

From the Frazier Turnaround, head to the right-hand Serene Lake Trail and go 0.8 mile to a junction. A mere 0.2 mile to the left is Middle Rock Lake, and you can follow the shore back to a higher and smaller lake beyond. The main trail continues to the right and to Lower Rock Lake, with its sunken logs and tree-lined shores. Stay on the main trail another 2.1 miles to Serene Lake, a larger lake with cliffs diving into the water. To do the full loop, continue another 0.9 mile through woods and up to the plateau. Go left on the Grouse Point Trail for 1.8 miles past viewpoints to Cache Meadow, the remains of an old guard station, and a four-way junction. Stay left on the Grouse Point Trail at this and the next junction as you climb out of the bowl, the trail leveling out finally on the 2.1-mile return to the Frazier Turnaround.

User Groups: Hikers, dogs, horses, and mountain bikes. No wheelchair facilities.
Permits: Permits are not required. Parking and access are free.
Maps: For a map of the Mount Hood National Forest, contact Mount Hood National Forest Headquarters, 16400 Champion Way, Sandy, OR, 97055, 503/668-1700. For a topographic map, ask the USGS for High Rock.
Directions: From Oregon City on I-205, take Exit 12 and go 18 miles east toward Estacada. Go through Estacada and continue 26 miles on Highway 224 to the bridge at Ripplebrook. Go left on Road 57 toward Timothy Lake for 7.4 miles, then turn left on Road 58 for 6.9 miles toward High Rock, then left on Abbott Road 4610 for 1.3 miles. Go straight on the unmaintained dirt Road 240 at the sign for Frazier Fork for 4.4 miles, then keep left at a fork by Frazier Fork campground and go 0.2 mile to the end of the road.
Contact: Mount Hood National Forest, Clackamas River Ranger District, 595 NW Industrial Way, Estacada, OR, 97023, 503/630-6861.

68 TIMOTHY LAKE

12.0 mi/6.0 hr 3 7

south of Mount Hood in Mount Hood National Forest

BEST

The Pacific Crest Trail follows the eastern shoreline of this tremendous lake within eyeshot of Mount Hood. The 1,500-acre lake is maintained as parkland by Portland General Electric because of the PGE-run dam at its far end. There are a host of campgrounds around it, including a primitive spot to pitch a tent at Meditation Point, not to mention windsurfing and fishing. There's also plenty to see while hiking the loop around the lapping shores, making this an ideal outing for the family.

From Little Crater Campground, start off on the 0.3-mile connection trail to the PCT, passing Little Crater Lake. Go left on the PCT another 0.3 mile, following Crater Creek to the junction of the loop trail. To follow the PCT, head to the left 3.6 miles, passing views to the mountain. At the next junction, stay along the lakeshore for another thre miles, passing through the many campgrounds to a crossing of the lake's outlet on a log boom. Continue 1.2 miles along the shore to a 0.3-mile side trail out to Meditation Point, then the remaining three miles to the end of the loop.

User Groups: Hikers, dogs, horses, and mountain bikes. There are several wheelchair access points.

Permits: Permits are not required. Parking and access are free.

Maps: For a map of the Mount Hood National Forest, contact Mount Hood National Forest Headquarters, 16400 Champion Way, Sandy, OR, 97055, 503/668-1700. For a topographic map, ask the USGS for Timothy Lake.

Directions: From Portland, drive U.S. 26 toward Mount Hood. Drive past Wapinitia Pass 3.4 miles to a turnoff between mileposts 65 and 66. At a sign for Timothy Lake, turn onto Skyline Road 42 for four miles. Turn right on Abbott Road 58 for 1.4 miles to Little Crater Campground and park at the far end of the campground loop by the trail sign.

Contact: Mount Hood National Forest, Barlow Ranger District, 780 NE Court Street, Dufur, OR, 97021, 541/467-2291.

69 LOWER DESCHUTES RIVER

4.2-8.0 mi/2.0-4.0 hr 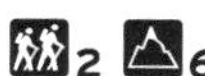 

east of The Dalles in Deschutes River State Recreation Area

An old railroad once ran along this penultimate stretch of the Deschutes River before it joins at last with the Columbia River at the easternmost edge of the Columbia River Gorge National Scenic Area. Now the railroad is gone, but the grade remains, and its path through this dry, rocky land is now a state park with many options for hiking, both easy and more challenging. Along the river, three rapids—Moody, Rattlesnake, and Colorado—tumble through this sagebrush-dotted canyon. For something a bit more wild, there are also a number of trails between the old railroad grade and the river. The bike path makes for good mountain biking, as well as easy hiking.

The railroad grade is the easiest, and makes for an eight-mile out-and-back trail to Gordon Canyon and an old corral. A loop trail up the bluff begins 1.4 miles out and heads up the canyon to a high viewpoint near Ferry Springs, then connects back down, about 2.5 miles in all. Other trails skirt the riverbank, some dropping down to beaches on the river and close-up views of the rapids.

User Groups: Hikers, dogs on leash only, horses, and mountain bikers. Limited wheelchair access.

Permits: Permits are not required. Parking and access are free.

Maps: For a free park brochure, call Oregon Parks and Recreation, 800/551-6949, or download a free map at www.oregonstateparks.org. For a topographic map, ask the USGS for Wishram and Emerson.

Directions: Drive past the Dalles Dam on I-84 to Exit 97 for Deschutes Park. Follow park signs two miles on Highway 206, and after crossing the Deschutes River turn right into the park. Park at the last lot.

Contact: Oregon Parks and Recreation Department, 1115 Commercial Street NE, Salem, OR, 97301, 800/551-6949, www.oregonstateparks.org.

70 TABLE ROCK

7.6 mi/3.5 hr 

east of Salem in Table Rock Wilderness

This small, seemingly insignificant wilderness area in the Cascade Mountains actually claims two formidable rock outcrops: Rooster

HIKING

Rock and 4,881-foot Table Rock, which is entirely climbable and has views to spare. You'll see 10 full Cascade Peaks from here, and all you'll have to do is make it around a couple landslides. These woods are rich with Douglas fir and western hemlock and are home to two endangered plants: Oregon sullivantia and the Gorman's aster. You may even spot the elusive spotted owl.

Getting to the trailhead is part of the hike, as two landslides damaged the road quite a bit, making it impassable for all but on foot. Park before the first landslide and hike in 1.3 miles to the trailhead on the right. From there, climb 1.9 miles on the Table Rock Trail to a junction. To the left, 0.4 mile, is access to the peak of Table Rock, a good destination in and of itself with views north to Mount Rainier and west to the Willamette Valley. If you're up for more, go to the right after bagging the peak for 1.4 miles to view the sheer lava cliffs of Rooster Rock.

User Groups: Hikers, dogs, and horses. No mountain bikes. No wheelchair facilities.

Permits: A free self-issue Wilderness Permit is required and is available at the trailhead. Parking and access are free.

Maps: For a map of the Mount Hood National Forest, contact Mount Hood National Forest Headquarters, 16400 Champion Way, Sandy, OR, 97055, 503/668-1700. For a topographic map, ask the USGS for Rooster Rock.

Directions: From Molalla (east of I-5 at Woodburn), drive 0.5 mile on Highway 211 toward Estacada, and turn right on South Mathias Road for 0.3 mile, then left on South Feyrer Park Road for 1.6 miles, then right on South Dickey Prairie Road for 5.3 miles. At a junction with South Molalla Forest Road, turn right and cross the Molalla River and follow this paved road 12.8 miles to a fork, and go left on Middle Fork Road for 2.6 miles, then right at a sign for Table Rock Wilderness. After two miles, go left, following wilderness pointers. Go the last 2.4 miles to the landslide.

Contact: Bureau of Land Management, Salem District Office, 1717 Fabry Road SE, Salem, OR, 97306, 503/375-5646.

71 WHETSTONE MOUNTAIN

4.8 mi/2.5 hr

southeast of Estacada in Bull of the Woods Wilderness

Here's an easy way to get into the high country, overlooking the dense forests of the Opal Creek Wilderness and Bull of the Woods Wilderness. This moderately paced trail up Whetstone Mountain has views extending from Mount Rainier to the Three Sisters, with Mount Jefferson a prominent viewpoint. The mountain, like many others in the region, was a Native American site for vision quests. Find your own peace of mind here in this easy summit.

From the trailhead, head into the old-growth woods 1.3 miles on the Whetstone Mountain Trail, passing a little pond that is one of the sources for Whetstone Creek. At a junction, go right on a faint path for 1.1 miles, turning right at a signboard for the summit trail. You'll see the Bull of the Woods Lookout, and clear out over the Willamette Valley to the Coast Range.

User Groups: Hikers, dogs, and horses. No mountain bikes allowed. No wheelchair facilities.

Permits: A free self-issue Wilderness Permit is required and is available at the trailhead. Parking and access are free.

Maps: For a map of the Mount Hood National Forest, contact Mount Hood National Forest Headquarters, 16400 Champion Way, Sandy, OR, 97055, 503/668-1700. For a topographic map, ask the USGS for Battle Ax.

Directions: From I-205 near Oregon City, take Exit 12 and go east 18 miles to Estacada. Go through town and continue 26 miles on Highway 224 to the Ripplebrook bridge. Go straight on Road 46 for 3.6 miles, turn right on Road 63 for 3.5 miles, and turn right on

Road 70 for nine miles. Then follow signs for the Whetstone Mountain Trail, going left on Road 7030 for 5.6 miles, then right on Road 7020 for 0.7 mile. Just prior to the end of the road, turn left onto Road 028 to a parking area.

Contact: Mount Hood National Forest, Clackamas River Ranger District, 595 NW Industrial Way, Estacada, OR, 97023, 503/630-6861.

72 BAGBY HOT SPRINGS

3.0 mi/1.5 hr 1 6

south of Estacada in Mount Hood National Forest

The hike into Bagby Hot Springs is pleasant enough without its famous destination: a series of bathhouses that channel the thermal spring water down a series of flumes into cedar tubs. Really, it defies short explanation, and the trail in is a lovely walk through springtime rhododendron flowers and white trilliums along the Hot Springs Fork of the Collawash River. There's also a historic Guard Station being restored to its early 20th-century glory. From the trailhead, cross Nohorn Creek and follow the Bagby Trail into the woods 1.5 miles, crossing the Fork, and arriving at the hot springs complex. This trail continues into the Bull of the Woods Wilderness and its many destinations.

User Groups: Hikers and dogs. No horses or mountain bikes allowed. No wheelchair facilities.

Permits: Permits are not required. A federal Northwest Forest Pass is required to park here; the cost is $5 a day or $30 for an annual pass. You can buy a day pass at the trailhead, at ranger stations, or through private vendors.

Maps: For a map of the Mount Hood National Forest, contact Mount Hood National Forest Headquarters, 16400 Champion Way, Sandy, OR, 97055, 503/668-1700. For a topographic map, ask the USGS for Bagby Hot Springs.

Directions: From I-205 near Oregon City, take Exit 12 and go east 18 miles to Estacada. Go through town and continue 26 miles on Highway 224 to the Ripplebrook bridge. Go straight on Road 46 for 3.6 miles, turn right on Road 63 for 3.5 miles, and turn right on Road 70 for six miles to a parking lot on the left.

Contact: Mount Hood National Forest, Clackamas River Ranger District, 595 NW Industrial Way, Estacada, OR, 97023, 503/630-6861.

73 PANSY LAKE

2.3 mi/1.0 hr 1 8

south of Estacada in Bull of the Woods Wilderness

This easy exploration of the Bull of the Woods Wilderness visits green Pansy Lake, named for a nearby mining claim called the Pansy Blossom Mine, where Robert Bagby mined copper. Though the claim is a thing of the past, you can make a claim to a beautiful meadowed basin beneath Pansy Mountain, with options for camping and further hiking.

The easiest access is to follow the Pansy Lake Trail in from the road 0.9 mile to a junction. A right-hand trail goes into Pansy Basin on an abandoned trail. The left-hand trail goes promptly uphill to another junction; go straight 0.2 mile to Pansy Lake, where you can follow the trail to the right along the lakeshore.

User Groups: Hikers, dogs, and horses. No mountain bikes allowed. No wheelchair facilities.

Permits: A free self-issue Wilderness Permit is required and is available at the trailhead. Parking and access are free.

Maps: For a map of the Mount Hood National Forest, contact Mount Hood National Forest Headquarters, 16400 Champion Way, Sandy, OR, 97055, 503/668-1700. For a topographic map, ask the USGS for Bull of the Woods.

Directions: From I-205 near Oregon City, take Exit 12 and go east 18 miles to Estacada. Go through town and continue 26 miles on Highway 224 to the Ripplebrook bridge. Go straight on Road 46 for 3.6 miles, turn right on Road 63 for 5.6 miles, and turn right on Road 6340 for 7.8 miles, following signs for Pansy Basin Trail. Turn right on Road 6341 for 3.5 miles and park at a pullout on the right side. The trail begins across the road.
Contact: Mount Hood National Forest, Clackamas River Ranger District, 595 NW Industrial Way, Estacada, OR, 97023, 503/630-6861.

HIKING

74 BULL OF THE WOODS LOOKOUT

6.4 mi/3.5 hr 7 9

south of Estacada in Bull of the Woods Wilderness

This trail passes Pansy Lake (see previous listing) but continues up to the 1942 Bull of the Woods Lookout, which is sometimes staffed. It then follows a loop up and down a mountain cradling little Dickey Lake. Views extend out to Mount Jefferson, and to many more as well.

Follow the Pansy Lake Trail in from the road 0.9 mile to a junction. The right goes into Pansy Basin on an abandoned trail; take the left-hand trail, which goes promptly uphill to another junction. This time go straight 0.2 mile to Pansy Lake, taking the left-hand trail another 0.8 miles toward Twin Lakes. At the next junction, go uphill to the left on the Mother Lode Trail 1.9 miles, going left at a signed junction onto the Bull of the Woods Trail to the lookout tower. To complete the loop, continue past the tower 1.1 miles to a barely marked junction, then descend 1.3 miles on the Dickey Lake Trail, passing a short side trail to Dickey Lake, back to the Pansy Lake Trail, staying right at junctions back to the road.

User Groups: Hikers, dogs, and horses. No mountain bikes allowed. No wheelchair facilities.
Permits: A free self-issue Wilderness Permit is required and is available at the trailhead. Parking and access are free.
Maps: For a map of the Mount Hood National Forest, contact Mount Hood National Forest Headquarters, 16400 Champion Way, Sandy, OR, 97055, 503/668-1700. For a topographic map, ask the USGS for Bull of the Woods.
Directions: From I-205 near Oregon City, take Exit 12 and go east 18 miles to Estacada. Go through town and continue 26 miles on Highway 224 to the Ripplebrook bridge. Go straight on Road 46 for 3.6 miles, turn right on Road 63 for 5.6 miles, and turn right on Road 6340 for 7.8 miles, following signs for Pansy Basin Trail. Turn right on Road 6341 for 3.5 miles and park at a pullout on the right side. The trail begins across the road.
Contact: Mount Hood National Forest, Clackamas River Ranger District, 595 NW Industrial Way, Estacada, OR, 97023, 503/630-6861.

75 DICKEY CREEK

11.0 mi/5.5 hr 4 8

south of Estacada in Bull of the Woods Wilderness

Want to visit an old-growth forest? Try the groves along the wilderness of Dickey Creek. To get here, you must hike *down* first, an unwelcome prospect for many. Still, the lakes you'll find back in these woods in the carved-out flanks of Big Slide Mountain make it worth the price of admission.

The Dickey Creek Trail begins as an old road then changes to trail, the first 0.8 mile heading down nearly 500 feet into an old-growth grove of Douglas fir. From here you'll pass a pond and follow Dickey Creek 2.1 miles to a crossing. Now you'll begin climbing nearly 1,400 feet in 2.6 miles to the shore of

Big Slide Lake, with the mountain looming above. There are campsites and a small island to explore, and the Bull of the Woods Lookout is on the ridge above.

User Groups: Hikers, dogs, and horses. No mountain bikes allowed. No wheelchair facilities.

Permits: A free self-issue Wilderness Permit is required and is available at the trailhead. Parking and access are free.

Maps: For a map of the Mount Hood National Forest, contact Mount Hood National Forest Headquarters, 16400 Champion Way, Sandy, OR, 97055, 503/668-1700. For a topographic map, ask the USGS for Bull of the Woods.

Directions: From I-205 near Oregon City, take Exit 12 and go east 18 miles to Estacada. Go through town and continue 26 miles on Highway 224 to the Ripplebrook bridge. Go straight on Road 46 for 3.6 miles, turn right on Road 63 for 5.6 miles, and turn right on Road 6340 for 2.8 miles following signs for Dickey Creek Trail. Turn left on Road 140 for one mile, and turn right at a T-junction 0.5 mile to the trailhead at road's end.

Contact: Mount Hood National Forest, Clackamas River Ranger District, 595 NW Industrial Way, Estacada, OR, 97023, 503/630-6861.

76 HAWK MOUNTAIN

10.4 mi/5.0 hr

south of Estacada in Mount Hood National Forest

There is something romantic about a fire watchtower, with isolation and nature combining to form a kind of idyllic life. It took a certain kind of person to live alone on a mountaintop for a summer. There are many books written by authors who did this, from Jack Kerouac to Edward Abbey. With new techniques for spotting fires, however, many of these lookouts have been abandoned and many of the original structures lost—this lonely cabin atop Hawk Mountain remains, however. Today you can visit this cabin, look out over Mount Jefferson, and get a sense of how lookouts lived. This trail up Rho Ridge (short for "Rhododendron") crosses two meadows and provides a first-hand look.

From the Graham Pass trailhead, follow the Rho Ridge Trail 1.1 miles, connecting with abandoned Road 33, to a junction with Road 270. Go right for one mile, staying right at a junction with Road 280 and left at a junction with Road 290. Take a right on the continuation of the trail along Rho Ridge for 2.7 miles, crossing another dirt road, to Round Meadow. A left-hand trail leads 0.4 mile to the old lookout cabin atop Hawk Mountain.

User Groups: Hikers, dogs, horses, and mountain bikes. No wheelchair facilities.

Permits: Permits are not required. Parking and access are free.

Maps: For a map of the Mount Hood National Forest, contact Mount Hood National Forest Headquarters, 16400 Champion Way, Sandy, OR, 97055, 503/668-1700. For a topographic map, ask the USGS for Breitenbush Hot Springs.

Directions: From I-205 near Oregon City, take Exit 12 and go east 18 miles to Estacada. Go through town and continue 26 miles on Highway 224 to the Ripplebrook bridge. Go straight on Road 46 for 3.6 miles, turn right on Road 63 for 8.8 miles. At a sign for Graham Pass, turn left on Road 6350 for 1.2 miles, then go right for 4.5 miles on the gravel road, then fork left staying on Road 6350. In one mile, park in a lot at a four-way junction.

Contact: Mount Hood National Forest, Clackamas River Ranger District, 595 NW Industrial Way, Estacada, OR, 97023, 503/630-6861.

77 LITTLE NORTH SANTIAM RIVER

9.0 mi/4.0 mi

northeast of Mill City in Willamette National Forest

Cascading through a boulder-lined bed, this tributary of the Santiam watershed flows through old-growth forests and over waterfalls squeezing between the lava canyon. The 4.5-mile Little North Santiam Trail, built by volunteers from Salem, sometimes scrambles down to swimming holes and beaches and ends at a campground upstream. Go as far as you like and return as you came; there's plenty to see.

From Elkhorn Road, start in 0.7 mile to a side trail down to a series of waterfalls. From here, a 2.6-mile stretch crosses Winter Creek and climbs to 1,800 feet and back down to a series of inaccessible pools and a beach. The final 1.2 miles crosses Cedar Creek and ends at the Shady Grove Campground.

User Groups: Hikers, dogs, and bicycles. No horses allowed. No wheelchair facilities.

Permits: Permits are not required. A federal Northwest Forest Pass is required to park here; the cost is $5 a day or $30 for an annual pass. You can buy a day pass at the trailhead, at ranger stations, or through private vendors.

Maps: For a map of the Willamette National Forest, contact Willamette National Forest Headquarters, 3106 Pierce Parkway, Suite D, Springfield, OR, 97477, 541/225-6300. For a topographic map, ask the USGS for Lyons.

Directions: Drive east from Salem on OR 22 for 23 miles to Mehama and turn left on Little North Fork Road for 14.5 miles. Beyond milepost 13, turn right on Elkhorn Drive, cross the river, and 0.4 mile later park on the left at a pullout.

Contact: Willamette National Forest, Detroit Ranger District, HC73, Box 320, Mill City, OR, 97360, 503/854-4239.

78 HENLINE MOUNTAIN

5.6 mi/4.0 hr

northeast of Mill City in Opal Creek Wilderness

From the lookout site beneath Henline Mountain, the ridges and peaks of the Cascades ripple into the distance like frozen waves, their folded ridges flowing down to the Little North Santiam River. The lookout site is not on the peak of Henline, but who's counting? A 1.1-mile trail, rough as it is, continues past this lookout to the 4,650-foot peak, but the view from this destination is in itself worth the climb. This is also an initial foray into the Opal Creek Wilderness.

Prepare to climb steadily and steeply for the 2.8-mile trail to the old lookout point. You'll gain 2,200 feet in this short distance, so give yourself plenty of time.

User Groups: Hikers and dogs. No horses or mountain bikes allowed. No wheelchair facilities.

Permits: A free self-issue Wilderness Permit is required and is available at the trailhead. Parking and access are free.

Maps: For a map of the Willamette National Forest, contact Willamette National Forest Headquarters, 3106 Pierce Parkway, Suite D, Springfield, OR, 97477, 541/225-6300. For a topographic map, ask the USGS for Elkhorn.

Directions: Drive east from Salem on OR 22 for 23 miles to Mehama and turn left on Little North Fork Road for 16.3 miles to a fork. Go to the left on Road 2209 for one mile and park on the right near the trailhead.

Contact: Willamette National Forest, Detroit Ranger District, HC73, Box 320, Mill City, OR, 97360, 503/854-4239.

79 OPAL CREEK

7.1 mi/2.5 hr

northeast of Mill City in Opal Creek Wilderness

BEST

Let's just say the Opal Creek Wilderness is famous to some and infamous to others. Author David Seideman's 1993 book, *Showdown at Opal Creek: The Battle for America's Last Wilderness* amply details the 1980s controversy over the designation of this area as wilderness. What ensued here involved armed standoffs between federal agencies and the owners of the private land that stood between the National Forest and the proposed logging area, which houses some enormous stands of Douglas fir and Western red cedar. Senator Mark Hatfield stepped in to protect the area and it has now been preserved. The mining town back here called Jawbone Flats, where the owners made their stand, remains, and now that the furor is over ,the whole town has become the Opal Creek Ancient Forest Research Center. This trail follows the original road along the Little North Santiam River, passing an abandoned mill, slipping into the mining town, and setting off along Opal Creek towards the wilderness area.

From the locked gate, follow the old dirt road 3.5 miles. You'll scurry along some amazing half-bridges, where the road clings to the cliff-face, then arrive at the site of the Merton Mill and its hodgepodge of lumber bric-a-brac, and a side trail down to Sawmill Falls. You'll pass Slide Falls on the way, too. At Jawbone Flats, take a right-hand junction to a footbridge over heavily photographed Opal Pool. To return via a loop, go right for 1.4 miles back to a crossing over the river and return via the road. To extend your trip, however, you can go left on the Opal Creek Trail 1.5 miles to a stand of enormous red cedars that are staggering to see. The trail eventually reaches Beachie Creek and peters out.

User Groups: Hikers and dogs. No horses or mountain bikes allowed. No wheelchair facilities.

Permits: A free self-issue Wilderness Permit is required and is available at the trailhead. Parking and access are free.

Maps: An Opal Creek Wilderness map is available from Geo-Graphics. For a map of the Willamette National Forest, contact Willamette National Forest Headquarters, 3106 Pierce Parkway, Suite D, Springfield, OR, 97477, 541/225-6300. For a topographic map, ask the USGS for Battle Ax.

Directions: Drive east from Salem on OR 22 for 23 miles to Mehama and turn left on Little North Fork Road for 16.3 miles to a fork. Go to the left on Road 2209 for 4.2 miles and park on the shoulder at the locked gate.

Contact: Willamette National Forest, Detroit Ranger District, HC73, Box 320, Mill City, OR, 97360, 503/854-4239.

80 FRENCH CREEK RIDGE

8.2 mi/3.5 hr

north of Detroit in Opal Creek Wilderness

This long ridge over the Opal Creek Wilderness passes a number of rock formations and peaks on its way to Mount Beachie, entering stands of rare Alaska cedar and offering views to Mount Jefferson, craggy Three-Fingered Jack, and the Three Sisters.

From the message board, start into the forest on the French Creek Ridge Trail, passing Marten Buttes, for 2.4 miles to a series of rock formations at a pass. Ignoring a side trail to the right, continue 1.7 miles past a pond and through a brush-lined path to the viewpoint on Mount Beachie.

User Groups: Hikers, dogs, and horses. No mountain bikes allowed. No wheelchair facilities.

Permits: A free self-issue Wilderness Permit is required and is available at the trailhead. Parking and access are free.

Maps: An Opal Creek Wilderness map is available from Geo-Graphics. For a map of the Willamette National Forest, contact

Willamette National Forest Headquarters, 3106 Pierce Parkway, Suite D, Springfield, OR, 97477, 541/225-6300. For a topographic map, ask the USGS for Battle Ax.

Directions: Drive 50 miles east of Salem on OR 22 to Detroit Lake. Just before the Breitenbush River turn left on French Creek Road 2223 and go 4.2 miles to a fork at pavement's end. Go right on Road 2207 for 3.7 miles and park at a large lot on the right.

Contact: Willamette National Forest, Detroit Ranger District, HC73, Box 320, Mill City, OR, 97360, 503/854-4239.

81 BATTLE AX

5.6-6.4 mi/3.0-3.5 hr

north of Detroit in Bull of the Woods Wilderness

This mountain has such a rugged name, don't you think? Some say it's because of its sharp shape, others because of a brand of chewing tobacco around during the time of the gold prospectors. Either way, it's earned its moniker. This peak, the tallest in the Bull of the Woods Wilderness, has views extending as far as Diamond Peak in the southern Cascades and Mount Hood to the north. Beneath it, Elk Lake looks like a big puddle among the trees. Atop its rocky peak, a profusion of alpine flowers root down and thrive.

After parking at the fork in the road approaching Elk Lake Campground, walk the remaining 0.4 mile of road to the trailhead on the right. Strike out on the Bagby Hot Springs Trail for two miles, passing a number of ponds and steadily climbing to a junction. Go left 1.3 miles to the 5,558-foot peak of Battle Ax. To make a loop of this hike, continue forward and descend the mountain down a series of switchbacks 1.5 mile to the end of the road at Beachie Saddle. Walk the road back down 0.8 mile to the trailhead, then the remaining distance to your vehicle.

User Groups: Hikers, dogs, and horses. No mountain bikes allowed. No wheelchair facilities.

Permits: A free self-issue Wilderness Permit is required and is available at the trailhead. Parking and access are free.

Maps: An Opal Creek Wilderness map is available from Geo-Graphics. For a map of the Willamette National Forest, contact Willamette National Forest Headquarters, 3106 Pierce Parkway, Suite D, Springfield, OR, 97477, 541/225-6300. For a topographic map, ask the USGS for Battle Ax.

Directions: Drive 50 miles east of Salem on OR 22 to Detroit Lake. Cross the Breitenbush River and turn left on paved Road 46 for 4.4 miles to a sign for Elk Lake. Turn left on Road 4696 for 0.8 mile, then turn left onto Road 4697 and go 4.7 miles, then turn left yet again at a sign for Elk Lake. The next two miles are rough and difficult. At a fork for the Elk Lake Campground, passenger cars without clearance should park and hikers will need to continue on foot up the road another 0.4 mile to the trailhead. However, high-clearance vehicles can continue up the road and park on the shoulder.

Contact: Willamette National Forest, Detroit Ranger District, HC73, Box 320, Mill City, OR, 97360, 503/854-4239.

82 PHANTOM BRIDGE

4.6 mi/2.0 hr 2 8

north of Detroit in Willamette National Forest

This rare and intimidating rock arch spans a 50-foot-deep gorge that will unnerve even the bravest. Maybe just a view of it is enough. The trail itself stretches away from French Creek Ridge, rounding Dog Rock and Cedar Lake before climbing to the arch. Below, the Opal Creek Wilderness drifts into the distance, with Opal Lake, source of the creek, within view.

Park in the lot at the end of Road 2223 and walk back down the road about 100 feet to the trailhead. In 1.3 miles you'll arrive at

Cedar Lake and a junction. Go left up the ridge another 0.7 mile to an old trailhead lot, then continue the remaining 0.3 mile to the Phantom Bridge.

User Groups: Hikers, dogs, horses, and mountain bikes. No wheelchair facilities.

Permits: Permits are not required. Parking and access are free.

Maps: For a map of the Willamette National Forest, contact Willamette National Forest Headquarters, 3106 Pierce Parkway, Suite D, Springfield, OR, 97477, 541/225-6300. For a topographic map, ask the USGS for Battle Ax.

Directions: Drive 50 miles east of Salem on OR 22 to Detroit Lake. Just before the Breitenbush River, turn left on French Creek Road 2223 and go 4.2 miles to a fork at pavement's end. Go right on Road 2207 for 3.7 miles and park at a large lot on the right.

Contact: Willamette National Forest, Detroit Ranger District, HC73, Box 320, Mill City, OR, 97360, 503/854-4239.

83 DOME ROCK AND TUMBLE LAKE

5.2 mi/2.5 hr 2 7

north of Detroit in Willamette National Forest

From the edge of Detroit Reservoir, the Tumble Ridge Trail heads straight into the neighboring mountains, climbing steeply to the spire of Needle Rock and the vista of Dome Rock. Hidden up Tumble Creek is Tumble Lake, with a waterfall. Though you could hike in this way, there is an easier point of entry that makes for a quicker hike to these sights.

From the upper trailhead on Road 2223, go in 0.4 mile to a junction. To access Dome Rock, go left 0.5 mile to a second junction, then left another 0.5 mile to the 4,869-foot peak. To access Tumble Lake, go right at this first junction, crossing a meadow down into a gully for 1.2 miles to the shore. Follow the shore to the left 0.3 mile to see the outlet creek and waterfall.

User Groups: Hikers, dogs, and mountain bikes. No horses allowed. No wheelchair facilities.

Permits: Permits are not required. Parking and access are free.

Maps: For a map of the Willamette National Forest, contact Willamette National Forest Headquarters, 3106 Pierce Parkway, Suite D, Springfield, OR, 97477, 541/225-6300. For a topographic map, ask the USGS for Battle Ax and Detroit.

Directions: Drive 50 miles east of Salem on OR 22 to Detroit Lake. Just before the Breitenbush River turn left on French Creek Road 2223 and go 4.2 miles to a fork at pavement's end. Fork left onto Road 2223 for 3.9 miles, watching carefully for a post on the left that marks the trailhead. Park on the right.

Contact: Willamette National Forest, Detroit Ranger District, HC73, Box 320, Mill City, OR, 97360, 503/854-4239.

84 STAHLMAN POINT

5.0 mi/2.5 hr 1 8

south of Detroit Reservoir in Willamette National Forest

If you're in the area and looking for a quick view of the surrounding country, incorporating the Detroit Reservoir and Mount Jefferson, head up this fairly easy 2.5-mile trail that climbs 1,300 feet to an old lookout site. Below, sailboats drift on the massive lake and the mountain broods in the distance. Watch for fish-hunting osprey, which nest in the area.

User Groups: Hikers and dogs. No horses or mountain bikes allowed. No wheelchair facilities.

Permits: Permits are not required. Parking and access are free.

Maps: For a map of the Willamette National Forest, contact Willamette National Forest Headquarters, 3106 Pierce Parkway, Suite D,

Springfield, OR, 97477, 541/225-6300. For a topographic map, ask the USGS for Detroit.
Directions: Drive 50 miles east of Salem on OR 22 to the town of Detroit. Go 2.5 miles east of town, then turn right on Blowout Road 10 for 3.5 miles to the large parking area on the left side of the road.
Contact: Willamette National Forest, Detroit Ranger District, HC73, Box 320, Mill City, OR, 97360, 503/854-4239.

85 COFFIN MOUNTAIN LOOKOUT

3.0 mi/2.0 hr 1 9

south of Detroit in Willamette National Forest

From a distance, it's easy to see how Coffin Mountain got its name. This square and prominent peak atop a wall of cliffs certainly resembles a giant's final resting place, but those cliffs are deceptive; along the backside, an easy trail climbs to a staffed lookout tower—a 16-square-foot box that, if you're lucky, you may be able to visit. You'll see why these fire towers are still staffed on the way up: the trail passes through an old burn being repopulated by young noble fir and sub-alpine fir. From the trailhead, follow the old bulldozer road and finally trail up 1.5 miles to the peak.
User Groups: Hikers, dogs, and mountain bikes. No horses allowed. No wheelchair facilities.
Permits: Permits are not required. Parking and access are free.
Maps: For a map of the Willamette National Forest, contact Willamette National Forest Headquarters, 3106 Pierce Parkway, Suite D, Springfield, OR, 97477, 541/225-6300. For a topographic map, ask the USGS for Coffin Mountain.
Directions: Drive east of Salem 69 miles on OR 22. Beyond Marion Forks 2.9 miles, go right on Straight Creek Road for 4.2 miles to a sign for Coffin Mountain Trailhead, and turn right for 3.8 miles on Road 1168 to the trailhead sign and parking area on the left.
Contact: Willamette National Forest, Detroit Ranger District, HC73, Box 320, Mill City, OR, 97360, 503/854-4239.

86 BACHELOR MOUNTAIN

3.8 mi/2.5 hr 1 9

south of Detroit in Willamette National Forest

Just beyond the towering cliffs of Coffin Mountain sits the slightly higher Bachelor Mountain. By coupling this trail with the Coffin Mountain Lookout hike (previous listing), both peaks are easy to bag in a single day (or even in a couple of hours). This trail traverses the Buck Mountain Burn, which in the 1970s reduced many of the trees to the white snags you see today.

From the trailhead, follow the ridge 1.2 miles to a junction with the Bruno Meadows Trail. Stay to the left and climb the final 0.7-mile rocky path up 500 feet to the peak.
User Groups: Hikers, dogs, horses, and mountain bikes. No wheelchair facilities.
Permits: Permits are not required. Parking and access are free.
Maps: For a map of the Willamette National Forest, contact Willamette National Forest Headquarters, 3106 Pierce Parkway, Suite D, Springfield, OR, 97477, 541/225-6300. For a topographic map, ask the USGS for Mount Bruno.
Directions: Drive east of Salem 69 miles on OR 22. Beyond Marion Forks 2.9 miles, go right on Straight Creek Road for 4.2 miles to a sign for Coffin Mountain Trailhead, and turn right for 4.5 miles on Road 1168 then turn left on Road 430, driving 0.5 mile to its end.
Contact: Willamette National Forest, Detroit Ranger District, HC73, Box 320, Mill City, OR, 97360, 503/854-4239.

87 OLALLIE LAKE AND POTATO BUTTE

7.2 mi/3.0 hr 2 7

east of Detroit in Olallie Lakes Scenic Area

A long stretch of power lines marks the boundary for the Olallie Lake Scenic Area, and the transformation to this lake-strewn plateau is abrupt. The Olallie Lake Scenic Area sits in the shadow of Mount Jefferson and offers many options for hiking. To start into the Scenic Area from the west, try this hike; it passes four big lakes and a couple smaller ones, finally topping it off with 5,280-foot Potato Butte, with views over the dense forest to the towering peak of Jefferson.

From the road, the Red Lake Trail crosses a clear-cut and joins a dirt road. Go left a short distance, then right on a spur road to find the continuation of the trail. Once you go under the power lines, you enter the Scenic Area. The first 1.6 miles of the trail reaches Red Lake. The next 1.3 miles passes Averill, Wall, and Sheep Lakes and arrives at a junction. Go left 0.7 mile past a few small ponds and up several steep switchbacks to the top of Potato Butte.

User Groups: Hikers, dogs, horses, and mountain bikes. No wheelchair facilities.

Permits: Permits are not required. Parking and access are free.

Maps: For a map of the Mount Hood National Forest, contact Mount Hood National Forest Headquarters, 16400 Champion Way, Sandy, OR, 97055, 503/668-1700. For a topographic map, ask the USGS for Olallie Butte.

Directions: From I-205 near Oregon City, take Exit 12 and go east 18 miles to Estacada. Go through town and continue 26 miles on Highway 224 to the Ripplebrook bridge. Go straight on Road 46 for 26.7 miles toward Detroit. Beyond the turnoff for Olallie Lake 4.9 miles, turn left on Road 380 for 0.9 mile to a point where the road becomes unmaintained. From Salem, follow OR 22 east to Detroit and go left on Breitenbush Road 46 for 18.2 miles to the right-hand turnoff for Road 380.

Contact: Mount Hood National Forest, Clackamas River Ranger District, 595 NW Industrial Way, Estacada, OR, 97023, 503/630-6861.

88 SOUTH BREITENBUSH GORGE

6.2 mi/2.0 hr 

east of Detroit on the South Breitenbush River

The South Breitenbush River comes roaring down from the flanks of Mount Jefferson into this cool, green old-growth forest. Long ridges tower over the water, including nearby Devils Peak. At one point in the forest, the light pours down through a large swath of blowdown, the trees leveled by a 1990 windstorm. But the forest goes on, and in the midst of a particular glade the river squeezes into a 40-foot gorge running along for 100 yards. Fallen trees crisscross the lava walls, making for precarious bridges suitable, at best, for small mammals. The gorge is a perfect destination, though continuing onward will eventually bring you to Roaring Creek—another great turnaround point—and the slopes of Jefferson itself.

Begin at the site of an historic guard station, descending into the forest to the river, heading upstream for 1.2 miles, crossing the North Fork Breitenbush along the way, to a trail junction. Go straight along the river another 1.4 miles to a sign and spur trail on the right for "South Breitenbush Gorge." To continue on to Roaring Creek is only another 0.5 mile up the trail, and it's worth it for views of both the river and this lovely creek.

User Groups: Hikers and dogs. No horses or mountain bikes allowed. No wheelchair facilities.

Permits: Permits are not required. Parking and access are free.

Maps: For a map of the Willamette National Forest, contact Willamette National Forest

Headquarters, 3106 Pierce Parkway, Suite D, Springfield, OR, 97477, 541/225-6300. For a topographic map, ask the USGS for Breitenbush Hot Springs.
Directions: Drive 50 miles east of Salem on OR 22 to Detroit. Cross the Breitenbush River and turn left on Road 46 for 11.2 miles. Turn right on a gravel road and after 0.3 mile park on the left at the site of the old guard station.
Contact: Willamette National Forest, Detroit Ranger District, HC73, Box 320, Mill City, OR, 97360, 503/854-4239.

89 TOP LAKE AND DOUBLE PEAKS

5.3 mi/3.0 hr 1 8

east of Detroit in Olallie Lakes Scenic Area

The 6,000-year-old remnant of a glacier-carved plateau has left mile after mile of lakes scattered across the Olallie Lake Scenic Area like pearls from a broken necklace. To see for yourself, try this loop past several lakes to Double Peaks, a 5,998-foot summit towering above the lake basin and looking out to Olallie Butte and Mount Jefferson.

Follow the Red Lake Trail 1.1 miles through mountain hemlocks and lodgepole pines, keeping right at a junction to Timber Lake, to Top Lake and a three-way junction. Go left 0.4 mile, switchbacking up to the Pacific Crest Trail and then going left to Cigar Lake. At the next junction, leave the PCT and go right steeply up 0.8 mile to Double Peaks. To return via the loop, go back to the PCT, following it left 0.5 mile past Cigar Lake to a four-way junction with the Red Lake Trail. Stay straight on the PCT another 1.4 miles to the road at Head Lake, going right 0.3 mile back to the car.
User Groups: Hikers, dogs, and horses. No mountain bikes allowed. No wheelchair facilities.
Permits: Permits are not required. Parking and access are free.
Maps: For a map of the Mount Hood National Forest, contact Mount Hood National Forest Headquarters, 16400 Champion Way, Sandy, OR, 97055, 503/668-1700. For a topographic map, ask the USGS for Olallie Butte.
Directions: From I-205 near Oregon City, take Exit 12 and go east 18 miles to Estacada. Go through town and continue 26 miles on Highway 224 to the Ripplebrook bridge. Go straight on Road 46 for 21.8 miles toward Detroit. Turn left on Road 4690 at the Olallie Lake turnoff, following this road 8.1 miles, turning right on Road 4220 for 5.1 miles, turning right at an intersection with the Olallie Lake Resort. Go 0.3 mile to a message board on the right for the Red Lake Trail and park on the shoulder. From Salem, follow OR 22 east to Detroit and go left on Breitenbush Road 46 for 23.5 miles to the Olallie Turnoff.
Contact: Mount Hood National Forest, Clackamas River Ranger District, 595 NW Industrial Way, Estacada, OR, 97023, 503/630-6861.

90 MONON LAKE

3.9 mi/2.0 hr 1 7

northeast of Detroit in Olallie Lakes Scenic Area

Olallie Lake is a popular destination and rightfully so. With its big campgrounds and unparalleled view of nearby Olallie Butte, it makes for a great destination. But nearby Monon Lake, the second-biggest lake after Olallie, has its own beauty. Unfortunately, a 2001 fire blackened the shores of this scenic lake, but it is slowly recovering as the undergrowth begins its triumphant resurgence. These mountains, after all, evolved with forest fires, so you can get an edifying look at how a forest regenerates, even after such a devastating burn as this one.

From the campground, go 0.5 mile to the right along Olallie Lake to a junction with the Olallie Lake Trail, going right. You'll pass

Nep-Te-Pa and Mangriff Lakes and arrive at Monon Lake. Go right for a 2.9-mile loop around the lake, with 0.3 mile of it on the road, then rejoin the Olallie Trail. At the last junction, you can go left to return to the car or extend the day by going right 0.4 mile along Olallie Lake to another junction. Going left extends this trail another 0.9 mile to the Paul Dennis Campground; going right heads 0.4 mile into the Warm Springs Reservation to the shore of Long Lake.

User Groups: Hikers, dogs, horses, and mountain bikes. No wheelchair facilities.

Permits: Permits are not required. Parking and access are free.

Maps: For a map of the Mount Hood National Forest, contact Mount Hood National Forest Headquarters, 16400 Champion Way, Sandy, OR, 97055, 503/668-1700. For a topographic map, ask the USGS for Olallie Butte.

Directions: From I-205 near Oregon City, take Exit 12 and go east 18 miles to Estacada. Go through town and continue 26 miles on Highway 224 to the Ripplebrook bridge. Go straight on Road 46 for 21.8 miles toward Detroit. Turn left on Road 4690 at the Olallie Lake turnoff, following this road 8.1 miles, turning right on Road 4220 for seven miles, turning left at the Peninsula Campground entrance and following signs for the boat ramp. From Salem, follow OR 22 east to Detroit and go left on Breitenbush Road 46 for 23.5 miles to the Olallie Turnoff.

Contact: Mount Hood National Forest, Clackamas River Ranger District, 595 NW Industrial Way, Estacada, OR, 97023, 503/630-6861.

91 PARK RIDGE

7.4 mi/5.0 hr

east of Detroit in Mount Jefferson Wilderness

Jefferson Park is one of the most spectacular places in the Cascade Mountains. Don't let the word "Park" fool you though, for this is no city park with picnic tables. Rather, "Park" designates a mountain meadow, and this one is unsurpassed for its beauty, especially in early summer when the flower show begins. There are a number of ways in, and this one—despite the final two miles of rough roads—comes in from the north, up and over Park Ridge and down to Russell Lake and the jeweled expanse of lakes, alpine scenery, and islands of windswept trees. There's even a side trail to climb 6,095-foot Pyramid Butte on the way.

From the trailhead, follow the Pacific Crest Trail to the left for 0.6 mile to a junction. To continue to Jefferson Park, stay on the PCT for five miles to cross over Park Ridge and arrive at Russell Lake and the meadows. For a climb up Pyramid Butte, go right 1.1 miles, then right again to the peak. Coming back down, go one mile, staying right and rejoining the PCT.

User Groups: Hikers, dogs, and horses. No mountain bikes allowed. No wheelchair facilities.

Permits: A free self-issue Wilderness Permit is required and is available at the trailhead. Parking and access are free.

Maps: You can purchase a Mount Jefferson Wilderness Map from Geo-Graphics. For a map of the Mount Hood National Forest and the Mount Jefferson Wilderness, contact Mount Hood National Forest Headquarters, 16400 Champion Way, Sandy, OR, 97055, 503/668-1700. For a topographic map, ask the USGS for Olallie Butte Mount Jefferson.

Directions: From I-205 near Oregon City, take Exit 12 and go east 18 miles to Estacada. Go through town and continue 26 miles on Highway 224 to the Ripplebrook bridge. Go straight on Road 46 for 21.8 miles toward Detroit. Turn left on Road 4690 at the Olallie Lake turnoff, following this road 8.1 miles, turning right on Road 4220 for 10.5 miles, noting that the final two miles of this road are extremely rough and require high-clearance vehicles. Past Breitenbush Lake, turn left to the Pacific Crest Trail lot. From Salem, follow OR 22 east to Detroit and go left on

Breitenbush Road 46 for 23.5 miles to the Olallie turnoff.

Contact: Mount Hood National Forest, Clackamas River Ranger District, 595 NW Industrial Way, Estacada, OR, 97023, 503/630-6861.

92 TRIANGULATION PEAK

4.2 mi/2.0 hr 1 9

east of Detroit in Mount Jefferson Wilderness

A fitting name for a peak on which a fire watchtower once stood, Triangulation Peak offers an impressive view of Mount Jefferson not only from its peak, but from the mouth of a secret cave accessible by a cross-country scramble over the flanks of the peak. Along the way, the trail passes the towering monolith of Spire Rock and enters a series of alpine meadows covered with fish-filled lakes. For intrepid travelers, this trail also provides access deeper into Mount Jefferson Wilderness Area.

From the trailhead, start out 1.5 easy miles on the Triangulation Trail paralleling an old road and entering the Wilderness area. At a junction by Spire Rock's pillar, which rises from the trees and tempts rock climbers, go right to climb the remaining 500 feet and 0.6 mile. To find Boca Cave, beware of steep cliffs and watch your step. From the peak, hike down to a saddle and go right and cross-country to a second and lower peak. From here, a scramble trail descends along the right of a rock outcrop. The path ends at a cliff edge. Go to the right around the cliff and descend a steep forested slope to a 100-foot-deep cavern with a view of Mount Jefferson.

User Groups: Hikers, dogs, and horses. No mountain bikes allowed. No wheelchair facilities.

Permits: A free self-issue Wilderness Permit is required and is available at the trailhead. Parking and access are free.

Maps: You can purchase a Mount Jefferson Wilderness Map from Geo-Graphics. For a map of the Willamette National Forest and the Mount Jefferson Wilderness, contact Willamette National Forest Headquarters, 3106 Pierce Parkway, Suite D, Springfield, OR, 97477, 541/225-6300. For a topographic map, ask the USGS for Mount Bruno.

Directions: Drive 56 miles east of Salem on OR 22. One mile past Idanha, turn left on McCoy Creek Road 2233 for 9.2 miles. At a building, go right and continue 1.3 miles and park at spur Road 635. The trailhead is 100 feet down the spur road.

Contact: Willamette National Forest, Detroit Ranger District, HC73, Box 320, Mill City, OR, 97360, 503/854-4239.

93 JEFFERSON PARK

10.2 mi/5.0 hr 3 10

south of Detroit in Mount Jefferson Wilderness

BEST

By far one of the most beloved places in Oregon, Jefferson Park is an alpine dream. Wildflowers dot the seemingly endless expanses of meadows, spotted here and there by mountain lakes and islands of wind-bent trees. Looming above it is Oregon's second-highest mountain, 10,497-foot Mount Jefferson. There are a number of ways into Jeff Park, as it's known, and this route is by far one of the most scenic. Climbing through an old-growth forest, the trail has expansive views of the mountain as it climbs and crosses the Sentinel Hills, passing rock fields where pikas dart in and out of their dens, and arriving at a virtual wonderland of lakes and undulating land.

The Whitewater Trail is easy to follow, climbing through the forest 1.5 miles to a junction. Go right along the Sentinel Hills 2.7 miles to a junction with the Pacific Crest Trail, then follow it 0.9 mile to the start of Jefferson Park. If you continue on the PCT another 0.7 mile, you'll come to Russell Lake, and side trails lead to other lakes: Scout, Rock, Bays, and Park.

User Groups: Hikers, dogs, and horses. No

mountain bikes allowed. No wheelchair facilities.

Permits: You can purchase a Mount Jefferson Wilderness Map from Geo-Graphics. A free self-issue Wilderness Permit is required and is available at the trailhead. A federal Northwest Forest Pass is required to park here; the cost is $5 a day or $30 for an annual pass. You can buy a day pass at the trailhead, at ranger stations, or through private vendors.

Maps: For a map of the Willamette National Forest and the Mount Jefferson Wilderness, contact Willamette National Forest Headquarters, 3106 Pierce Parkway, Suite D, Springfield, OR, 97477, 541/225-6300. For a topographic map, ask the USGS for Mount Jefferson.

Directions: Drive 61 miles east of Salem on OR 22. Beyond Detroit about 10 miles and between mileposts 60 and 61, turn left on Whitewater Road 2243 and drive 7.4 miles to its end at a parking area.

Contact: Willamette National Forest, Detroit Ranger District, HC73, Box 320, Mill City, OR, 97360, 503/854-4239.

94 PAMELIA LAKE AND GRIZZLY PEAK

10.0 mi/5.0 hr 3 9

south of Detroit in Mount Jefferson Wilderness

This popular trail has become, in the last umpteen years, too popular. What could it be? The stroll along Pamelia Creek? The shores of Pamelia Lake, with staggering Mount Jefferson reflected in its waters? Or possibly the side hike up domineering Grizzly Peak? Alas, it is all of these. To deal with the onslaught of hikers, the Forest Service requires hikers to obtain a free permit in advance. This helps to ease the congestion and allow for this fragile area, especially the lakeshore, to recover from overuse.

The first 2.2 miles of trail follow Pamelia Creek into the dense forest. At a junction you have several options. Go straight to the lakeshore, and you can circle it to the right for a view of Mount Jefferson. Go right at the junction following a sign for Grizzly Peak to climb 2.8 miles to the 5,799-foot summit.

User Groups: Hikers, dogs, and horses. No mountain bikes allowed. No wheelchair facilities.

Permits: A free Limited Entry Permit is required for overnight and day visits to the Pamelia Lake area; contact the USFS for information. A federal Northwest Forest Pass is required to park here; the cost is $5 a day or $30 for an annual pass. You can buy a day pass at the trailhead, at ranger stations, or through private vendors.

Maps: You can purchase a Mount Jefferson Wilderness Map from Geo-Graphics. For a map of the Willamette National Forest and the Mount Jefferson Wilderness, contact Willamette National Forest Headquarters, 3106 Pierce Parkway, Suite D, Springfield, OR, 97477, 541/225-6300. For a topographic map, ask the USGS for Mount Jefferson.

Directions: Drive 62 miles east of Salem on OR 22. Beyond Detroit about 12 miles, between mileposts 62 and 63, turn left on Pamelia Road 2246 for 3.7 miles to the trailhead lot at the end of the road.

Contact: Willamette National Forest, Detroit Ranger District, HC73, Box 320, Mill City, OR, 97360, 503/854-4239.

95 MARION LAKE AND MARION MOUNTAIN

11.2 mi/5.5 hr

east of Marion Forks in Mount Jefferson Wilderness

Like nearby Pamelia Lake, this popular lake in the Mount Jefferson Wilderness shows obvious signs of overuse. The trail is well trammeled, and on a summer day you can expect to have company. None of this makes this big lake any less lovely. Anglers ply the waters, hikers climb over boulders to views of Three-Fingered Jack, and campers linger in the woods on cool mornings. Marion Lake isn't the only destination; you'll also see Marion Falls and Marion Mountain (did I mention this is Marion County?) along this hike. Granted, for some parts you will have to enter the notorious B&B Complex Burn, a devastating fire that roared through this wilderness in 2003, reducing much of it to ash.

The first 2.2 miles on the Marion Lake Trail are an easy walk through the forest, passing Lake Ann and its subterranean outlet. At a junction, go right on the Marion Lake Outlet Trail for 0.6 mile, watching on the right for the 0.2-mile side trail down to Marion Falls. At the next junction, you have a choice: left for a 0.7-mile trail along Marion Lake, which connects to a left-hand 0.3-mile trail back toward Lake Ann; or, if you're feeling sturdy, to the right, crossing Marion Creek and heading toward Marion Mountain on the Blue Lake Trail. The first mile enters the burn. At a pond-side junction, go right on the Pine Ridge Trail for 0.8 mile to a fork and a small sign for Marion Mountain. The remaining 0.8 mile climbs to the site of an old lookout with views to Three-Fingered Jack and Mount Jefferson.

User Groups: Hikers, dogs, and horses. No mountain bikes allowed. No wheelchair facilities.

Permits: A free self-issue Wilderness Permit is required and is available at the trailhead. A federal Northwest Forest Pass is required to park here; the cost is $5 a day or $30 for an annual pass. You can buy a day pass at the trailhead, at ranger stations, or through private vendors.

Maps: You can purchase a Mount Jefferson Wilderness Map from Geo-Graphics. For a map of the Willamette National Forest and the Mount Jefferson Wilderness, contact Willamette National Forest Headquarters, 3106 Pierce Parkway, Suite D, Springfield, OR, 97477, 541/225-6300. For a topographic map, ask the USGS for Marion Lake.

Directions: Drive 66 miles east of Salem on OR 22 to Marion Forks. Between mileposts 66 and 67 turn left on Marion Creek Road 2255 and drive 5.4 miles to the lot at road's end.

Contact: Willamette National Forest, Detroit Ranger District, HC73, Box 320, Mill City, OR, 97360, 503/854-4239.

96 CARL LAKE AND SOUTH CINDER PEAK

9.4-13.4 mi/4.5-6.0 hr  

north of Sisters in Mount Jefferson Wilderness

In 2003, the massive B&B Complex Fire (actually two forest fires that merged into one epic conflagration) swept through the Mount Jefferson Wilderness, torching many beloved places. Still, many areas were spared, including rock-rimmed Carl Lake. This camping-friendly lake also gives access to a number of great hikes, astonishing huckleberry fields, and a momentous view from the barren South Cinder Peak.

From the trailhead, march into the burned area which ends before the 1.9-mile walk to Cabot Lake and its side trail. From here the trail begins to switchback up into the high country, passing several ponds on the 2.8-mile walk to Carl Lake. Circle the lake for a variety of perspectives on the surrounding mountain country. The hike from here to South Cinder Peak is a challenge, requiring a 1.5-mile climb past Shirley Lake and along a deep valley to the Pacific Crest Trail. Go left on the PCT for 0.2 mile, then follow a path up the red cinder butte for views to Mount Jefferson and south to the Three Sisters.

User Groups: Hikers, dogs, and horses. No mountain bikes allowed. No wheelchair facilities.

Permits: A free self-issue Wilderness Permit is required and is available at the trailhead. A federal Northwest Forest Pass is required to park here; the cost is $5 a day or $30 for an annual pass. You can buy a day pass at the trailhead, at ranger stations, or through private vendors.

Maps: You can purchase a Mount Jefferson Wilderness Map from Geo-Graphics. For a map of the Deschutes National Forest and Mount Jefferson Wilderness, contact Deschutes National Forest Headquarters, 1001 SW Emkay Drive, Bend, OR, 97702, 541/383-5300.For a topographic map, ask the USGS for Marion Lake.

Directions: Drive 12 miles west of Sisters on U.S. 20 to a "Wilderness Trailheads" sign near milepost 88. Drive north on Jack Lake Road 12 for 4.4 miles and turn left on Road 1230 for 1.6 miles to pavement's end and seven miles on gravel to road's end at a large lot.

Contact: Deschutes National Forest, Sisters Ranger District, P.O. Box 249, Sisters, OR, 97759, 541/549-7700.

97 METOLIUS RIVER

5.4 mi/2.0 hr 

north of Sisters in Deschutes National Forest

The Metolius River rushes aboveground at 50,000 gallons a minute from an underground spring at the base of Black Butte. From there, the river makes a full display of itself with its ethereal blues and white water rushing through a forest of ponderosa pine and Douglas fir, where eagles wait in the branches for a chance at fish. This trail passes among songbirds amid some real scenery: islands of flowers entirely growing on fallen logs and a cascade of springs—including a waterfall splashing right out of the rock.

The easy West Metolius Trail is out-and-back from the Lower Canyon Creek Campground, heading 2.7 miles downstream to Wizard Falls and a fish hatchery. You can continue this hike as far downstream as far as you'd like, and can even cross the river and explore the opposite shore along a trail there, though there is no loop available in the form of a second bridge to return you to the starting point.

User Groups: Hikers and dogs. No horses or mountain bikes allowed. No wheelchair facilities.

Permits: Permits are not required. Parking and access are free.

Maps: For a map of the Deschutes National Forest, contact Deschutes National Forest Headquarters, 1001 SW Emkay Drive, Bend, OR, 97702, 541/383-5300. For a topographic map, ask the USGS for Candle Creek.

Directions: Drive U.S. 20 west of Sisters nine miles, passing Black Butte. Near milepost 91, turn right at a sign for Metolius River and drive onto Road 1419 for 4.8 miles. At a stop sign, go straight on Road 1420 another 3.3 miles and turn right at a sign for Canyon Creek Campground, driving one mile to the end of the road.

Contact: Deschutes National Forest, Sisters Ranger District, P.O. Box 249, Sisters, OR, 97759, 541/549-7700.

98 COVE PALISADES STATE PARK

7.2 mi/2.5 hr 

southwest of Madras in Cove Palisades State Park

BEST

In a dramatic canyon where three rivers—the Deschutes, the Crooked, and the Metolius—meet, an impressive array of cliff walls nestle the combined flow into the massive Lake Billy Chinook reservoir. One way to get the views of two arms of the canyon and The Island (actually a peninsula, whose towering plateau-expanse makes it the next best thing to an island) is to hike the Tam-A-Lau Trail to The Peninsula, a broad desert atop a plateau with views over Cove Palisades State Park. If you're lucky, you can spot the bald eagles that roost nearby, and on a clear day you'll certainly see Mount Jefferson on the horizon.

From the lot, follow the Tam-A-Lau Trail

0.5 mile through massive tumbled boulders, crossing the two entrance roads to a junction, going to the right. The next 1.3 miles climbs the canyon wall up a series of switchbacks to a junction with some old roads. Keep to the left and follow the trail along the lip of The Peninsula 1.2 miles to the tip above the strange formation of Steamboat Rock. For a longer loop, follow this trail around the plateau another 2.4 miles, returning to the Tam-A-Lau Trail.

User Groups: Hikers and dogs only. No wheelchair facilities.

Permits: Permits are not required. A $3 day-use fee is collected at the parking entrance, or you can get an annual Oregon Parks and Recreation pass for $25; contact Oregon Parks and Recreation, 800/551-6949.

Maps: For a free park brochure, call Oregon Parks and Recreation, 800/551-6949 or download a free map at www.oregonstateparks.org. For a topographic map, ask the USGS for Round Butte Dam.

Directions: Drive 15 miles north of Redmond on U.S. 97, going up and over Culver Butte, to a sign for The Cove State Park. Follow the Culver Highway and signs for the park into the canyon. Follow this road over a suspension bridge above the Crooked River, passing a turnout for the Crooked River Petroglyph, the park headquarters, and campgrounds. Turn right at a sign for the Tam-A-Lau Trail. Park in the big lot at the end of the road.

Contact: Oregon Parks and Recreation Department, 1115 Commercial Street NE, Salem, OR, 97301, 800/551-6949, www.oregonstateparks.org.

Index

OUTDOORS

"Well written, thoroughly researched, and packed full of useful information and advice. These guides really do get you into the outdoors."

—GORP.COM

ALSO AVAILABLE AS FOGHORN OUTDOORS ACTIVITY GUIDES:

250 Great Hikes in California's National Parks
California Golf
California Waterfalls
California Wildlife
Camper's Companion
Easy Biking in Northern California
Easy Hiking in Northern California
Easy Hiking in Southern California
Georgia & Alabama Camping
Maine Hiking
Massachusetts Hiking
New England Biking
New England Cabins & Cottages
New England Camping
New England Hiking
New Hampshire Hiking
Southern California Cabins & Cottages
Tom Stienstra's Bay Area Recreation
Utah Camping
Vermont Hiking
Washington Boating & Water Sports

MOON OREGON'S COLUMBIA RIVER GORGE CAMPING & HIKING

Avalon Travel
a member of the Perseus Books Group
1700 Fourth Street
Berkeley, CA 94710, USA
www.moon.com

Editors: Elizabeth Hollis Hansen, Sabrina Young
Series Manager: Sabrina Young
Senior Research Editor: Kathie Morgan
Research Editor: Glenn Mayeda
Copy Editor: Valerie Sellers Blanton
Graphics Coordinators: Elizabeth Jang, Domini Dragoone
Production Coordinators: Elizabeth Jang, Domini Dragoone
Cover Designer: Kathryn Osgood
Interior Designer: Darren Alessi
Map Editor: Mike Morgenfeld
Cartographers: Michelle Trame, Brice Ticen, Kat Bennett
Illustrations: Bob Race

ISBN-13: 978-1-59880-574-1

Front cover photo: Indian paintbrush at south face of Mount Hood © Troy Farr/Dreamstime.com
Title page photo: oak tree in mountain meadow, Columbia River Gorge © Rick Carlson/123rf.com

Printed in the United States of America

ABOUT THE AUTHORS

© JOHN BEATH

Tom Stienstra

For 30 years, Tom Stienstra's full-time job has been to capture and communicate the outdoor experience. Tom writes a weekly outdoors column that is distributed across America. He has won more than 100 national and regional writing awards, and has twice been named National Outdoors Writer of the Year. His television show, *The Great Outdoors,* is broadcast weekly on CBS/CW. His first edition of *Pacific Northwest Camping* was acclaimed by the *Portland Oregonian.*

Tom takes part in all facets of the outdoors, and as a pilot and airplane owner, can cover great distances quickly in the pursuit of adventure. He lives with his wife Stephani at their ranch in the "State of Jefferson," near the Oregon border.

You can contact Tom directly via his website at www.tomstienstra.com. His guidebooks include:

Moon Oregon Camping
Moon Washington Camping
Moon Pacific Northwest Camping
Moon West Coast RV Camping
Moon California Camping
Moon California Hiking (with Ann Marie Brown)
Moon California Fishing
Moon California Recreational Lakes & Rivers
California Wildlife
Moon Northern California Cabins & Cottages
Tom Stienstra's Bay Area Recreation

© ANDY BUDOR

Sean Patrick Hill

Sean Patrick Hill is a freelance writer, poet, and teacher who has spent many weekends and summers exploring the best of Oregon's mountains, deserts, and coastlines. Born and raised in upstate New York, Hill moved to Oregon after graduating from the University of Buffalo. He lived in Eugene, Bend, and then Portland, graduating with a masters in writing from Portland State University. For two summers he worked with the Oregon Youth Conservation Corps, leading teenage crews into the Cascade Mountains to do everything from maintaining trails to building bridges to counting frogs. Later, as an AmeriCorps volunteer, he organized tree plantings in local parks, clean-ups of riverside environments, and field trips into the wilderness for high school students.

Hill has written outdoor travel articles for *The Oregonian, The Source Weekly, Columbia Gorge Magazine,* and *Oregon Coast.* His poetry appears widely in online and print journals, and his first book of poems, *The Imagined Fields,* will be published this year.

Made in the USA
Lexington, KY
26 August 2012